# GREAT AMERICAN
# STATESMEN AND HEROES

# GREAT AMERICAN STATESMEN AND HEROES

Catherine Millard

Illustrator: Maxwell Edgar

Horizon Books
3825 Hartzdale Drive
Camp Hill, PA 17011

ISBN: 0-88965-120-5

Printed in the United States of America

96  97  98  99  00    6  5  4  3  2

Cover illustration © by Karl Foster


Unless otherwise noted, Scripture quotations
are from the New American Standard Bible,
© The Lockman Foundation, 1960, 1962, 1963,
1968, 1971, 1972, 1973, 1975, 1977.

*Taken from the bronze statue of "Armed Freedom,"*
*atop our U.S. Capitol dome. Original by Thomas Crawford. She holds a*
*sheathed sword in her right hand, a wreath in her left. Thirteen stars*
*representing our 13 original states, crown her head.*

# INTRODUCTION

This book was born out of the need to provide a useful compendium of godly American statesmen and heroes. Because their lives were anchored in Scripture, they provided the foundation and framework that built this country into the greatest nation the world has ever known.

Communist officials have long understood the need to reach the youth of a nation in order to bring about a social revolution. This is done through the rewriting of textbook curricula, focusing particularly upon history, in order to redirect impressionable young minds. In Hitler's Germany it was JUGEND (Youth Government Organization); in Romania, UNIUNEA TINERETULUI COMUNIST (Communist Youth League), in Hungary, KOMMUNISTA ISJUSAGI SZOVETSEG (Hungarian Association of Communist Youth). The results were identical — millions who embrace a false ideology.

Today in the United States, there has been a subtle, but carefully orchestrated attempt to gain control of the minds of our youth, and particularly to teach them a revisionary, godless, anti-Christian history of America, devoid of its true identity. You will find documentation of this travesty in my book, *The Rewriting of America's History*.

For *Great American Statesmen and Heroes*, I have abstracted from this former book true historical sketches of America's godly heroes, in addition to many others which have been added. The book includes statesmen and heroes from the discovery of America to the Development Period, from numerous states in the union.

Catherine Millard

"In the name of God, Amen. We, whose names are underwritten. . . having undertaken, for the glory of God, and advancement of the Christian faith . . . a voyage to plant the first colony in the northern parts of Virginia, do, by these presents, solemnly and mutually, in the presence of God and one another, covenant and combine ourselves together into a civil body politic. . ."

The MAYFLOWER Compact
of the 1620 Pilgrims.
In the year of our Lord,
November 11, 1620.

# TABLE OF CONTENTS

Introduction

## Chapter IV  *Development*

# CHAPTER I
Discovery

*After the original painting "Christopher Columbus — Discovery"*
*by Constantino Brumidi, in the ceiling of the President's Room,*
*U.S. Capitol, Washington, D.C. For many years the Presidents*
*used this room as the Ceremonial Chamber for signing documents.*

# CHRISTOPHER COLUMBUS
## "Christ-bearer to unknown Coastlands"
## (1451 - 1506)

### Columbus, the Bible and Prayer

Through the ages of history, many great inventors, scientists and visionaries have acknowledged the Bible and the leading of the Holy Spirit as the basis for their contributions which revolutionized the world of their day. Columbus was no exception. The following lengthy quotation from the Introduction to Christopher Columbus' *Book of Prophecies* summarizes not only his deep commitment to the gospel mandate, but also points to the Bible as the very source of his inspiration:

> At a very early age I began to sail upon the ocean. For more than forty years, I have sailed everywhere that people go. I prayed to the most merciful Lord about my heart's great desire, and He gave me the spirit and the intelligence for the task: seafaring, astronomy, geometry, arithmetic, skill in drafting spherical maps and placing correctly the cities, rivers, mountains and ports. I also studied cosmology, history, chronology and philosophy.

> It was the Lord who put into my mind (I could feel His hand upon me) the fact that it would be possible to sail from here to the Indies. All who heard of my project rejected it with laughter, ridiculing me. There is no question that the inspiration was from the Holy Spirit, because he comforted me with rays of marvelous illumination from the Holy Scriptures, a strong and clear testimony from the 44 books of the Old Testament, from the four Gospels, and from the 23 Epistles of the blessed Apostles, encouraging me continually to press forward; and without ceasing for a moment they now encourage me to make haste.

> Our Lord Jesus desired to perform a very obvious miracle in the voyage to the Indies, to comfort me and the whole people of God. I spent seven years in the royal court, discussing the matter with many persons of great reputation and wisdom in all the arts; and in the end they concluded that it was all foolishness, so they gave it up. But since things generally came to pass that were predicted by our Savior Jesus Christ, we should also believe that this particular prophecy will come to pass. In support of this, I offer the gospel text, Matt. 24:35, in which Jesus said that all things would pass away, but not his marvelous Word. He also affirmed that it was necessary that all things be fulfilled that were prophesied by himself and by the prophets.

> I said that I would state my reasons: I hold alone to the sacred and Holy Scriptures, and to the interpretations of prophecy given by certain devout persons.

> It is possible that those who see this book will accuse me of being unlearned in literature, of being a layman and a sailor. I reply with the words of Matt. 11:25: "Lord, because thou has hid these things from the wise and prudent, and hath revealed them unto babes."

> The Holy Scripture testifies in the Old Testament by our Redeemer Jesus

Christ, that the world must come to an end. The signs of when this must happen are given by Matthew, Mark and Luke. The prophets also predicted many things about it.

Our Redeemer Jesus Christ said that before the end of the world, all things must come to pass that had been written by the prophets.

The prophets wrote in various ways. Isaiah is the one most praised by Jerome, Augustine and by the other theologians. They all say that Isaiah was not only a prophet, but an evangelist as well. Isaiah goes into great detail in describing future events and in calling all people to our holy catholic faith.

Most of the prophecies of Holy Scripture have been fulfilled already... I am a most unworthy sinner, but I have cried out to the Lord for grace and mercy, and they have covered me completely. I have found the sweetest consolations since I made it my whole purpose to enjoy His marvelous presence.

For the execution of the journey to the Indies I did not make use of intelligence, mathematics or maps. It is simply the fulfillment of what Isaiah had prophesied. All this is what I desire to write down for you in this book.

No one should fear to undertake any task in the name of our Savior, if it is just and if the intention is purely for His holy service. The working out of all things has been assigned to each person by our Lord, but it all happens according to His sovereign will even though He gives advice. He lacks nothing that it is in the power of men to give him. Oh what a gracious Lord, who desires that people should perform for Him those things for which He holds Himself responsible! Day and night moment by moment, everyone should express to Him their most devoted gratitude.

I said that some of the prophecies remained yet to be fulfilled. These are great and wonderful things for the earth, and the signs are that the Lord is hastening the end. The fact that the gospel must still be preached to so many lands in such a short time — this is what convinces me.[1]

## Columbus Acclaimed as One of the World's Greatest Christian Heroes

Christopher Columbus was highly esteemed and praised by King Ferdinand and Queen Isabel of Spain, who funded his expedition. He was acclaimed as a man of fervent Christian faith by all who knew him, and heralded as the discoverer of America — one of the world's greatest Christian heroes, by his contemporaries. He considered himself chosen of the Lord, to "bring the Gospel to unknown coastlands," and cited Isaiah 66:19 as his prophetic Scripture:

> "And I will set a sign among them and will send survivors from them to the nations: Tarshish, Put, Lud, Meshech, Rosh, Tubal and Javan, to the distant coastlands that have neither heard My fame nor seen My glory. And they will declare My glory among the nations."
>
> Isaiah 66:19

## Columbus' Burden for Lost Souls

Columbus' letter to Lord Raphael Sansix, dated May 3, 1493 is entitled, *Concerning the Islands Lately Discovered*, and gives insight, once again, into the soul of this great American hero, his intense love of the Lord, his life of prayer, and his desire to bring the life-saving gospel of Jesus Christ to these distant shores. It is hereunder excerpted:

> ...But great and wonderful is this thing, neither attributable to our merits, but to the holy Christian Faith, and to the piety and religion of our sovereigns: because what the human understanding was unable to attain, that thing the Divine understanding granted to human creatures. For God is accustomed to hearken to His servants, and those who love His precepts, even to the accomplishment of impossibilities, as it hath befallen us in the present case, who have accomplished those things, which hitherto the strength of mortals hath not attained. For if others have written or spoken anything of these Islands, all have done so by quibbles or conjectures, no one affirms that he has seen them. Whence the whole matter seemed almost a fable.
>
> Let, therefore, the King and Queen, our Sovereigns, and their most happy Realms; together with all Christian regions, — let us all give thanks to our Lord Jesus Christ the Saviour, who hath bestowed on us so great a triumph:... Let Christ exult on earth, as He exults in Heaven, foreseeing as He does, that so many souls of people heretofore lost, are now about to be saved. Let us also rejoice, both by reason of the exultation of our faith, and by reason of the increase of our temporal things, of which things not only Spain but all Christendom will be partakers. These things, as they have been promptly achieved, so are they briefly related...[2]

## Hardships at Sea

There were many hardships and difficulties on his four expeditions to the new world, especially in the latter trips, such as storms at sea, ships worm-eaten and not able to stay afloat, and mutinies.

## God's Timely Help in the Midst of Tribulation

Perhaps one of Columbus' most insightful and moving letters was the one he wrote from Jamaica on July 7, 1503 during his last voyage to America. It depicts his inner soul, his human frailty in perilous times, and God's timely help in the midst of tribulation. It is here excerpted:

> ...In January the mouth of the river had closed. In April the ships were all worm-eaten and would not stay afloat. The river now formed a canal through which we drew three of them, empty, with great difficulty. The boats were sent in again for salt and water; the sea rose and became turbulent, which prevented their coming out. The Indians were many in number and began a battle which ended in slaughter. My brother and the other people were all in a ship that remained inside. I was outside, all alone, on that wild coast, with a high fever and utterly exhausted. All hope of escape had left me; I worked myself to the highest part of the ship, and with sobs and in tremulous tones called for help upon the war-captains of your Highnesses, in every direction, but never an answer did I get. Worn out, I fell asleep groaning. A voice full of

pity I heard saying: 'Oh, fool that thou art and slow to believe in and serve thy God, the Lord of all! What more did He do for Moses or for David His servant? Since the day of thy birth hath He ever watched over thee. When thou didst reach an age that seemed well to Him, marvelously He made thy name resound throughout the earth. The Indies, that are so rich a part of the world, He hath given thee for thine own. Thou didst distribute them as it pleased thee, and He gave thee power to do so. To the barriers of the seas that were closed with such mighty chains, hath He given thee the keys; and thou wast obeyed in so many lands and didst receive such just fame among Christians. What more did He do for the people of Israel when He took them out of Egypt? Or for David, who, from a shepherd He made King of Judea? Turn to Him, and see thine error. His mercy is infinite; ... vast and many are the gifts that He can bestow. Abraham was more than one hundred years old when he begat Isaac; and Sarah, was she a young girl? Thou callest for uncertain help — answer: who has afflicted thee so greatly and so often, God, or the world? The privileges bestowed by the Lord are never taken away and His promises are never broken; ... His every promise is faithfully kept and fulfilled in overflowing measure ... I have told thee what thy Creator hath done for thee, and what He doth for all of His children: now behold the reward that hath been thine for the dangers and hardships that thou hast suffered while serving others!' Thus in a dazed state did I listen; but I could make no answer to words so true except to weep for my errors. The speaker, whoever he might be, closed by saying: 'Fear not; have faith; all thy tribulations are written upon marble, and not without cause...'[3]

## Columbus' Primary Goal in Life

The above shows a humble man who knew God, and whose purpose in life was to serve Him. What a rich Christian heritage can be traced to the year of our Lord 1492, when Christopher Columbus, "Christ-bearer to the Uncharted Isles," brought the gospel of Jesus Christ to America.

Even in his final instructions to his son Don Diego, he desired to further the gospel of Jesus Christ to the lost.

## Columbus' Last Will and Testament, and the Christian School

In his famed Mayorazgo (Testament of Founding Hereditary Family Estate), dated Thursday, 22nd February, 1498, are these directions for maintaining and sustaining a Christian school on the Island of Espanola:

> Also I order to said Don Diego, my son, or to him who will inherit said mayorazgo, that he shall help to maintain and sustain on the Island Espanola four good teachers of the holy theology with the intention to convert to our holy religion all those people in the Indias, and when it pleases God that the income of the mayorazgo will increase, that then also be increased the number of such devoted persons who will help all these people to become Christians. And may he not worry about the money that it will be necessary to spend for

the purpose...[4]

Thus we see that Columbus' primary allegiance was to God and not gold, as some modern-day revisionist historians have indicated. His vision and burden remained the same — "to bring the Gospel to unknown coastlands."

*After the original painting "Discovery of the Mississippi by de Soto A.D. 1541" in the Main Rotunda, U.S. Capitol, Washington, D.C. The cross of Christ is being erected in the foreground, to the right.*

# HERNANDO DE SOTO
## Explorer
## (c.1500 - 1542)

### De Soto's Trust in Almighty God

On July 9th, 1539, Hernando de Soto, discoverer of Florida, wrote to the Justice and Board of Magistrates of Santiago, Cuba, informing them of his activities in "this new country." His original letter gives a clear view of this hero's faith in Christ, and his trust in Almighty God, who, according to de Soto, "...has directed all, through His bounteous goodness, in such a way that He appears to have this enterprise altogether under His especial care..." It is hereunder reprinted, in order to understand de Soto's true identity:

..After our arrival, I received information of there being here a Christian, who was in the power of a cacique; and I sent Baltazar de Gallegos, with forty cavalry and as many infantry, to endeavor to get him. He met him, in company with 8 or 10 Indians, a day's journey from this place, and brought him to me. We were not a little glad to have him; for he speaks the language of the country, and although he has forgotten his own, it directly returned to him. His name is Joan Ortiz, a native of Sevilla, and a hidalgo... This interpreter affords us the means of being understood, and without him, I know not what we should do. Glory to God, who has directed all, through his bounteous goodness, in such a way, that he appears to have this enterprise altogether under his especial care, that it should be for his service, as I have besought that it might be, and have so dedicated it to Him... I enjoin it upon you to make the utmost exertions to maintain the quiet and well-being of the public, and the proper administration of justice, consulting always with the Licenciado, that everything may be so done, according to law, that God and the king may be served, myself gratified, and everyone be content and pleased with the performance of his trust;... That our Lord may guard and increase your happiness, is my wish, and your worships deserving.

At the town and port of Espiritu Santo, in the Province of Florida. July the 9th, in the year 1539.

The Servant of your worships,
El Adelantado D. Hernando de Soto.[1]

The above displays de Soto's awe and reverence for Almighty God, as well as his servant heart, both towards God and his superiors. Hernando's deep concern for the well-being and safety of the people of Santiago, Cuba, after his departure, is heart-warming and reassuring. De Soto finishes his letter by giving God all the glory as author of the blessings and happiness which He bestows upon His own.

## The Indians' Treatment of the Christians

In the same rare book, we find the detailed *Memoir of Hernando de Escalante Fontaneida*, translated from the original Spanish manuscript. This accurate account of de Soto's voyage gives further insight into the Christian dimensions of his expedition, together with the Indians' treatment of the Christians. As I wish to remain within the context of the original narrative, it is hereunder extracted, as follows:

> ...Many Spaniards have saved their lives by finding before them these associates (Christian companions). For the natives who took them would order them to dance and sing; and as they were not understood, and the Indians themselves are very artful (for the most so of any are the people of Florida), they thought the Christians were obstinate, and unwilling to do so. And so they would kill them, and report to their cacique that for their craft and disobedience they had been slain, because they would not do as they were told; which was the answer, as I have said, made to the cacique when he would ask why they had killed them. One day, I, a negro, and two others, Spaniards recently made captives, being present, the cacique, in conversation with his vassals and the great chiefs of his train about what I have just mentioned, asked me, I being mas ladino (better acquainted with the language than anyone), saying: "Escalante, tell us the truth, for you well know that I like you much: When we require these, your companions, to dance and sing, and do other things, why are they so dissembling and obstinate that they will not? Or is it that they do not fear death, or will not yield to a people unlike them in their customs? Answer me; and if you do not know the reason, ask it of those newly taken, who for their own fault are prisoners now, a people whom once we held to be gods come down from the sky." And I, answering my lord and master, told him the truth: "Sir, as I understand it, they are not contrary, nor do they behave badly on purpose; but it is because they cannot comprehend you, which they earnestly strive to do." He said it was not true; that often he would command them to do things; and sometimes they would obey him, and at others they would not, however much they might be told... The cacique, discovering the truth, said to his vassals, that when they should find Christians thus cast away, and take them, they must require them to do nothing without giving notice that one might go to them who should understand their language...[2]

Here we learn of the Indians' exploitation and slaying of the Christians. Many modern-day textbooks and history books would have the youth of America believe the opposite to be true. One reads volumes of twentieth century revisionist accounts decrying de Soto's — and other great American explorers' and discoverers' — cruelty, abuse and extermination of the natives; majoring upon their despoiling of the Indians' culture and "idyllic" way of life. True historic records, however, such as the one just cited on Hernando de Soto, show these accounts to be without evidence and a revision of history.

## De Soto arrives in Florida Unarmed and Defenseless

The original narrative goes on to document de Soto's arrival in Florida, on May 25, 1539, on the Festival of Espiritu Santo (the Holy Spirit). Interestingly enough, the governor and a few others went ashore, unarmed and defenseless, which counters the myth of his conquering with the sword:

> ...The danger of the Governor at this time was great, and not less the anxiety of those on board the ships, because of his defenseless condition; for had he come to be in any extremity they would have been unable to yield him assistance...[3]

## The Gospel of Christ Preached to the Indians

A third account of de Soto's expedition is entitled *A Narrative of the Expedition of Hernando de Soto into Florida by a gentleman of Elvas.* Translated from the Portuguese in 1609, it was originally published at Evora in 1557. This historic document gives a vivid account of the Gospel of Jesus Christ being preached to the Indians on the Isle of Cuba. Here the Governor was besought by two blind men who wanted him to restore their sight. But the Governor answered that:

> ...in the high heavens was He that had power to give them health, and whatsoever they could ask of Him; whose servant he was; and that this Lord made the heavens and the earth, and man after His own likeness, and that He suffered upon the cross to save mankind, and rose again the third day, and that he died as he was man, and as touching His divinity, He was, and is immortal; and that He ascended into heaven, where He standeth with His arms open to receive all such as turn unto Him: and straightway he commanded him to make a very high cross of wood, which was set up in the highest place of the town; declaring unto him, that the Christians worshipped the same in resemblance and memory of that whereon Christ suffered. The Governor and his men kneeled down before it, and the Indians did the like. The Governor willed him, that from thenceforth, he would worship the same and should ask whatever they stood in need of, of that Lord that he told him was in heaven...[4]

The foregoing portrays the true Christian identity, mind-set, values and goals of Hernando de Soto in his expedition to Cuba and Florida in the year of our Lord, 1539. It shows a man whose Lord and Master is Jesus Christ, the Son of God, who heals, restores sight to the blind and answers the prayers of His own.

MIDNIGHT BURIAL OF DE SOTO IN THE MISSISSIPPI

*After the frieze by Constantino Brumidi*
*within the inner dome of the Main Rotunda of the U.S. Capitol.*

# CAPTAIN JOHN SMITH
## Leader of the 1607 Jamestown Settlement in Virginia
## (1580 - 1631)

The **First Charter of Virginia**, dated April 10, 1606, provides Americans with the true identity of our great nation, the 1607 Jamestown settlers having laid down their lives to bring Protestant Christianity to these shores. It is hereunder excerpted:

> ...We, greatly commending, and graciously accepting of, their desires for the furtherance of so noble a work, which may, by the Providence of Almighty God, hereafter tend to the Glory of his Divine Majesty, in propagating of Christian Religion to such people, as yet live in darkness and miserable ignorance of the true knowledge and worship of God...[1]

Captain John Smith, leader of the 1607 Christian expedition and settlement in Virginia, was both Governor and Admiral. In describing Virginia's earliest history, Thomas Jefferson cites the reputed historian Sir William Keith as a foremost authority. Keith gives us this account of Captain Smith's imprisonment and near execution by the Indians:

## A Prisoner of Powhatan

> ...The Captain was conducted to a long room, where forty tall fellows were appointed for his guard; and soon after that a great quantity of bread, venison, and other eatables were set before him; and when the prisoner had done eating as much as satisfied him, the remainder was carefully put by 'til midnight, when they brought in a fresh quantity, eating only themselves what was left at noon; and thus they continued to do every twelve hours, which made the Captain suspect that they intended to fatten him up for a sacrifice; and while under this desperate uncertain condition, he was ready to perish with cold, an Indian called Mancassater brought him his gown, in grateful return for some beads, and other toys, he had received from the Captain, at his first arrival in Virginia... Last of all, the prisoner was carried to Weronocomaco, the seat of their great Emperor Powhatan, to whom they were formally introduced, as he sat, in a solemn manner, on a wooden bench before a great fire, covered with a robe of raccoon skins. There sat on each side of the Emperor a young woman, and on each side of the room, two rows of men, and as many women behind them, with all their hands and shoulders painted red; at the Captain's entrance before this prince, all the people gave a shout, and the Queen of Appomatock was appointed to bring water to wash his hands, and another brought him a bunch of feathers, instead of a towel, to dry them. After this, having feasted the prisoner in the grandest manner they could, a long consultation was held amongst them; at the conclusion whereof, two great stones were placed before the Emperor Powhatan; then as many as could, laid hands on the prisoner, and dragging him towards the stones, they put his head on them, and immediately prepared themselves with great clubs to knock out his brains; but at this very

JAMESTOWN, VIRGINIA

*Captain John Smith, after the original bronze sculpture next to 1607 Jamestown Settlers' Church, Jamestown Island, Virginia.*

instant, Pocahontas, the king's favourite daughter, after she found no entreaties could prevail, flew to the block; and taking Captain Smith's head in her arms, she laid her own upon it to save him from death; which surprising event moved the Emperor to tell the prisoner that he should live to make hatchets for him, and bells and other ornaments for his daughter Pocahontas... He told him that now they were good friends together, he intended to send him to Jamestown, from whence he desired the Captain would order two great guns and a grindstone to be sent to him; for which Powhatan would give him in return the country Capahowosiok, and for ever esteem him as his son Nantaquand...[2]

## Captain John Smith's Testimony
Captain Smith gave the following bold testimony:

Powhatan, please to know that I worship only one God and serve but one king. I am not therefore here as your subject but as a friend to serve you in what I can...[3]

## The Religion of the Indians
We also read of the practise of child sacrifice among the Indians, this being an abomination to the Living God. Captain Smith relates this fact for posterity in these terms:

...Their solemn sacrifices of children, which they call Blackboyes.[4]

Smith continues his narrative on the Indians' "strange" religion in his *Historie of Virginia*, thus:

| | |
|---|---|
| **Their god:** | ...But their chief god they worship is the devil. Him they call Okee, and serve more of fear than love. They say they have conference with him, and fashion themselves as near to his shape as they can imagine...[5] |
| **How the world was made:** | ...They believe there are many gods, which they call Mantoac, but of different sorts and degrees. Also that there is one chief god that hath been from all eternity, who as they say when he purposed first to make the world, made first other gods of a principle order, to be as instruments to be used in the creation and government to follow: And after the sun, moon and stars, as petty gods; and the instruments of the other order more principal. First (they say) were made waters, out of which by the gods were made all diversity creatures that are visible or invisible. |
| **How man was made:** | For mankind they say a woman was made first, which by the working of one of the gods conceived and brought forth children; and so they had their beginnings, but how many years or ages since they know not; having no records but only tradition from father to son. |

| | |
|---|---|
| **How they use their gods:** | They think that all the gods are of human shape, and therefore represent them by images in the forms of men; which they call Kewasowok: one alone is called Kewasa; them they place in their temples, where they worship, pray, sing, and make many offerings. The common sort think them also gods... |
| **The subtlety of their priests:** | What subtlety soever be in the Werowances, and priests: this opinion worketh so much in the common sort, that they have great respect to the governors; and as great care to avoid torment after death, and to enjoy bliss. Yet they have divers sorts of punishments according to the offense, according to the greatness of the fact. And this is the sum of their religion, which I learned by having special familiarity with their priests, wherein they were not so sure grounded, nor gave such credit, but, through conversing with us, they were brought into great doubts their own, and no small admiration of ours: of which many desired to learn more than we had means for want of utterance in their language to express... |
| **Their consultations:** | When they intend any wars, the Werowances usually have the advice of their priests and conjurers, and their allies and ancient friends, but chiefly the priests determine their resolution. Every Werowance, or some lusty fellow, they appoint Captain over every nation. They seldom make war for lands or goods, but for women and children, and principally for revenge. |
| **Their enemies:** | They have many enemies, namely, all their westerly countries beyond the mountains, and the heads of the rivers... |
| **Their charms to cure:** | They have many professed physicians, who, with their charms and rattles, with an infernal rout of words and actions, will seem to suck their inward grief from their navals, or their grieved places...[6] |

Smith then quotes this phrase to show the powerlessness of their charms:

> But 'tis not always in physician's skill, to heal the patient that is sick and ill; For sometimes sickness on the patient's part, Proves stronger far than all physician's art.[7]

## The Religion of the 1607 Jamestown Settlers:

Robert Hunt was the chaplain appointed by the Church of England to oversee the Jamestown Church. At his death, the colonists paid homage to him with these words, inscribed upon Hunt's memorial on Jamestown Island:

> ...He was an honest, religious and courageous Divine. He preferred the service of God in so good a voyage to every thought of ease at home. He endured every privation, yet none ever heard him repine. During his life our factions were ofte healed, and our greatest extremities so comforted that they seemed easy in comparison with what we endured after his memorable death. We all received from him the Holy Communion together, as a pledge of reconciliation, for we all loved him for his exceeding goodness. He planted the First Protestant Church in America and laid down his life in the foundation of America.[8]

## The Indians' Desire of Salvation

Under the subtitle **Their Desire of Salvation**, Smith relates that even the natives were in awe and admiration of the colonists' Christian lives, that is, their life of prayer, obedience to the Lord, longsuffering and forgiveness; all of which drew them to the true God of the Bible and Jesus Christ His Son:

> ...The King Wingina where we dwelt would oft be with us at prayer. Twice he was exceeding sick and like to die. And doubting of any help from his priests, thinking he was in such danger for offending us and our God, sent for some of us to pray, and be a means to our God, he might live with Him after death. And so did many other in like case. One other strange accident (leaving others) will I mention before I end, which moved the whole country that either knew or heard of us, to have us in wonderful admiration. There was no town where they had practised any villany against us (we leaving it unpunished, because we sought by all possible means to win them by gentleness) but within a few days after our departure, they began to die; in some towns twenty, in some forty, in some sixty, and in one a hundred and twenty, which was very many in respect to their numbers. And this happened in no place (we could learn) where we had been, but where they had used some practice to betray us. And this disease was so strange, they neither knew what it was, nor how to cure it; nor had they known the like time out of mind; a thing specially observed by us, as also by themselves, in so much that some of them who were our friends, especially Wingina, had observed such effects in four or five towns, that they were persuaded it was the work of God through our means: and that we by Him might kill and slay whom we would, without weapons, and not come near them. And thereupon, when they had any understanding, that any of their enemies abused us in our journies, they would entreat us, we would be a means to our God, that they, as the others that had dealt ill with us, might die in like sort: although we showed them their requests were ungodly and that

our God would not subject Himself to any such requests of men, but all things as He pleased came to pass: and that we, to show ourselves His true servants, ought rather to pray for the contrary. Yet because the effect fell out so suddenly after, according to their desires, they thought it came to pass by our means, and would come give us thanks in their manner, that though we satisfied them not in words, yet in deeds we had fulfilled their desires...[9]

The above accounts point out the contrast between Christianity as embraced by the 1607 settlement in Virginia, and the false religions practised by Indian tribes such as the Werowances. Once again, we find that these original historic documents of early Virginia dispel the modern mythological textbook and history book accounts of the "noble savage;" indoctrinated, exploited and massacred by the colonists.

# POCAHONTAS
## Indian Christian Princess
## (c.1595 - 1617)

Pocahontas is one of the most unique heroines of our nation's history. Let us understand the reasons for her claim to fame, as recorded for us in the annals of America's original history books. She was the favorite daughter of the Emperor Powhatan of the Indians in Virginia. Pocahontas and Captain John Smith, leader of the 1607 settlement in Jamestown, Virginia, were good friends. She saved his life twice, her first allegiance being to her fellow-believers before her own family, after accepting Jesus Christ as her Lord and Savior, the Redeemer of her soul.

POCAHONTAS SAVING THE LIFE
OF CAPT. JOHN SMITH

*After the frieze painted by Constantino Brumidi within the inner dome of the Main Rotunda, U.S. Capitol, Washington, D.C.*

## Pocahontas became *Rebecka,* and married John Rolfe

She was baptized in 1613 and took the Christian name, Rebecka. In April, 1614, she married John Rolfe, council member of the Jamestown Colony. Her husband took her and their infant son, Thomas, to England, in the year 1616.

The famed historian Sir William Keith, in his *History of Virginia*, writes these lines regarding their trip and her meeting once again with Captain John Smith:

Maloaks als Rebecka daughter to the mighty Prince Powhatan Emperour of Attanoughkomouck als Virgin converted and baptized in the Chriſtian faith, an Wife to the worſ Mr Tho: Rolff.

*After the only original extant portrait of Pocahontas in America. Painted by the artist Brooke in 1616, it is displayed in the Portrait Gallery of the Smithsonian Institution, Washington, D.C.*

...Mr. John Rolfe, and his wife, the Princess Pocahontas, who had been baptized by the name of Rebecka, went along in the same ship with Sir Thomas Dale, and landed at Plymouth on 12th of June. As soon as Captain Smith at London, who was then ready to sail for New England, heard that his incomparable friend Pocahontas was arrived, lest he should not have the opportunity to see her before his departure, he presented a petition to the Queen in her behalf, setting forth at large all the particular circumstances of his obligations to Pocahontas, but she, happily arriving at London before the Captain left that place, he went to visit her, and for a considerable time the good lady would not condescend to speak to him, or so much as to look towards him; for, it seems, she had been told in Virginia, that Captain Smith was actually dead; and was therefore greatly offended to find she had been so grossly imposed on; and at last, when she was prevailed with to talk to him, she upbraided him with his forgetfulness of the great friendship she had formerly showed to him, and behaved herself in every other respect, so much becoming a person of high birth and rank, that she was treated at court and everywhere else with marks of great distinction; but sometime afterwards she fell sick at Gravesend, as she waited there to embark on her return to Virginia; and after a few days' illness, *died, with all the tokens of piety and religion that became a good Christian*; leaving behind her only one son, Thomas Rolfe, whose posterity, in Virginia, at this day, live in very good repute, and inherit lands by descent from her..."[1]

From the above we see that Pocahontas, whose name meant "Bright Stream between Two Hills,"[2] gained a new name at her conversion to Christianity, that of "Rebecka," the godly name given to Isaac's wife in the Old Testament Scriptures.

## Pocahontas Leaves an Inheritance to her Descendants

We also learn of the great friendship she maintained with Captain John Smith, and her beautiful, Christian death. We further understand that Pocahontas left an inheritance of lands to her own descendants. This fact is quite contrary to modern-day history book accounts which decry the 1607 settlers as having taken land from the Indians by force; misusing and abusing them — even to the point of robbing them of their inheritance and culture!

How different is this true historical record of Pocahontas, the Indian Christian Princess, compared to these recent revisionist fables. Americans can be justly proud of their rich Christian beginnings, stemming from Virginia, "the cradle of the Republic."

# CHAPTER II
## Colonial

# WILLIAM BRADFORD
## And the 1620 Pilgrims
## (1590 - 1657)

William Bradford was governor of Plymouth Colony, the second permanent English settlement in America. It was founded on Cape Cod Bay in Massachusetts in 1620. He was also an author, and his history, *Of Plimoth Plantation*, is the primary means of our knowledge of that noble Pilgrim band who came to America to establish a biblical way of life furthering the gospel of Jesus Christ in the new world. His history covers the period of their persecution in England for their faith in Christ; their resettlement in Holland; their arrival in America in 1620, and their settled years to 1646.[1]

## Cotton Mather's Account of Governor William Bradford

Bradford was born in 1590 in an obscure town in Yorkshire, England. "Here, and in some other places," writes Cotton Mather, to whom we are indebted for what is known of Bradford's early life,

> ...he had a comfortable inheritance left him of his honest parents who died while he was yet a child and cast him on the education, first of his grandparents, and then of his uncles, who devoted him, like his ancestors, into the affairs of husbandry. Long sickness kept him as he would afterwards thankfully say, from the vanities of youth and made him the fitter for what he was afterwards to undergo. When he was about a dozen years old, the readings of the Scriptures began to cause great impressions upon him; and those impressions were much assisted and improved when he came to attend the ministry of Reverend Mr. Richard Clifton, not far from his abode; he was then also further befriended by being brought into the company and fellowship of such as were then called professors. Nor could the wrath of his uncles, nor the scoff of his neighbors, now turned upon him as one of the Puritans, divert him from his pious inclinations.

When about 18 years of age, Bradford, with the company who had separated from the established church, went to Holland. He was twice arrested for having fled from England; but an explanation of his reasons secured his early release, and he was permitted to join his friends at Amsterdam. While there, he became apprenticed to a Frenchman engaged in the manufacture of silks. On coming of age, he promptly converted the property left him in England into money and engaged in business for himself at Leyden, Holland. Here he continued until, with a portion of Mr. Robinson's church, he embarked on the *Mayflower* for New England. No doubt Bradford was an equal sharer in the many trials of the colonists on land. He was chosen the second governor of the

EMBARKATION OF THE PILGRIM FATHERS - 1620

*After the original painting, "Embarkation of the Pilgrim Fathers"*
*by Charles West Cope.*

colony in 1621, and continued in that office with the exception of five years, until his death in 1657. Mather continues:

> He was a person for study as well as action; and hence, not withstanding the difficulties through which he passed in his youth, he attained unto a noble skill in languages. He was also well skilled in history, in antiquity; and in philosophy and for theology, he became so versed in it, that he was an irrefragable disputant against the errors, especially those of Anabaptism, which with anxiety he saw rising in his colony; wherefore he wrote some significant things for the confutation of those errors. At length he fell sick, and so continued through a winter and spring, and died on the 9th of May, following, in the 69th year of his age. The opportunities which governor Bradford had for writing the history of the Plymouth Colony were superior to those of any other colonist and although his duties as Chief Magistrate would seem to afford him little leisure for writing, yet he thereby acquired an entire familiarity with every subject of a public nature in any way connected with the colony. This, taken in connection with the high character which he has always enjoyed, has caused this work to be regarded as of the first authority, and as entitled to take precedence over anything else relating to the history of the Pilgrims.

## Of Plymouth Plantation — The Original Manuscript

The history of Plymouth Plantation is fascinating. After the death of its author, the manuscript written by Bradford passed into the hands of his nephew, Nathaniel Morton, who drew quite copiously from it for the facts in his "New England's Memorial." It afterwards came into the possession of Thomas Prince, who made use of it in his *Chronological History of New England*. On the death of Prince, it was left in the New England Library, in the tower of the Old South Church, Boston. When Boston was occupied by the British in 1775-76, the church was used by the British soldiers for a riding school, and it is quite likely that Bradford's manuscript history was among the spoils carried to Nova Scotia. In 1855, the manuscript, which had long been given up for lost, was found in Fulham Library, among a rare collection belonging to the Bishop of London. How it ever got from Boston to London still remains a mystery. The original manuscript was returned to Massachusetts in 1897.[2]

## The Pilgrims Separate from the Established Church of England

In England during the 1600's, the only recognized church was the Church of England, which had turned away from the simple gospel message of Jesus Christ. Bradford documented the split that took place among professing Christians as follows:

The one side laboured to have ye right worship of God and discipline of Christ established in ye church, according to ye simplicitie of ye gospell, without the mixture of men's inventions, and to have and to be ruled by ye laws of God's word, dispensed in those offices, and by those officers of Pastors, Teachers, and Elders, etc. according to ye Scriptures. The other partie, though under many colours and pretences, endeavored to have ye episcopall dignities (affter ye popish maner) with their large power and jurisdiction still retained; with all those courts, cannons, and ceremonies, togeather with all such livings, revenues, and subordinate officers, with other such means as formerly upheld their antichristian greatnes, and enabled them with lordly and tyranous power to persecute ye poore servants of God. This contention was so great, as neither ye honour of God, the commone persecuton, nor ye mediation of Mr. Calvin and other worthies of ye Lord in those places, could prevaile with those thus episcopally minded, but they proceeded by all means to disturbe ye peace of this poor persecuted church, even so farr as to charge (very unjustly, and ungodily, yet prelatelike) some of their cheefe opposers, with rebellion and high treason against ye Emperour, and other such crimes...

Governor Bradford goes on to give the lamentable results of this schism:

...Religion hath been disgraced, the godly greeved, afflicted, persecuted, and many exiled, sundrie have lost their lives in prisones and otherways. On the other hand, sin hath been countenanced, ignorance, profannes, and atheisme increased, and the papists encouraged to hope againe for a day...so that in England at this day the man or woman that begins to profes Religion, and to serve God, must resolve with him selfe to sustaine mocks and injuries even as though he lived amongst ye enimies of Religion...

The historian weighs all these cataclysmic happenings in the scales of Scripture, and concludes:

...but it is ye Lord's doing, and ought to be marvelous in our eyes!...Every plante which mine heavenly father hath not planted (saith our Saviour) shall be rooted up. (Matt. 15:13)...Behold, I come unto ye, O proud man, saith the Lord God of hosts; for thy day is come, even the time that I will visite thee. Jer. 50:31...

and:

When the Lord brougt againe the captivitie of Zion, we were like them that dreame. Psa: 126:1. The Lord hath done greate things for us, wherof we rejoyce. v. 3. They that sow in teares, shall reap in joye...

## William Bradford Gives Much Credit to True Men of God — John Robinson, William Brewster, Richard Clifton

Bradford gives much credit to the preachers and true men of God, such as John Robinson, William Brewster, Richard Clifton and others. Through them, people saw their sinful conditions, repented and

"THE PURITAN"
BY AUGUSTUS SAINT-GAUDENS 1848-1907

*After the original bronze statue in Springfield, Massachusetts.*
*He holds a Bible in his left hand.*

received God's grace to change their lives. But they soon met with persecution and scorn which, Bradford tells us, they bore with much patience. Furthermore, God revealed to them that the "lordly and tyrannous power of ye prelates ought not to be submitted unto: which was contrary to the freedome of the gospell, would load and burden men's consciences, and by their compulsive power make a prophane mixture of persons and things in ye worship of God."

## Their Afflictions are "Fleebites" Compared to Later Sufferings

The afflictions took a turn for the worse; Bradford likens their former problems to "fleebites" in comparison to their latter sufferings. In 1607, concluding that it was impossible to continue the worship of God in England, they agreed to resettle in Holland where they had heard they would have freedom of religion. It was not any easy undertaking, as Bradford describes below:

> Being thus constrained to leave their native soyle and countrie, their lands and livings, and all their friends and famillier acquaintance, it was much, and thought marvelous by many. But to goe into a countrie they knew not (but by hearsay), wher they must learne a new language, and get their livings they knew not how, it being a dear place, and subjecte to ye miseries of warr, it was by many thought an adventure almost desperate, a case intolerable, and a miserie worse than death. Espetially seeing they were not acquainted with trade nor traffique, (by which ye countrie doth subsiste), but had only been used to a plaine countrie life, and ye inocente trade of husbandrey. But these things did not dismay them (though they did sometimes trouble them) for their desires were sett on ye ways of God and to enjoye His ordinances; but they rested in His Providence, and knew whom they had believed...

## The Pilgrims' Departure From Holland – Rooted in the Word of God

Life in Holland was very difficult. There were extremely long hours for the adults and the children alike. They feared the corruption of their children by the native youth. Difficulties finally drove them to leave Holland. Bradford describes their departure from Holland being rooted in their love of God:

> So being ready to departe, they had a day of solleme humiliation, their pastor taking his texte from Ezra 8:21: "And ther at ye river, by Ahava, I proclaimed a fast, that we might humble ourselves before our God and seeke of Him a right way for us, and for our children, and for all our substance." Upon which they spente a good parte of ye day very profitably and suitable to their presente occasion. The rest of the time was spent in powering out prairs to ye

Lord with greate fervencie, mixed with abundence of tears. And ye time being come that they must departe, they were accompanied with most of their brethren out of ye citie, unto a towne sundrie miles off called Delfes-Haven, wher the ship lay ready to receive them. So they lefte ye goodly and pleasante citie, which had been ther resting place near 12. years; but they knew they were pilgrimes (Hebrews 11), but lift their eyes to ye heavens, their dearest cuntrie, and quieted their spirits...

What could now sustaine them but ye spirite of God and His grace? May not and ought not the children of these fathers rightly say: Our fathers were Englishmen which came over this great ocean, and were ready to perish in this wilderness; (Deuteronomy 26:5,7) but they cried unto ye Lord, and He heard their voyce, and looked on their adversitie, etc. Let them therefore praise ye Lord, because He is good, and His mercies endure for ever. (107 Psalm: v. 1,2,4,5,8) Yea let them which have been redeemed of ye Lord, show how He hath delivered them from ye hand of ye oppressour. When they wandered in ye deserte wilderness out of ye way, and found no citie to dwell in, both hungrie, and thirstie, their sowle was overwhelmed in them. Let them confess before ye Lord His loving kindnes, and His wonderful works before ye sons of men.

# The Pilgrims' Arrival in Massachusetts, November 11, 1620

They arrived at Cape Cod, Massachusetts, on November 11, 1620. Ocean storms had blown them off course. Thus, they arrived in Massachusetts rather than their originally intended Virginia destination, King James having granted a charter to the Virginia Company for its incorporation (First Charter of Virginia, April 10, 1606.)

## The Pilgrims' 1618 Leyden Agreement –
## Seven Articles of Faith and Practice

It is interesting to note that these Pilgrims had written up an agreement entitled *The Leyden Agreement of 1618* subscribed by John Robinson and William Brewster. The following excerpt clearly establishes their priorities.

## Seven articles which the Church of Leyden sent to the Counsel of England to be considered of their judgment occasioned about their going to Virginia. Anno 1618.

1. To the confession of faith published in the name of the Church of England and to every article thereof we do with the reformed churches where we live and also elsewhere assent wholly. 2. As we do acknowledge the doctrine of faith there taught, so do we the fruits and effects of the same doctrine to the begetting of saving faith in thousands in the land (conformists and reformists as you are called) with whom also as with our brethren, we do desire to keep spiritual communion in peace and will practise in our parts all lawful things. 3. The King's Majesty we acknowledge for Supreme Governor

in his Dominion in all causes and over all persons, and none may decline or appeal from his authority or judgment in any cause whatsoever, but in all things obedience is due unto him, either active, if the thing commanded be not against God's Word, or passive if it be, except pardon can be obtained. 4. We judge it lawful for his Majesty to appoint bishops; civil overseers, or officers in authority under him, in the several provinces, dioses, congregations or parishes to oversee the churches and govern them civilly according to the Laws of the Land, unto whom you are in all things to give an account, and by them, to be ordered according to Godliness. 5. The authority of the present bishops in the land, we do acknowledge so far forth as the same is indeed derived from his Majesty unto them and as you proceed in his name, whom we will also therein honor in all things and him in them. 6. We believe that no sinod, classes, convocation or assembly of Ecclesiastical officers has any power or authority at all but as the same by the Magistrate given unto them. 7. And lastly, we desire to give unto all Superiors due honor to preserve the unity of the Spirit, with all who fear God, to have peace with all men what in us lieth, and wherein we err to be instructed by any.

Subscribed by John Robinson and William Brewster.[3]

The *1618 Leyden Agreement* only further validates the Christian identity and purpose of the 1620 Pilgrims, who subsequently finding themselves about to arrive upon land with no established form of government as it would have been, had they landed in Virginia, saw the necessity to establish some type of governmental order among themselves before landing. The result was the *Mayflower Compact*, a charter which they drew up and signed, electing their own officers, and binding themselves to work together for their common Christian faith and their common good. From this simple mutual agreement, took form the first American Commonwealth, the beginning "of government of the people, by the people, for the people." This document, establishing the Pilgrims' priorities, read as follows:

## The Famed Mayflower Compact

### THE COMPACT

In the Name of God, Amen. We, whose names are underwritten, the loyal subjects of our dread sovereign Lord King James, by the grace of God, of Great Britain, France and Ireland King, defender of the faith, etc., having undertaken, for the glory of God, and advancement of the Christian faith, and honor of our king and country, a voyage to plant the first colony in the northern parts of Virginia, do, by these presents, solemnly and mutually, in the presence of God and one of another, covenant and combine ourselves together into a civil body politic, for our better ordering and preservation, and furtherance of the ends aforesaid; and by virtue hereof to enact, constitute and frame such just and equal laws, ordinances, acts, constitutions, and offices, from time to time, as shall be thought most meet and convenient for the general good of the colony; unto which we promise all due submission and obedience. In witness whereof we have hereunder subscribed our names at Cape Cod the 11 of November, in the year of the reign of our sovereign lord, King James of England, France, and Ireland and the eighteenth, and of Scotland the fifty-fourth, Anno Dom. 1620.[4]

It had been a difficult journey. Bradford tells us that, of the 103 Mayflower Pilgrim disembarking passengers, 51 of these died during the first New England winter. However, this stalwart band of settlers who had braved the dangerous seas and inhospitable New England shores, to live their lives in harmony with God's Holy Scriptures, persevered in prayer, obedience and praise to Almighty God.

## John Quincy Adams' 1802 Oration on the Pilgrims' Unique Form of Government

In an oration of 1802 commemorating the landing of the 1620 Pilgrims, John Quincy Adams, sixth U.S. president, noted the greatness of this unique new form of government:

> ...One of these remarkable incidents is the execution of that instrument of government by which they formed themselves into a body politic, the day after their arrival upon the coast, and previous to their first landing. This is perhaps the only instance, in human history, of that positive, original social compact, which speculative philosophers have imagined as the only legitimate source of government. Here was a unanimous and personal assent by all the individuals of the community, to the association by which they became a nation. It was the result of circumstances and discussions, which had occurred during their passage from Europe, and is a full demonstration that the nature of civil government, abstracted from the political institutions of their native country, had been an object of their serious meditation...The importance of these circumstances will not be duly weighed without taking into consideration the state of opinions then prevalent in England. The general principles of government were there little understood and less examined. The whole substance of human authority was centered in the simple doctrine of royal prerogative, the origin of which was always traced in theory to divine institution. Twenty years later the subject was more industriously sifted, and for half a century became one of the principle topics of controversy between the ablest and most enlightened men in the nation. The instrument of voluntary association executed on board the Mayflower, testifies that the parties to it had anticipated the improvement of their nation...[5]

## Governor William Bradford's Death

In 1657, William Bradford, Pilgrim father, relinquished his soul into the hands of his blessed Redeemer, Jesus Christ, whom he had served faithfully throughout his life.

## Bradford's Epitaph —
## His Godly Admonitions to All Americans

A marble obelisk at Burial Hill, in Plymouth, marks his grave with a Latin inscription bearing the phrase:

**"What our fathers with so much difficulty attained, do not basely relinquish."**

The inscription on the south side reads: "H.I. William Bradford of Austerfield, Yorkshire, England. Was the son of William and Alice Bradford. He was Governor of Plymouth Colony from 1621 to 1633; 1635 to 1637; 1639 to 1643; 1645 to 1657."

An inscription to the north side follows: "Under this stone rest the ashes of William Bradford, a zealous puritan and sincere Christian Governor of Plymouth Colony from 1621 to 1657, (the year he died) aged 69, except 5 years, which he declined."

Since Bradford was a student of Old Testament Hebrew, it is appropriate that a Hebrew inscription, beautifully reiterating his life, is engraved upon his tombstone:

**"Let the right hand of the Lord awake"**

PILGRIMS GOING
TO CHURCH

THOMAS HOOKER
CONNECTICUT.

*After the original statue in the State Capitol of Connecticut, at Hartford.*
*He holds a Bible in his left hand.*

# THOMAS HOOKER
### Founder of Connecticut
### (1586 - 1647)

Thomas Hooker, the founder of Connecticut, and one of New England's greatest men of God, was born in 1586 in Markfield, Leicestershire, England. He died at Hartford, Connecticut, in 1647.[1]

## Hooker Persecuted for the Cause of Christ

Hooker was a fellow of Emmanuel College, Cambridge, after which he became the assistant to a minister in Chelmsford. Archbishop Laud ordered him to refrain from preaching the Gospel of Christ, his preaching being considered outside the format of the established Church of England. He then taught school in Little Braddon; John Eliot, missionary to the Indians, becoming his assistant. Under intense persecution, Hooker left for Holland, embarking on a ship bound for New England in 1633.[2]

## Hooker arrives in America

After arriving in America, he was appointed as pastor of the church at Newtown, (Cambridge), his spiritual influence in the colony being immeasurable. In 1636, Thomas Hooker founded Connecticut, the new colony encompassing the towns of Hartford, Windsor and Weathersfield.[3]

PILGRIMAGE OF THOMAS HOOKER
TO THE CONNECTICUT VALLEY
1636

*As depicted in a 1909 public school history book.*
*He holds a Bible under his left arm.*

# Hooker draws up the First Written Constitution Made by the People for the People in History

The Fundamental Orders of Connecticut — the first written Constitution — made by the people and for the people in the history of civilization, limiting the powers of government, was drawn up by Hooker and adopted by the assembly of planters of the three towns of Connecticut, on January 14, 1638.[4]

# Thomas Hooker Influential in Both the Church and the State

It can be said that the birthplace of the American republican form of government is Hartford.[5] Hooker was influential in both the church and in government, his *Survey of the Summe of Church Discipline* forming an accurate exposé of the way of the churches of New England. To this work John Cotton's writing on Congregationalism is added. Hooker's *Survey of the Summe of Church Discipline* was first printed in London in 1648, shortly after his death.[5]

# Hooker's Greatest Work:
# *A Survey of the Summe of Church Discipline*

The preface to this work, considered to be his greatest: A *Survey of the Summe of Church Discipline (wherein the Way of the Churches of New England is warranted out of the Word, and all Exceptions of Weight, which are Made against it, Answered...)* gives insight into this great American statesman's understanding of the church and how it strayed away from the true gospel; but was finally brought to deliverance by the Reformation.

> ...Sometimes God makes an eclipse of the Truth at midday, that so He might express his wrath from Heaven, against the unthankfulness, prophaneness and atheism of a malignant world. Hence it was he let loose those hellish delusions, immediately after the Ascension of our Saviour; that though His life and conversation gave in evidence beyond gainsaying, that He was true man: though the miracles and wonders He wrought in His life and death, resurrection and ascension, were witnesses undeniable, that He was true God: yet there arose a wretched generation of heretics, in the first, second and third hundred years, who adventured not only against the express verdict of the Scripture, but against sense and experience, fresh in the observation and tradition of living men, with more than Satanical impudency to deny both the natures of our blessed Saviour. Some denied the Deity of our Saviour, and would have Him mere man... First, they began to encroach upon the Priestly Office of our Saviour, and not only to pray for the dead, and to attribute too much to the martyrs and their worth; and to derogate from the merits, and that plentiful and perfect redemption wrought alone by the Lord Jesus. The Spouse

of Christ thus like the unwise virgins, was taken aside with the slumber of idolatry, till at last she fell fast asleep as the following times give in abundant testimony. Not long after, these sleeps were attended with suitable dreams, for not being content with the simplicity of the Gospel, and the purity of the worship appointed therein: They set forth a new and large edition of devised and instituted ceremonies, coined merely out of the vanity of men's carnal minds, which as so many blinds, were set up by the subtlety of Satan, merely to delude men, and mislead them from the Truth of God's worship, under a pretense of directing them more easily in the way of grace: and under a colour of kindling, they quenched all true zeal for, and love of the Truth... When God had revenged the contempt of the authority of His Son, by delivering up such condemners to the tyranny and slavery of Antichrist,... They then began to sigh for some deliverance from this spiritual, more than Egyptian bondage; and being thus prepared to lend a listening ear unto the truth, God sent them some little reviving in their extremities, a day-star arising in this their darkness...[6]

Here we see Hooker relating the lethargy, apathy and idolatry of the churches, which fell into the trap of liturgy and formats, as opposed to the simplicity and purity of the Gospel, and worship of God. "Instituted ceremonies" led the churches astray from the true worship of God to the delusions of Satan. Finally, however, after centuries of slavery to the spirit of Antichrist, the church awoke to serving Jesus Christ, its Lord and Redeemer.

## Hooker, Minister of the Gospel

In terms of Hooker's ministry of the gospel, his work entitled, *The Covenant of Grace Opened*, shows forth a masterful exposition of the grace of God. It is hereunder excerpted, for the reader to assess:

...The second is from that, Romans 4.11. 'Abraham received the sign of circumcision, as the seal of the righteousness of faith,' etc. that is, the righteousness of Christ received by faith, sealed by circumcision, that was the seal of the righteousness of faith by God's appointment... Hence it is plain, that what Abraham had was the covenant of the gospel of grace: It is proved thus, that which was the covenant of the righteousness of faith, is the covenant of the gospel; that this is so, we may see it by the Apostle, 'If it be of works, it is not of faith; if it be of faith, it is not of works.' *Romans 3*...[7]

His thesis is that we attain to righteousness in God's eyes, through faith in Christ and not by good deeds performed in our own strength. It is God's grace which draws us to Him, giving us the faith which gains favor for us in the sight of God: good deeds being a by-product of faith, and not a prerequisite to it.

Thomas Hooker has produced many more works of value on topics of biblical truth and Christian doctrine. Some of these are enumerated as follows:

— *The Soul's Humiliation*
— *The Soul's Implantation*
— *The Soul's Exhaltation*
— *The Poor Doubting Christian drawn to Christ*
— *The Application of Redemption by the effectual work of the Word, and the Spirit of Christ for the bringing home of Lost Sinners to God.*
— *A Comment upon Christ's Last Prayer in the 17th of John*

## Thomas Hooker's Death

After his death, John Cotton wrote these moving lines eulogizing his friend and fellow-Christian:

On my Reverend and dear Brother, Mr. Thomas Hooker, late Pastor of the Church at Hartford on Connecticut

...Christ in the Spirit, is more than Christ in the Flesh,
Our souls to quicken, and our States to bless;
Yet Christ in Spirit brake forth mightily,
In faithful Hooker's searching ministry.
Paul in the pulpit, Hooker could not reach,
Yet did He Christ in Spirit so lively preach;
That living hearers thought
He did inherit,
A double portion of Paul's lively spirit...
All these in Hooker's spirit did remain
A Son of Thunder, and a shower of rain,
A pourer forth of lively oracles
In saving souls, the sum of miracles,
Now blessed Hooker, thou art set on high;
Above the thankless world, and cloudy sky;
Do thou of all thy labor reap the crown,
Whilst we here reap the seed, which thou has sown.

J. Cotton[8]

## The Bible, Hooker's Blueprint to Life

Hence we see the character and inner strength of the founder of Connecticut, rooted firmly in Scripture. It can be said conservatively that Thomas Hooker, minister of the gospel and faithful pastor of the Church at Hartford, was a statesman of great caliber and ability. It is plain to see, however, from whence he derived his political ideals and standards — from the Bible — God's Word, biblical principles and values forming the basis for the government of that State. Connecticut can be rightly proud of her greatest son, Thomas Hooker, preacher of the gospel par excellence.

*After the original marble statue in the Main Rotunda
of the U.S. Capitol, Washington, D.C.*

# ROGER WILLIAMS
## and Freedom of Religion
## (1603 - 1683)

> From this grant I infer that the Sovereign, original, and foundation of civil power lies in the people...And if so, that a people may erect and establish what form of Government seems to them most meet for their civil condition: It is evident that such Governments as are by them erected and established, have no more power, nor for no longer time, than the civil power or people consenting and agreeing shall betrust them with. This is clear not only in reason, but in the experience of all Commonweales, where the people are not deprived of their natural freedom by the power of Tyrants.
>
> Roger Williams, 1644[1]

## Roger Becomes an Outcast for Preaching the Gospel

Roger Williams was born in Wales in 1603. After graduating from Oxford, he ministered through the Church of England, but, upon returning to the Word of God, and preaching the pure Gospel of Jesus Christ, he was labelled "a Puritan" and became an outcast of the established Anglican Church.

## America, "the Haven for Persecuted Christians"

Embarking on a ship for America, considered "the haven for persecuted Christians," he and his wife Mary, arrived on February 5, 1631 in this country.[2] Two months later, he became a teaching elder of the Church at Salem. Being, once again, offensive to the Governor and Assistants of Massachusetts Bay, he left for Plymouth, and assisted Reverend Ralph Smith of the church there. His preaching on Freedom of Religion and Biblical Truth caused some of his parishioners to be offended. He thus returned to Salem, settling there with his family. Roger Williams gained the reputation, both in America and England of "a godly man and a zealous preacher."[3] However, historians relate that the government of Massachusetts viewed him with jealousy from the moment he set foot in the colony. He boldly preached against violation of the Indians' rights, through the land patent, which the King of England had placed in the hands of that government. He also preached that the magistrate had no right "to deal in matters of conscience and religion."[4]

## Roger Banished from Massachusetts Bay

As a result of these activities, he was banished from Massachusetts Bay in the Fall of 1635. He was ordered to leave the colony, the time being extended to Spring, 1636. However, "the people being much taken with the apprehension of his godliness," in January following, the Governor and Assistants sent an officer to take him to a ship bound for England. Roger thus moved to Rehoboth, prior to the officer's arrival.[5]

## Persecuted in Rehoboth, he Founds Providence Settlement in 1636

Governor Winslow of Plymouth next informed him that he was within the jurisdiction of the Plymouth patent. He thus crossed the river and founded the Providence settlement in 1636, after which he joined the Baptists. Three years later, in March, 1639, Williams was baptized by Ezekiel Halliman at Providence.

## Roger Williams Represents the Colonies in England, Obtaining a Charter

In 1643, Roger Williams returned to England, representing the colonies of Providence, Rhode Island and Warwick; in order to seek a Charter of Incorporation. He finally procured one. It was signed on March 14, 1644, by the Earl of Warwick, who was both Governor and Admiral of the English Plantations.[6]

## Williams Excels in Languages, a God-given Talent

Williams had received meager funds to help him secure a new Charter for the colonies. He was obliged to labor to earn his living as well as to oversee the affairs of the colonies. He taught languages — a talent in which he excelled. He had mastered Greek, Latin, French and Dutch. Among his pupils was John Milton, then Secretary of the Council of State, who was in dire need of understanding the Dutch language, his country being at war with Holland. Williams' letter to John Winthrop in July, 1654, gives insight into his teaching profession:

> It hath pleased the Lord to call me for some time and with some persons, to practise the Hebrew, Greek, Latin, French and Dutch. The secretary of the Council, Mr. Milton, for my Dutch I read him, read me many more languages. Grammar rules begin to be esteemed a tyranny. I taught two young gentlemen, a Parliament man's sons, as we teach our children English by words, phrases, constant talk, etc.[7]

## Roger Williams' Dependence Upon God

Williams' dependence upon God is evidenced by this moving letter he wrote from England:

My dear friends, though it pleased God himself, by many favors to encourage me, yet please you to remember, that no man can stay here as I do, having a present employment there, without much self-denial, which I beseech God for more, and for you also, that no private respects, or gains, or quarrels, may cause you to neglect the public and common safety, peace and liberties. I beseech the blessed God to keep fresh in your thoughts what he hath done for Providence Plantations. My dear respects to yourselves, wives and children. I beseech the eternal God to be seen amongst you; so prays your most faithful and affectionate friend and servant,

Roger Williams

P.S. My love to all my Indian friends.[8]

## He is Elected President and Governor of Providence

He set sail for America in 1654, bringing back with him a letter from Sir Henry Vane, which is found in the records of Providence. It invited the planters of Providence Plantations to become united with one mind. This letter, together with Roger's counsels, brought peace and harmony to the colony, which had been divided in his absence. As a true leader and man of God, he was elected President and Governor of this colony by the "free vote of the freemen," a number of times.[9]

## His Christian Character Traits

Roger Williams was a man of moral excellence and integrity. He stood firmly upon his convictions, performed his duty at all costs and never allowed tyranny or praise to divert him from his biblical convictions. One fact speaks clearly in favor of his Christianity. After being banished from Massachusetts Bay, he was an injured, persecuted man. However, he made the best of every opportunity to befriend and expose the neighboring Indian tribes to the life-saving Gospel of Jesus Christ, never harboring revenge. He continually performed acts of kindness to his persecutors, helping the poor and miserable, and offering an asylum to the persecuted.[10] Williams' life was consistently conformed to his duty to God and man, gaining for himself the reputation of "the undaunted champion of Religious Freedom."[11]

## The Hireling Ministry Explained

One of his discourses is hereunder excerpted, in order to better understand this great American statesman's mindset and Christian convictions. It is entitled "The Hireling Ministry," an exposure of the corruptions of clergy paid to perform church offices, in contrast to voluntary trust, obedience, faith and service to Jesus Christ, through the empowering of the Holy Spirit, and prayer:

...First, where God hath been pleased to bring in one soul to Himself by the Hireling Ministry, many more have been brought home by the voluntary and more single preachings of some, whether public or private, by the endeavors of private Christians, by the reading of the Holy Scriptures, by godly example, by afflictions, &c. hence woeful experience hath made it evident, that many excellent men (in their persons, and the graces of God's spirit) have labored a score of years, and more in an Hireling way, without the birth of one child to God; while others singly out of love to Christ Jesus, have despised bargains and hire, and been more abundantly blessed with merciful success and fruitfulness. Hence sure it is that there have been, are many excellent prophets and Witnesses of Christ Jesus, who never entered (as they say) into the Ministry, to wit, Lawyers, Physicians, Soldiers, Tradesmen, and others of higher, and lower rank, who by God's Holy Spirit (breathing on their meditations on the Holy Scriptures, and other private helps) have attained, and much improved, an excellent spirit of knowledge, and utterance in the Holy Things of Jesus Christ, which spirit they ought to cherish, and further to improve to the praise of Christ...

Thirdly, it is the duty of all that are in Authority, and of all that are able, to countenance, encourage and supply such true Volunteers, as give and devote themselves to the service and Ministry of Christ Jesus in any kind: although it be also the duty and will be the practice of such, whom the Spirit of God sends upon any work of Christ's, rather to work as Paul did, among the Corinthians, and Thessalonians, than the work and service of their Lord and Master should not be neglected...[12]

## Williams' Outreach to the Indians— "A Key into the Language of America"

Leaving an indelible mark on posterity, Williams' A *Key into the Language of America* was composed in 1643 on his voyage to America. This work presents the character of the Indians in a new and favorable light, admirably calculated to facilitate communication with them, necessary to peaceful cohabitation. Of this famous work, Williams writes:

To my dear and well-beloved friends and countrymen, in Old and New England: I present you with a Key; I have not heard of the like, yet framed, since it pleased God to bring that mighty Continent of America to light; others of my countrymen, have often and excellently, and lately written of the country (and none that I know beyond the goodness and worth of it.) This Key, respects the native language of it, and happily may unlock some rarities concerning the natives themselves, not yet discovered...There is a mixture of this language North and South, from the place of my abode, about six hundred miles; yet within the 200 miles (aforementioned) their Dialects do exceedingly differ; yet not so, but (within that compasse) a man may by this help, converse with thousands of natives all over the country: and by such converse it may please the Father of Mercies to spread civility (and in His own most holy season) Christianity; for one candle will light ten thousand, and it may please God to bless a little leaven to season the mighty lump of those peoples and territories...[13]

## Roger's Indian Translation of God's Account of Creation in Genesis, First Book of the Bible

Ever focused upon bringing the Word of God to lost souls, Williams prefaces his translation of the Genesis account of Creation. It is hereunder excerpted:

> ...I shall propose some proper expressions concerning the Creation of the world, and man's estate, and in particular theirs also, which from myself many hundreds of times, great numbers of them have heard with great delight, and great convictions: which who knows (in God's Holy season) may rise to the exalting of the Lord Jesus Christ in their conversion and salvation?

| | |
|---|---|
| Nétop Kunnatótemous. | Friend, I will aske you a Question. |
| Nntótema. | Speak on. |
| Tocketunnántum? | What thinke you? |
| Awaun Keesiteouwin Kéesuck? | Who made the Heavens? |
| Aûke Wechêkom? | The Earth, the Sea. |
| Mittauke, | The World. |

Some will answer Tattá, I cannot tell, some will answer Manittôwock, the Gods.

| | |
|---|---|
| Tà suóg Manittôwock, | How many Gods bee there? |
| Maunaúog Mishaúnawock | Many, great many. |
| Netop macháge, | Friend, not so. |
| Paúsuck naúnt manit, | There is onely one God. |
| Cuppíssittone, | You are mistaken. |
| Cowauwaúnemem, | You are out of the way. |

A phrase which much pleaseth them, being proper for their wandring in the Woods, and similitudes greatly please them.

| | |
|---|---|
| Kukkakótemous, wachitquáshouwe. | I will tell you, presently. |
| Kuttaunchemókous. | I will tell you newes. |
| Paûsuck naúnt manít kéesittin keesuck, &c. | One Onely God made the Heavens &c. |
| Napannètashèmittan naugecautúmmonabnshque, | Five thousand years agoe, and upwards. |
| Naúgom naúnt wukkesittinnes wameteâgun | He alone made all things. |
| Wuche mateag, | Out of nothing. |
| Quttatashuchuckqunnacaus-keesitinneswâme, | In six days He made all things. |
| Nquittaqúnne, Wuckéesitin weqâi, | The first day Hee made the Light. |
| Neesqunne, Wuckeesitin Keésuck, | The second day Hee made the Firmament. |
| Shúckqunne wuckéesitin Aúkekà wechèkom, | The third day Hee made the Earth and sea. |
| Yóqunne wuckkéesitin Nippaúus kà Nanepaúshat, | The fourth day He made the Sun and the Moon. |

| | |
|---|---|
| Neenash-mamockíuwash wêquanantiganash, | Two great Lights. |
| Kà wáme anócksuck, | And all the Starres. |
| Napannetashúckqunne | The fifth day Hee made all the fowle. |
| Wuckéesittinpussuck-seesuckwâme, | |
| Keesuckquíuke, | In the Ayre or Heavens |
| Kawámeaúmúasuck, Wechekommiuke, | And all the Fish in the Sea. |
| Quttatashúkqunne Wuckkeés-ittin | The sixth day Hee made all the Beasts |
| penashímwock wamè, | of the Field. |
| Wuttàke wuckèwuckeesittin pausuck Enìn, or, Eneskéetomp, | Last of all He made one Man. |
| Wuche mishquòck, | Of red Earth. |
| Kawesuonckgonnakaûnes Adam, tuppautea mishquock, | And call'd him Adam, or red Earth. |
| Wuttáke wuchè | And the afterward, while |
| Cawit mishquock, | Adam or red Earth slept. |
| Wuckaudnúmmenes manit peetaúgonwuche Adam, | God tooke a rib from Adam, or red Earth. |
| Kà wuchè peteaúgon Wuk-keessitínnes pausuck squàw, | And of that rib He made One woman. |
| Kà pawtouwúnnes Adâm-uck | And brought her to Adam...[14] |

## Roger's Poem on Salvation, Through Christ Jesus

*His Key into the Language of America* finishes with a heart-rending poem, prefaced with this eternal Truth, as found in the Bible:

O, how terrible is the look the speedy and serious thought of death to all the sons of men? Thrice happy those who are dead and risen with the Son of God, for they are past from death to life, and shall not see death (a heavenly sweet paradox or riddle), as the Son of God hath promised them.

More particular:

The Indians say their bodies die,
Their souls they do not die;
Worse are then Indians such, as hold the soul's mortality
Our hopeless body rots, say they,
Is gone eternally,
English hope better, yet some's hope
Proves endless misery
Two worlds of men shall rise and stand
'Fore Christ's most dreadful bar;
Indians and English naked too,
That now most gallant are.
True Christ most Glorious then shall make
New Earth, and Heavens new,
False Christs, false Christians then shall quake,

O blessed then the true.[15]

## Roger Williams—Man of Prayer

A magnificent prayer to Almighty God concludes his masterful translation of their Indian language:

> Now, to the most High and most Holy, Immortal,
> Invisible, and the only Wise God, who alone is
> Alpha and Omega, the Beginning and the Ending,
> the First and the Last, who Was, and Is, and is
> to Come; from Whom, and to Whom are
> all things; by Whose gracious assistance
> and wonderful supportment in so many varieties of
> hardship and outward miseries,…be Honor,
> Glory, Power, Riches, Wisdom, Goodness and
> Dominion ascribed by all His in Jesus Christ
> to Eternity, Amen.
>
> > Finis.[16]

## Williams' Love for the Indians

This American hero shows his deep love of the Indians in his statement that "God was pleased to give me a painful, patient Spirit to lodge with them, in their filthy smoky holes (even while I lived in Plymouth and Salem) to gain their tongue."[17]

## Roger Williams' Greatest Work—
### *The Bloudy Tenent, of Persecution, for Cause of Conscience*

Williams' 1644 work: *The Bloudy Tenent, of Persecution, for Cause of Conscience,* was published in 1644 by Gregory Dexter. It was written in answer to Cotton's work upholding the right and enforcing the duty of the civil magistrate to regulate the doctrines of the church. This able Christian apologist prefaces his case as follows:

> Whether Persecution for cause of Conscience be not against the Doctrine of Jesus Christ the King of Kings. The Scriptures and reasons are these.
>
> Because Christ commandeth that the tares and wheat (which some understand are those that walke in the truth, and those that walke in lies) should be let alone in the world, and not plucked up untill the harvest, which is the end of the world, Matt. 13.30.38.&c.
>
> The same commandeth Matth. 15.14. that they that are blinde (as some interpret, led on in false religion, and are offended with him for teaching true religion) should be let alone, referring their punishment unto their falling into the ditch.
>
> Againe, Luke 9.55.56. hee reproved his disciples who would have had fire come downe from heaven and devour those Samaritans who would not receive Him, in these words: Ye know not what manner of Spirit ye are of, for

the Son of Man is not come to destroy men's lives but to save them....All civill states with their officers of justice in their respective constitutions and administrations are proved essentially civill and therefore not Judges, Governours or Defendours of the spirituall or Christian state and worship...[18]

The above work encapsulates Williams' stance for freedom of religion, being the first great American Christian statesman to preach and advocate, *Separation of Church from Interference by the State.*

## Chosen as Rhode Island's Greatest Hero in the U.S. Capitol's Hall of Fame

This man of God died in April, 1683, at Providence, and was buried in his family burial ground, with every testimony of respect that the colony could manifest. He was father of six children: Mary, Freeborn, Providence, Mercy, Daniel and Joseph. Roger Williams finds his place in America's Hall of Fame, having been chosen by the citizens of Rhode Island to represent them as their greatest hero in our United States Capitol.

# WILLIAM PENN
## Founder of Pennsylvania
## (1644 - 1718)

William Penn, founder of Pennsylvania, was born in 1644. He was the son of Vice-Admiral Sir William Penn, a well known personage in the British navy who was the recipient of favor from the king.[1]

## William's Acceptance of Christ as His Savior at Age 22

Admiral Penn had planned a great military career for his son. At age 22, however, Penn was converted from Atheism to Christianity after hearing Thomas Loe's famous sermon: "The Sandy Foundation Shaken." Young William joined the Friends Society of Quakers.

The Quakers endured great persecution due to the fact that they rejected empty religious formats and the imposed hierarchy of a state-controlled church.

Penn found himself imprisoned three times for preaching the Word of God.[2] His supposed unsoundness to the interpretations of the established Church of England caused him to be imprisoned in the Tower of London. Asked by the Bishop of London to recant in exchange for his liberty, Penn replied: "My prison shall be my grave before I shall budge a jot. For I owe obedience to no mortal man."[3]

## Penn's Greatest Works Written from Prison

Many of his great works were written while in prison, including his most noted and valuable work, "No Cross, No Crown," which illustrates his godly character. It gives insight into William Penn's own conversion account, and the basis for his longing to establish a Christian colony in the New World, free from persecution. It also explains his willingness to risk everything, leaving family and possessions behind, in order to serve Christ. Following are excerpts:

> ...Christ's cross is Christ's way to Christ's crown. This is the subject of the following discourse, first written during my confinement in the Tower of London in the year 1668, now reprinted with great enlargement of matter and testimonies, that thou mayest be won to Christ, or if won already, brought nearer to Him. It is a path which God in his everlasting kindness guided my feet into, in the flower of my youth, when about two and twenty years of age. He took me by the hand and led me out of the pleasures, vanities and hopes of the world. I have tasted of Christ's judgments, and of his mercies, and of the world's frowns and reproaches. I rejoice in my experience, and dedicate it to thy service in Christ.

WILLIAM PENN

*After the painting of William Penn at age 22,*
*presented by his grandson, Granville Penn of Stoke Poges –*
*Original in the Historical Society of Pennsylvania*

Though the knowledge and obedience of the doctrine of the cross of Christ be of infinite moment to the souls of men, being the only door to true Christianity and the path which the ancients ever trod to blessedness, yet it is little understood, much neglected, and bitterly contradicted, by the vanity, superstition, and intemperance of professed Christians.

The unmortified Christian and the heathen are of the same religion, and the deity they truly worship is the god of this world. What shall we eat? What shall we drink? What shall we wear? And how shall we pass away our time? Which way may we gather and perpetuate our names and families in the earth? It is a mournful reflection, but a truth which will not be denied, that these worldly lusts fill up a great part of the study, care and conversation of Christendom. The false notion that they may be children of God while in a state of disobedience to his holy commandments, and disciples of Jesus though they revolt from his cross, and members of his true church, which is without spot or wrinkle, notwithstanding their lives are full of spots and wrinkles, is of all other deceptions upon themselves the most pernicious to their eternal condition for they are at peace in sin and under a security in their transgression.[4]

Other works written by Penn include:

| 1668 | Truth Exalted |
| 1668 | The Sandy Foundation Shaken |
| 1668 | Innocency with her Open Face |
| 1670 | A Seasonable Caveat Against Popery |
| 1671 | Great Case of Liberty of Conscience |
| 1675 | Treatise on Oaths |
| 1675 | England's Present Interests Considered |
| 1679 | Address to Protestants of all Persuasions |
| 1681 | Examination of Liberty Spiritual |
| 1686 | Persuasive to Moderation |
| 1692 | Fruits of Solitude |
| 1692 | Essay towards the Present and Future Peace of Europe |
| 1695 | Rise and Progress of the People called Quakers |
| 1696 | Primitive Christianity Revived |

# William Penn's "A Summons or Call to Christendom" — His Call for Revival in the Church

William Penn's sermons are profound and stirring, lifting up hearts and kindling souls to great heights of spiritual worship. His dynamic sermon entitled, "A summons or call to Christendom—In an earnest expostulation with her to prepare for the Great and Notable Day of the Lord that is at the Door," is alive with the Holy Spirit's pleading for repentance and spiritual growth among believers:

...O Christendom! Thou has long sat as Queen that should never know sorrow; great have been thy pretences, and large thy profession of God, Christ, Spirit and Scriptures; come, let me expostulate with thee and thy children in the fear and presence of Him that shall bring every word and work to judgment. God is pure, and the pure in heart only see Him. Now, are you pure? Do you see Him? God is spirit, and none can worship Him aright but such as come to His spirit, and obey it. Do you so? Christ is the gift of God, have you received Him into your hearts? If not, you are not true Christians. The spirit of truth leadeth into all truth; and the children of God are born of it, and led by it. But are you led into all the holy ways of truth, born of this eternal spirit? Then you follow not the spirit of this world; nor do your own wills, but the will of God. You profess the holy Scriptures; but what do you witness and experience? What interest have you in them? Can you set to your seal they are true by the work of the same spirit in you that gave them forth in the holy ancients? What is David's roarings and praises to thee that livest in the lusts of this world? What is Paul's and Peter's experiences to thee that walkest after the flesh?

O you that are called Christians, give ear a little unto me, for I am pressed in Spirit to write to you. Read with patience and consider my words; for behold what I have to say unto you concerneth your eternal good.

God hath so loved the world that He hath sent His only begotten Son into the world that those that believe on Him should have eternal life. And this Son is Christ Jesus, the true light that lighteth everyone coming into the world; and they that abide not in Him, the light, dwell in darkness, in sin, and are under the region and shadow of death. Yea, dead in sin and see not their own states, neither perceive the sad conditions of their own souls. They are blind to the things of God's kingdom, and insensible of true and spiritual life and motion, what it is to live to God. And in that state are alienated from God without true judgment and living knowledge; and under the curse. For in Jesus Christ, the light of the world, are hid all the treasures of wisdom and knowledge; redemption and glory; they are hid from the worldly Christian, from all that are captivated by the Spirit and lusts of the world; and whoever would see them (for therein consist the things that belong to their eternal peace) must come to Christ Jesus the true light in their consciences, bring their deeds to Him, love Him and obey Him; whom God hath ordained a light to lighten the Gentiles, and for His salvation to the ends of the earth...[5]

## William Penn Inherits Pennsylvania as a Debt Paid Back to His Father by the King

In 1670 Admiral Penn died. Penn's father had lent King Charles II a large sum, and the king was happy to acquit this debt to the son, by a grant of land in America, to be founded as a refuge for persecuted Christians.[6] Hence it was, that in 1681, Penn received a Royal Charter making him proprietor of the territory between New York and Maryland west of the Delaware River. Penn called the land "Sylvania" (Woodland), but the king insisted on adding the prefix "Penn" in honor of the Admiral.[7]

To William Penn, Pennsylvania was not only to be a place of refuge for his fellow persecuted Quakers, but also a Christian commonwealth demonstrating liberty, justice and peace.

## Penn Founds "Philadelphia – City of Brotherly Love." His Bible and Psalter

While serving a nine-month term in the Tower of London, Penn had dreamed of starting a colony in the new world, where biblical truth could be sought, free from persecution. In 1681, he arrived with his followers on board the ship "Welcome," founding shortly thereafter "Philadelphia, City of Brotherly Love." His leather-bound Bible and Psalter, which accompanied him, is in the Penn Mutual Collection, opposite Independence Hall. On the title page to his Book of Psalms, Penn had written:

> Set forth and allowed to be sung in all churches, of all the people together, before and after morning and evening prayer, and moreover in private houses for their godly solace and comfort, laying apart all ungodly songs and ballads: which tend only to the nourishing of vice and corrupting of youth.[8]

It is interesting to note that in this Latin Bible, the section which is the most underlined is the Book of Exodus, which tells about the Israelites' escape from Egypt. This is a point of significance, in view of the English Quaker exodus to Pennsylvania, likening their removal to America with that of the Israelites' deliverance from bondage and slavery.

## Penn's Stand Against Slavery

Penn called his undertaking a "Holy Experiment" of which he was governor and proprietor. Of his undertaking, it is recorded that,

> ...His province was the first to raise its voice against slavery...[9]

## Penn's Famed 1681 "Letter to the Indians"

Following are excerpts from Penn's famed Letter to the Indians dated August 18, 1681, which he sent ahead of him, prior to meeting them in conference:

> My Friends:
> There is one great God and Power that hath made the world and all things therein, to whom you and I and all people owe their being and well-being, and to whom you and I must one day give an account, for all that we doe in the world; This great God hath written His law in our hearts by which we are taught and commanded to love and help and doe good to one another and not to doe harm and mischief one unto another... I shall shortly come to you myself at which time we may more freely and largely confer and discourse of these matters. Receive those presents and tokens which I have sent to you as a testimony to my goodwill to you and my resolution to live justly, peaceably and friendly with you.
> I am, your loving friend, William Penn.[10]

## Penn's Excellent Relationship with the Indians

Celebrated artist Benjamin West's renowned painting, "Penn's Treaty with the Indians," signed in 1682, celebrates his excellent relationship with them which was never marred by war while he was governor of Pennsylvania. It is on permanent display at the Pennsylvania Academy of Fine Arts in Philadelphia.

## His *Fundamental Constitutions of Pennsylvania* Extol Christianity

In formulating his government, the first Constitution to Penn's *Fundamental Constitutions of Pennsylvania* clearly enunciates the foundations of the colony as being Christian:

> I Constitution
> Considering that it is impossible that any People or Government should ever prosper, where men render not unto God, that which is Gods, as well as to Caesar, that which is Caesars; and also perceiving that disorders and Mischiefs that attend those places where force in matters of faith and worship, and seriously reflecting upon the tenure of the new and Spirituall Government, and that both Christ did not use force and that he did expressly forbid it in his holy Religion, as also that the Testimony of his blessed Messengers was, that the weapons of the Christian warfare were not Carnall but Spirituall; And further weighing that this unpeopled Country can never be planted if there be not due encouragement given to Sober people of all sorts to plant, and that they will not esteem any thing a sufficient encouragement where they are not assured but that after all the Hazards of the Sea, and the troubles of a Wilderness, the Labour of their hands and Sweet of their browes may be made the forfeit of their Conscience, and they and their wives and Children ruin'd because they worship God in some different way from that which may be more generally owned. Therefore, in reverrence to God the Father of lights and Spirits the Author as well as object of all divine knowledge, faith and worship, I do hereby declare for me and myn and establish it for the first fundamental of the Government of my Country that every Person that does or shall reside therein shall have and enjoy the Free Possession of his or her faith and exercise of worship towards God, in such way and manner As every Person shall in Conscience believe is most acceptable to God and so long as every such Person useth not this Christian liberty to Licentiousness, that is to say to speak loosely and prophainly of God Christ or Religion, or to Committ any evil in their Conversation, he or she shall be protected in the enjoyment of the aforesaid Christian liberty by the civill Magistrate (very good).

## William Penn's Frame of Government Extols the Scriptures

From William Penn's well-known "Frame of Government" come these words of wisdom:

> That all persons ... having children ... shall cause such to be instructed in reading and writing, so that they may be able to read the Scriptures and to

write by the time they attain to 12 years of age.

## Penn's Famed 1701 *Charter of Privileges* — a Christian Document

In 1701, Penn issued a *Charter of Privileges* in which he stressed the importance of Freedom of Conscience. He stated:

> Almighty God being the only Lord of Conscience... and Author as well as object of all Divine Knowledge, faith and worship, who only doth enlighten the minds and persuade and convince the understandings of people, I do hereby grant and declare: that no person or persons, inhabiting in this province or territory who shall confess and acknowledge our Almighty God and Creator, Upholder and Ruler of the world; and profess Him or themselves obliged to live quietly under civil government, shall be in any case molested or prejudiced in his or her person or estate... And that all persons who also profess to believe in Jesus Christ, the Savior of the World, shall be capable to serve this government in any capacity, both legislatively or executively.[11]

## Freedom of Religion Under the Banner of Christianity

Having experienced persecution for his faith in Christ and his preaching of the Gospel, Penn stood firm upon the issue of religious liberty. Following is a tribute to him for his tolerance of the Catholic Church:

## St. Joseph's Church

In the heart of historic Philadelphia, not far from Independence Hall, is the site of old St. Joseph's Church, the city's first Roman Catholic Church. It was originally built in the 1700s when Catholic worship was prohibited by law in Britain and America, the present structure dating to 1838. A bronze plaque on the wrought-iron gate outside old St. Joseph's Church told the following poignant story:

> When in 1733, St. Joseph's Roman Catholic Church was founded... it was the only place in the entire English-speaking world where public celebration of the Mass was permitted by law. In 1734, the Provincial Council of Pennsylvania, defending the liberty of worship granted by William Penn to this colony, successfully withstood the demand of the Governor of the Province that this church be outlawed and such liberty be suppressed. Thus was established permanently in our nation the Principle of Religious Freedom which was later embodied into the Constitution of the United States of America.

## William Penn — Devoted Christian Husband and Father

Of his personal life, Penn was married at age 28 to Gulielma Maria Springett. On his first voyage with 100 other fellow-believers to settle

Pennsylvania, he was obliged to leave his family behind.[12] Not knowing what would befall him, Penn wrote the following affectionate letter
to them:

My dear Wife and Children:

My love, which neither sea nor land nor death itself can extinguish or
lessen toward you, most endearly visits you with eternal embraces, and will
abide with you forever; and may the God of my life watch over you and bless
you, and do you good in this world and forever! Some things are upon my spirit
to leave with you in your respective capacities, as I am to the one a husband
and to the rest a father, if I should never see you more in this world.

My dear wife, remember thou wast the love of my youth, and much the joy
of my life; the most beloved as well as most worthy of all my earthly comforts;
and the reason of that love was more thy inward than thy outward excellencies,
which yet were many. God knows, and thou knowest it, I can say it was a match
of Providence's making; and God's image in us both was the first thing, and
the most amiable and engaging ornament in our eyes. Now I am to leave thee,
and that without knowing whether I shall ever see thee more in this world;
take my counsel into thy bosom and let it dwell with thee in my stead while
thou livest.

First: Let the fear of the Lord and a zeal and love to his glory dwell richly
in thy heart; and thou wilt watch for good over thyself and thy dear children
and family, that no rude, light, or bad thing be committed; else God will be
offended, and He will repent Himself of the good He intends thee and thine.

Secondly: Be diligent in meetings for worship and business; stir up thyself
and others herein; it is thy duty and place; and let meetings be kept once a day
in the family to wait upon the Lord who has given us much time for ourselves.
And my dearest, to make thy family matters easy to thee, divide thy time and
be regular; it is easy and sweet; thy retirement will afford thee to do it; as in
the morning to view the business of the house and fix it as thou desirest, seeing
all be in order; that by thy counsel all may move, and to thee render an account
every evening. The time for work, for walking, for meals, may be certain—at
least as near as may be; and grieve not thyself with careless servants; they will
disorder thee; rather pay them and let them go if they will not be better by
admonitions; this is best to avoid many words, which I know wound the soul
and offend the Lord.

Thirdly: Cast up thy income and see what it daily amounts to; by which
thou mayest be sure to have it in thy sight and power to keep within compass;
and I beseech thee to live low and sparingly till my debts are paid; and then
enlarge as thou seest it convenient. Remember thy mother's example when
thy father's public-spiritedness had worsted his estate, which is my case. I
know thou lovest plain things, and art averse to the pomps of the world—a
nobility natural to thee...

Fourthly: And now, my dearest, let me recommend to thy care my dear
children; abundantly beloved of me as the Lord's blessings, and the sweet
pledges of our mutual and endeared affection. Above all things endeavor to
breed them up in the love and virtue, and that holy plain way of it which we
have lived in, that the world in no part of it get into my family. I had rather

they were homely than finely bred as to outward behavior; yet I love sweetness mixed with gravity and cheerfulness tempered with sobriety. Religion in the heart leads into this true civility, teaching men and women to be mild and courteous in their behavior, an accomplishment worthy indeed of praise...[13]

## Penn's Magnificent Prayer for Philadelphia

Of great significance to all Americans, is William Penn's magnificent *Prayer for Philadelphia*, delivered in 1684. It appears on a plaque within City Hall itself, the building upon which his magnificent statue stands with outstretched hand over the city he loved and prayed for:

And thou, Philadelphia, the Virgin settlement of this province named before thou wert born. What love, what care, what service and what travail have there been to bring thee forth and preserve thee from such as would abuse and defile thee. O that thou mayest be kept from the evil that would overwhelm thee. That faithful to the God of thy mercies, in the Life of Righteousness, thou mayest be preserved to the end. My soul prays to God for thee, that thou mayest stand in the day of trial, that thy children may be blest of the Lord and thy people saved by His Power.[14]

# ROBERT "KING" CARTER
## Builder of "Christ Church"
## (1663 - 1732)

### Carter — A Significant Figure of America's History

Robert "King" Carter was one of the most significant figures of America's founding period history. His property comprised 300,000 acres of land in colonial Virginia.[1] Born in 1663, his father died when he was only 6, his older brother John Carter II becoming his guardian. As stipulated in his father's will, he began his schooling under an indentured servant with some schooling.[2] He was then sent to England from 1672-1678, to board with a Mr. Bailey for his grammar school education.[3] Of his school days abroad, Carter writes:

> From my owne observations when I was in England, those boyes that wore the finest close and had the most money in their pocketts still went away, with the least learning in their heads.[4]

Carter's studies comprised grammar, rhetoric and logic, along with its roots in Latin, Greek and some Hebrew.

*Sanctuary of "Christ Church, 1732."*

ROBERT CARTER OF NOMINI HALL, REPRODUCED
FROM AN ORIGINAL PORTRAIT BELIEVED TO HAVE
BEEN PAINTED BY SIR JOSHUA REYNOLDS

## A Devoted Christian Husband and Father

Robert Carter was a devoted Christian husband and father of 12. He brought up his children in the love and admonition of the Lord Jesus Christ. Ritualism and hierarchy of the established church were of no importance to Carter who wished to impart biblical truth and high standards of morality to his offspring.[5]

## Builder of Christ Church, Virginia

He is remembered for the church which he built in the early 1700's, historic Christ Church in Lancaster County, Virginia, which is still maintained today.

## Robert Carter's Correspondence — "I am no Stranger to the Story of the Gospel."

Following are selected passages from Carter's personal correspondence. They disclose his adherence to the Gospel message of forgiveness and the sound guidance and counsel he offered his son.

To a Mr. Perry in England on July 22, 1720:

> ...My son, I find, upon the stool of repentance. It will be well he will come to his senses at last. He makes me large promises to retrench himself and that he will for the future call upon you for no more by the quarter than £37:10, and will make the best use of his time that he has to stay in England, by a close application to his study. These are agreeable promises if he keeps them. He hath sent me an account of How, the tailor's, for fifty-odd pound, which it seems I must pay. He expects it will cost him some money to be called to bar, which I must not grudge at. He begs of me to forget his past extravagances and desires I may not insist upon a particular account from him, and that he will give me no more occasion of future complaints. Upon these terms I am willing to shut up with him. Thus you see I am no stranger to the story of the Gospel. ...political jars here I hope will be laid aside for some time at least. All things at present carry the fact of peace, a most comprehensive word of all sublunary blessings.[6]

To John, his son, on July 23, 1720 (in relation to the letter above):

Dear Son John:

I have lately received your letters in Mr. Perry's packet of April date, in which you make me repeated promises to retrench your expenses and reduce them to the bounds I have set you—that is, to take no more from Mr. Perry than £37:10 per quarter, except the charge of calling you to the bar. You likewise promise me a strict improvement of your time that you have to spend in England, by a close application of your studies. May Heaven keep you fixed to this resolution without wavering. It will prove a cordial to your heart all the days of your life. Upon these hopes I shall pass over what's past, according to

CHRIST CHURCH—1732
VIRGINIA

*The church that Robert Carter built.*

your desire, and have ordered Mr. Perry to pay your tailor's bill of fifty-odd pound. Your relations here are in health; all that are capable, I believe, write to you themselves. Pray take a little more care of your brothers in England. The rest is to beg God's blessing upon you...[7]

## Carter's Outstanding Achievements

What were some of Carter's great achievements which so distinguish him in our nation's history?

A vestryman in Christ Church, the church he built for his parish, he also served as Justice of the Peace.[8] At the age of 28 he took his seat in the House of Burgesses at Jamestown as a member for Lancaster County. In 1696 he became Speaker of the House, and in 1697 filled the position of chairman of the Committee of Propriations and Grievances—the most important committee in that body.[9] After being elected member of the Council, in 1699 he became Colonial Treasurer, holding this position until 1704. He was highly esteemed and respected by all the Burgesses.[10] His duties as member of the Council, together with other leading men of the colony, comprised performing executive, legislative and judicial functions. Fellow members were William Byrd I, Edmund Jenings, Benjamin Harrison, James Blair and others.[11]

In 1715 Carter was appointed lieutenant commander of Lancaster and Northumberland counties. At the death of Governor Hugh Drysdale, "King" Carter, as president of the Council, assumed the administration of government, officially approved by George II in July 1726. This governorship Carter executed admirably for more than a year.[12] Among his impressive services to God and country, this American son also acted as rector and visitor of the College of William and Mary, being made a trustee of the college in 1729, and endowing the college with a handsome scholarship.[13]

## Robert "King" Carter's Epitaph —
## "He built at his Own Expense Christ Church —
## The Widowed and Orphaned Lament his Loss."

Buried in the yard at Christ Church where he had worshiped, his epitaph reads:

> Here lies Robert Carter, Esq., an honorable man, who exalted his high birth by noble endowments and pure morals. He sustained the College of William and Mary in the most trying times. He was Governor, Speaker of the House and Treasurer ... he built and endowed, at his own expense, this sacred edifice, a lasting monument of his piety to God. Entertaining his friends with kindness, he was neither a prodigal nor a thrifty host....At length, full of honor

and years, having discharged all the duties of an exemplary life, he departed from this world on the 4th day of August 1732, in the 69th year of his age. The wretched, the widowed, and the orphans, bereaved of their comforter, protector and father, alike lament his loss.[14]

# CHAPTER III
Revolutionary

*After the original marble statue in the Senate Connecting Corridor,*
*U.S. Capitol, Washington, D.C.*

# SAMUEL ADAMS
## Organizer of the American Revolution
## (1722 - 1803)

An inscription on the famed Adams statue in Boston, reads as follows:

Samuel Adams, 1722 - 1803, A Patriot
He organized the Revolution and
signed the Declaration of Independence
Governor, A true Leader of the People
A Statesman, Incorruptible and Fearless
Erected A.D. 1880
bequeathed to the City of Boston
by Jonathan Phillips

Further to this impressive memorial, we glean the following accomplishments by this Son of the American Revolution:

| | |
|---|---|
| 1722 | Born in Boston, September 16 |
| 1740 | Graduated at Harvard College |
| 1743 | Takes his Master's Degree from Cambridge |
| 1747-48 | Organizes a Political club and Newspaper |
| 1764 | Drafts the Boston Instructions |
| | Proposes a union of the Colonies in opposition to Parliament |
| 1765-74 | Member of the Legislature |
| 1765 | Writes the Massachusetts Resolves |
| 1766 | Conducts a Controversy with the Governor |
| 1768 | **Declares for Independence** |
| 1769 | Writes "An Appeal to the World" |
| 1770 | Demands the Removal of the Troops |
| 1772 | Author of "The Rights of the Colonists" |
| 1773 | Calls for a Continental Congress |
| | Opposes Landing of the Tea |
| 1774-81 | Member of the Continental Congress |
| 1775 | Member of the Provincial Congress |
| | Secretary of State, Councillor |
| 1776 | **Signs the Declaration of Independence** |
| 1777 | Member of the Board of War |
| 1779 | Member of the State Constitutional Convention |
| 1781-84 | President of the Massachusetts Senate |
| 1786 | Senator |
| 1787 | President of the Senate, and Councillor |
| 1788 | Member of the Convention to adopt the Federal Constitution |
| 1789-93 | Lieutenant Governor |
| 1793-97 | Governor |

## Samuel Adams — "the Visible Product of the Church."

What made Samuel Adams great? The historic annals of his own church, the Old South Meeting House in Boston, tell us that he was "the visible product of the New England Church."[1] Nothing else could have made him what he was. He was born and nurtured, trained and molded under its powerful and penetrating influence. Unquestionably, the biblical principles and republican government of these Christian churches, under life-changing ministries produced the sound, clear-thinking patriots whose wisdom laid the foundations of our freedoms.[2] The doctrine of the dignity of man, made in God's image, and hence, the equality of human rights and liberties, as God's inalienable gift to man, found its source in the Sacred Scriptures.[3]

## Adams — The Father of the American Revolution

Hence it is that Samuel Adams gained the reputation of being: The father of the American Revolution; the American Cato; the Chief Incendiary; Tribune of the People; the Cromwell of New England and The Last of the Puritans.[4] These titles all express the indelible stamp of a superior mind and extraordinary feats of wisdom and courage.

And what were the notable character traits which produced a great patriot and leader, pointing the way out of tyranny and oppression by an alien power? Brave as Adams was in resisting oppression by force of arms, he showed equal valor in refusing all offers to give up his beliefs for either advancement in salary or position. "Incorruptible," is a name which Samuel Adams has left to our nation. It is engraved upon our early history.[5]

Let the men of America take note today—in order that our politicians may see it; that our statesmen may comprehend its significance; and that our youth may inscribe its meaning upon the tablets of their hearts—and thus understand and merit their freedoms, once again.

## A Humble, Other-Centered Man

Samuel Adams was a humble and other-centered man, a great organizer. His rare ability to detect talent and bring it into public service, was one of the marked traits of this great American statesman.[6] This gave him increasing influence among the people who were not slow to see the purity of his motives, when they saw his selfless nature. Though the instigator of our independence, he always put others before himself, willing to give away the honors which he had earned. This is a magnificent tribute, both to his integrity of character and his intellectual superiority.[7]

## Thomas Jefferson Considers Adams –
## "the Fountain of Our More Important Measures"

Thomas Jefferson said of Adams, "I always considered him, more than any other member, the fountain of our more important measures." Men followed him because they saw that he was fit to lead. As Christ tells us in His Word, the Gospel: "He who would be first among you must be the servant of all" (Luke 22:26). Men looked up to him because they knew that their interests were in the hands of one whose life was regulated by his duty to God and man.[8]

## Samuel Adams, the Bible and Politics

In order to fully grasp the biblical mindset and value-system of this great American patriot, I quote from his famed Oration given at the State House (Independence Hall) on August 1, 1776. It is now housed in the Rare Book Collection of the Library of Congress in our nation's capital. Throughout this Address, Adams quotes the Holy Scriptures to undergird his thesis, which is that, "...Our Fore-fathers threw off the yoke of popery in religion; for you is reserved the honor of levelling the popery of politics. They opened the Bible to all, and maintained the capacity of every man to judge for himself in religion..."

> Countrymen, and Brethren,
> I would gladly have declined an honor to which I find myself unequal. I have not the calmness and impartiality which the infinite importance of this occasion demands. I will not deny the charge of my enemies that resentment for the accumulated injuries of our country, and an ardour for her glory, rising to enthusiasm, may deprive me of that accuracy of judgment and expression which men of cooler passions may possess... Truth loves an appeal to the common sense of mankind. Your unperverted understandings can best determine on subjects of a practical nature. The positions and plans which are said to be above the comprehension of the multitude may be always suspected to be visionary and fruitless. He who made all men hath made the truths necessary to human happiness obvious to all. Our Fore-fathers threw off the yoke of popery in religion; for you is reserved the honor of levelling the popery of politics. They opened the Bible to all, and maintained the capacity of every man to judge for himself in religion. Are we sufficient for the comprehension of the sublimest spiritual Truths, and unequal to material and temporal ones? Heaven hath trusted us with the management of things for Eternity, and man denies us ability to judge of the present, or to know from our feelings and experience what will make us happy —
> ...The hand of Heaven appears to have led us on to be perhaps humble instruments, and means in the great providential dispensation which is

completing. We have fled from the political Sodom; let us not look back lest we perish and become a monument of infamy and derision to the world... We cannot suppose that our opposition has made a corrupt and dissipated nation more friendly to America, or created in them a greater respect for the rights of mankind... Courage then, my countrymen! Our contest is not only whether we ourselves shall be free, but whether there shall be left to mankind, an asylum on earth, for civil and religious liberty? ... And, brethren and fellow-countrymen, if it was ever granted to mortals to trace the designs of Providence, and interpret its manifestations in favor of their cause, we may, with humility of soul, cry out, not unto us, not unto us, but to thy name be the praise... the gradual advances of our oppressors enabling us to prepare for our defense; the unusual fertility of our lands and clemency of the seasons— the success which at first attended our feeble arms, producing unanimity among our friends and reducing our internal foes to acquiescence — these are all strong and palpable marks and assurances, that Providence is yet gracious unto Zion, that it will turn away the captivity of Jacob. Our glorious Reformers, when they broke through the fetters of superstition, effected more than could be expected from an age so darkened: But they left much to be done by their posterity. They lopped off indeed some of the branches of popery, but they left the root and stock when they left us under the domination of human systems... and decisions, usurping the infallibility which can be attributed to Revelation alone. They dethroned one usurper only to raise up another. They refused allegiance to the pope, only to place the Civil Magistrate on the throne of Christ, vested with authority to enact laws, and inflict penalties in His Kingdom. And if we now cast our eyes over the nations of the earth we shall find, that instead of possessing *the pure Religion of the Gospel*, they may be divided either into infidels, who deny the Truth; or politicians, who make religion a stalking horse for their ambition; or professors who walk in the trammels of orthodoxy, and are more attentive to traditions and ordinances of men, than to oracles of Truth. The Civil Magistrate has everywhere contaminated Religion, by making it an engine of Policy; and Freedom of thought and the right of public judgment, in matters of conscience, driven from every other corner of the earth, direct their course to this happy country as their last asylum. Let us cherish the noble guests and shelter them under the wings of an Universal Toleration. Be this the seat of unbounded Religious Freedom. She will bring with her, in her train, Industry, Wisdom and Commerce. She thrives most when left to shoot forth in her natural luxuriance, and asks from human policy, only not to be checked in her growth by artificial encouragement... No man had once a greater veneration for Englishmen than I entertained. They were dear to me as branches of the same parental trunk, and partakers of the same Religion and Laws: I still view with respect the remains of the Constitution as I would a lifeless body which had once been animated by a great and heroic soul; But when I am raised by the din of arms; when I behold legions of foreign assassins paid by Englishmen to embrue their hands in our blood, when I tread over the uncoffined bones of my countrymen, neighbours and friends, when I see the locks of a venerable father torn by savage hands, and a feeble mother clasping her infants to her bosom, and on her knees imploring their lives from her own slaves whom Englishmen have allured to treachery and murder; when I behold my country, once the seat of industry, peace, and plenty, changed by Englishmen to a theatre of blood, and misery, Heaven forgive me, if I cannot root out those passions which it has implanted in my bosom, and detect submission to a people who have either ceased to be human, or have not virtue enough to feel their own wretchedness and servitude...[9]

The organizer of the American Revolution concludes his unforgettable Oration from Independence Hall with a rally to the cause of Independence:

...That these American states may never cease to be free and independent![10]

It is clear from the above words of Samuel Adams, that "the Bible set us, as Americans, free from the tyranny of popery and an alien power." This is the foundation stone of our liberties and freedoms. As Christ Jesus says Himself: "If you abide in My word, then you are truly disciples of mine, and you shall know the truth, and the truth shall make you free." (John 8:32)

## The Clarion Call of the American Revolution

I conclude this chapter on Samuel Adams with the clarion call of America's Revolution, given at the dedication of Samuel Adams' memorial in his church – the Old South Meeting House, Boston:

> God give us men!
> A time like this demands
> Strong minds, great hearts,
> true faith and ready hands;
> Men whom the lust of office
> does not kill;
> Men whom the spoils of office cannot buy;
> Men who possess opinions and
> a will;
> Men who have honor —
> Men who will not lie;
> Tall men, sun-crowned,
> Who live above the fog
> In public duty and in private thinking.[11]

# JOHN WITHERSPOON
## George Washington's close Friend and Sponsor
## (1723 - 1794)

## John Witherspoon —
## a Beacon on the Highway of American History

The life of John Witherspoon stands out like a beacon on the highway of history, giving us one of the most illuminating and interesting phases of the American Revolution. He was the spiritual inspiration behind the signing of the Declaration of Independence, his famed July 4, 1776 speech given to the Continental Congress causing its resolution.[1] His great eloquence dispelled any hesitation which his cosigners might have had. Just prior to the vote on signing the Declaration of Independence, one of the members of the Continental Congress argued, "We are not ripe for Revolution." Witherspoon responded with these words: "Not ripe, Sir, in my judgment we are not only ripe, but unless some action is taken, we will be rotting."[2]

## Witherspoon's Galvanizing Speech to the Continental Congress

His galvanizing speech followed. It so motivated members of the Continental Congress, that they rushed forward and signed this immortal document. His famed speech is here recorded:

> There is a tide in the affairs of men, a nick of time we now perceive before us. To hesitate is to consent to slavery. That noble instrument on your table, which insures immortality to its authors, should be subscribed this very morning by every pen in this House. For my part, of property I have some, of reputation more. That reputation is staked upon the issue of this contest, that property pledged, and although these gray hairs must soon descend into the sepulchre, I had infinitely rather they should descend thither by the hands of the public executioner than desert at this crisis the sacred cause of my Country.[3]

## Witherspoon was George Washington's
## Devoted Friend in Congress

During the War of Independence, John Witherspoon was George Washington's constant and devoted friend in Congress. He often went as a Commissioner of Congress to advise him, spending considerable time at Valley Forge, as he endeavored to lessen the suffering of the army.[4]

He was one of the firebrands of the American Revolution, being constantly reviled by the loyalists for his outspokenness. Whenever

JOHN WITHERSPOON

NEW JERSEY

*After the original bronze statue of John Witherspoon,*
*Connecticut Avenue and N Street, N.W., Washington, D.C.*

there was an anti-American demonstration, effigies of Washington and Witherspoon were burned side-by-side. Hence, Witherspoon was described as "Washington's twin."[5]

## America's Greatest Educator

His brilliance and caliber gained for him the reputation of being America's greatest educator; his patriotism was critical in igniting the American Revolution and in laying the foundation for Washington's appointment as Commander-in-Chief of the Continental Armies. In 1776, the Assembly asked him to draft a document denouncing the policies of the crown of England in the American colonies. Witherspoon thus declared the claims of parliament to be "unjust in the highest degree."[6]

## Witherspoon Declares a National Day of Prayer and Fasting

In self defense, the Americans were obliged to declare war. This they did in order to obtain their freedoms. At that time of intense crisis, Witherspoon became America's most fervent patriot.[7]

His wisdom, prudence and practical thinking led him to urge Congress to declare May 17, 1776 as a National Day of Prayer and Fasting, in order to beseech God's blessings upon their proceedings.[8]

Services were held in Princeton Chapel on that day, Witherspoon giving an Address on the state of affairs in the American colonies and boldly preaching independence from Great Britain. In Glasgow, however, Witherspoon was labelled "a rebel."[9]

His patriotism, zeal and brilliance of speech raised armies, won battles and initiated a unique form of government, which has been the admiration of the world for more than two centuries.

## President of Princeton College, Dean of the House of Burgesses and Minister of the Gospel

As President of Princeton College, he signified culture; as Dean of the colonial House of Congress, he personified the State and as a Minister of the Gospel, he preached the Word of God, with spiritual depth and fervor. The results were miraculous. Hesitation vanished, and from Massachusetts to Virginia, armies were organized. The Provincial Congress in New York, of which John Jay was a member, sent him a letter of encouragement, stating that,

> the reasons assigned by the Continental Congress are cogent and conclusive and while we lament the cruel necessity which has rendered the measure

unavoidable, we approve the same, and will, at the risk of our lives and fortunes, join with the other colonies in supporting it.[10]

## Witherspoon and the Sons of Freedom

The Sons of Freedom in New York tore down the equestrian statue of George III, which stood in Bowling Green, authorizing Witherspoon to melt the monument into bullets.

## Princeton becomes Temporary Capital of the United Colonies

When a section of the Continental Army mutinied and drove Congress from Philadelphia, Witherspoon invited his colleagues to resume their sessions in Nassau Hall on the Princeton College Campus, and upon their acceptance, Princeton became the temporary Capital of the United Colonies. Witherspoon thus guided the councils of the Continental Congress in the library of "Old Nassau" from June 26 to November 4, 1783.[11]

Nassau Hall was captured by the British in 1776, and was restored to the Americans in 1777, at the Battle of Princeton. This was the great turning point of the war. George Washington paid Witherspoon fifty guineas to utilize Princeton College as his barracks. Witherspoon, in turn, used these funds to have a full-length portrait of Washington painted. It now hangs in Nassau Hall in a frame which once adorned the image of King George II, shot away by an American cannon ball.[12] The Continental Congress honored Witherspoon in 1785 by adjourning their deliberations to attend the Commencement exercises. The Commander of the Continental Armies being present, he was given an ovation by both Congress and the students. Witherspoon imparted to his students a fervent spirit of patriotism. This was done by means of historic events, such as the story of Thomas Melville, a Princeton graduate, who took part in the Boston Tea Party. Another of his students, being accused of disloyalty by the colonists, simply displayed his Princeton diploma which was properly credentialled by Witherspoon.[13]

## James Madison, a Student of Witherspoon's

James Madison, father of the U.S. Constitution (which Witherspoon signed in 1787 as a delegate from New Jersey) had been one of his talented students. A noted historian states that,

It was from John Witherspoon that Madison imbibed the lesson of freedom in matters of conscience.[14]

## Congress is Spurred by Witherspoon
## to Obtain Recognition of Independence Abroad

Being spurred on by Witherspoon, Congress applied to the governments of many countries to recognize America's resolution that "the delegates should take steps such as they deem necessary for obtaining foreign alliances." Following this step, Benjamin Franklin was sent as Minister Plenipotentiary to the Court of France to intercede for America's autonomy, his activities during this mission being monitored by Witherspoon. The latter was also instrumental in planning the agenda of other American representatives overseas. The illustrious Marquis de Lafayette, who risked his life in the War for American Independence, responded to Witherspoon's appeal and supported him.

## Witherspoon the Diplomat, Politician and Biblical Scholar

Through his diplomatic successes, it became clear that Witherspoon understood the intricacies of politics, as well as the infallible truths contained in the Bible — the Word of God.[15]

In this War for Independence the great principles of freedom, affecting the entire known world, hung in the balance.

## A Statue is Erected in our Nation's Capital
## to Memorialize Witherspoon

To memorialize this foremost American Christian statesman, a statue was erected at Connecticut Avenue and N Street. Witherspoon's unforgettable speech of July 4, 1776 is inscribed upon its base. This striking memorial to a great American statesman and preacher was erected by the Presbyterian Church of the Covenant nearby, the pedestal being a gift of Congress. President Woodrow Wilson, at the dedication ceremonies, reflected upon John Witherspoon's dynamic role in gaining for us, the liberties and freedoms which we, as Americans, now enjoy.

> America was most willing to receive this redoubtable champion of an orthodox people, because he had established in Scotland a fame as a writer and a preacher which bespoke in him something more than the mere minister of the Gospel, bespoke in him the qualities of the statesman, of the man whose gift it is to lead, no matter what the sphere of leadership may be which he attempts.
>
> When he came to America he reorganized the course of study and revivified the whole administration of the college of New Jersey at Princeton, but he did more, as had been expected. It was only eight years before the signing of the Declaration of Independence, affairs were gathering for a very significant period of history. He was almost immediately sent to the Legislature

of New Jersey, the Colonial Assembly, and he was presently sent to the convention which framed the first Constitution of the state. Just before the signing of the Declaration of Independence he was made a Delegate to the Continental Congress, and added his voice to those counsels which brought about the promulgation of that great epoch-making document.

Then more important still, he, more assiduously than any other member, continued to lend his counsel throughout the Revolutionary war; and no man in it represented so consistently as he did the wise counsel which was necessary to sustain that difficult and sometimes discouraging contest. He, more than any other man in the Continental Congress, urged the maintenance of such measures as Washington felt to be indispensable for the support of his armies and the success of the cause. It was as if Washington himself spoke in council for the things which Washington in the field needed, when John Witherspoon stood upon his feet in the Continental Congress.

Then he returned to Princeton to pick up the scattered threads of the organization of that demoralized institution, which had gone to pieces like so many other things during the Revolution, and the closing work of his life was the rehabilitation of the college to which he had devoted so much of his thought and energy.

That, in the main outline, is the story of his life, but we are not interested in the historical and biographical detail so much as in the effort to recover a distinct image of the man and to make a reasonable assessment of the powers that were in him and the qualities which distinguished him.[16]

## Witherspoon Denounces the Theatre and Ungodly Play Acting

John Witherspoon's sterling character shines through his bold stance against what he terms "heathen idolatry," represented by the role-playing of immoral and degenerate characters on stage. In denouncing Theatre and its promotion of vice through reenactments of ungodly living and bad example, Witherspoon makes a sensible appeal to Christendom of his day, as follows:

Dear Christian Brethren,

We now address you, and recommend it to you, in the name of the Great God our Saviour, whose Disciples you are, to withhold all support from the Play-House.

In this recommendation, we are confident, that we are urging upon your attention a plain Christian duty. It is inconsistent with your holy calling to countenance the Theatre, because, in its origin and history it has been a public nuisance in society, in its present constitution it is criminal, under every form it is useless, and it must necessarily tend to demoralize any people who give it their support.

1. The Theatre owes its origin to the revelry which accompanied the celebration of the feast of Bacchus, the God of wine, in the licentious ages of heathen idolatry. Dramatic representations formed a part of that worship which the Athenians offered to this false God; and were perfectly in character with the worshippers themselves and the object of their adoration. The actors imitated whatever the poets thought proper to feign of their idol. Men and

women, in masquerade, appeared night and day before the public, practising the most gross immoralities, and indulging in every species of debauchery. The Goat, which is said to be injurious to the vine, and the name of which in Greek is Tragos, is the animal sacrificed on this occasion to Bacchus; and hence the revelry itself was called tragedy, and the actors tragedians. The feasts were celebrated during the vintage. So gratifying however did those shows prove to the public taste in Athens, that they were demanded more frequently than the season, to which they originally belonged, recurred. Thespis, accordingly, about five hundred and thirty-six years before the Christian era, embodied a company of actors, and carried them about with him on his cart to perform tragedies wherever an audience could be assembled. And afterwards under the direction of Æschylus, a public Theatre was erected ...[17]

## Witherspoon Traces the Origins of the Theatre to Bacchus, the God of Wine

From the above exposé, John Witherspoon has astutely traced the origins of the Theatre to Bacchus, the god of wine; the Athenians of the Apostle Paul's day offering dramatic plays as part of their worship to this false god of revelry and licentiousness. This is directly in opposition to the Word of God, which tells us that,

And you were dead in your trespasses and sins, in which you formerly walked according to the course of this world, according to the prince of the power of the air, of the spirit that is now working in the sons of disobedience. Among them we too all formerly lived in the lusts of our flesh, indulging the desires of the flesh and of the mind, and were by nature children of wrath, even as the rest. But God, being rich in mercy, because of His great love with which He loved us, even when we were dead in our transgressions, made us alive together with Christ (by grace you have been saved), and raised us up with Him, and seated us with Him in the heavenly places, in Christ Jesus, in order that in the ages to come He might show the surpassing riches of His grace in kindness toward us in Christ Jesus. For by grace you have been saved through faith; and that not of yourselves, it is the gift of God; not as a result of works, that no one should boast.
Ephesians 2:1-9

How much more treacherous is the theatre reenacted through films which beam vice and licentiousness hourly into millions of American homes; contaminating and indoctrinating innocent children at a very early age, and coaxing them into its alluring and subtle trap.

## Should a Christian Minister be involved in Civic and Community Affairs?

Witherspoon also set the stage for a Christian minister's involvement in civic and community affairs. His response to a newspaper article addressing the Georgia Constitution, shows sound reasoning and intelligent argument in favor of such involvement. It provides a provocative challenge to pastors and ministers in modern-day America, who would avoid such involvement, on the basis of violating Scripture:

## On the Georgia Constitution

Sir,

In your paper of Saturday last, you have given us the new Constitution of Georgia, in which I find the following resolution, "No clergyman of any denomination shall be a member of the General Assembly." I would be very well satisfied that some of the gentlemen who have made that an essential article of this constitution, or who have inserted and approve it in other constitutions, would be pleased to explain a little, the principles, as well as to ascertain the meaning of it.

Perhaps we understand pretty generally, what is meant by a clergyman, viz. a person regularly called and set apart to the ministry of the gospel, and authorized to preach and administer the sacraments of the Christian religion. Now suffer me to ask this question; Before any man among us was ordained a minister, was he not a citizen of the United States, and if being in Georgia, a citizen of the state of Georgia? Had he not then a right to be elected a member of the assembly, if qualified in point of property? How then has he lost, or why is he deprived of this right? Is it by offense or disqualification? Is it a sin against the public to become a minister? Does it merit that the person who is guilty of it should be immediately deprived of one of his most important rights as a citizen? Is not this inflicting a penalty which always supposes an offense? Is a minister then disqualified for the office of a senator or representative? Does this calling and profession render him stupid or ignorant? ... Do these all continue clergymen, or do they cease to be clergymen, and by that cessation return to, or recover the honorable privileges of laymen?[18]

Here, the only preacher-signer of the Declaration of Independence presents a powerful case in support of his argument. Broadly speaking, that of Christians holding public office.

It would behoove Christian pastors and educators throughout our nation to become well-acquainted with America's foundational historic documents, in order to preserve our freedoms – which are fast ebbing away. The former have been removed from public view and consciousness in recent years at an accelerated pace, without one word being uttered in their defense.

GEORGE WASHINGTON WITH
HIS RIGHT HAND UPON THE
BIBLE

*After the original bronze sculpture by Joseph Alexis Bailly in front of
Independence Hall, Chestnut Street, Philadelphia.*

# GEORGE WASHINGTON
## Man, or Giant among Men?
## (1732 - 1799)

George Washington was the son of Augustine Washington and his second wife, Mary Ball. He was a direct descendant of King John of England and nine of the 25 Baron Sureties of the Magna Charta. His father died in 1743 when the boy was 11 years old. Therefore, until age 16, he lived with his half brother, Augustine, on the family estate in Westmoreland County, 40 miles from Fredericksburg, Virginia.

### George Washington as a Boy

At the age of 15, this exceptional young man copied in meticulous handwriting the "110 Rules of Civility and Decent Behaviour in Company and Conversation."[1] These maxims were so fully lived out in George Washington's life that historians have regarded them as important influences in forming his character.

Here are some of these rules. They fall into several categories, beginning with the basics of personal grooming and advancing to the inner life of a well-rounded individual.

### I   Personal Grooming
5) If you cough, sneeze, sigh or yawn, do it not loud but privately; and speak not in your yawning, but put your handkerchief or hand before your face and turn aside.
15) Keep your nails clean and short, also your hands and teeth clean yet without showing any great concern for them.

### II   Manners in Interaction with Others
6) Sleep not when others speak, sit not when others stand, speak not when you should hold your peace, walk not on when others stop.
14) Turn not your back to others especially in speaking, jog not the table or desk on which another reads or writes, lean not upon anyone.

### III   Consideration and Concern for Others
18) Read no letters, books, or papers in company but when there is a necessity for the doing of it you must ask leave.
19) Let your countenance be pleasant but in serious matters somewhat grave.

### IV   Moral Behavior
22) Shew not yourself glad at the misfortune of another though he were your enemy.
109) Let your recreations be manfull not sinfull.

### V   Spiritual Life
108) When you speak of God, or His attributes, let it be seriously and with reverence. Honor and obey your natural parents although they be poor.

110)  Labour to keep alive in your breast that little spark of celestial fire called conscience.

## Washington Defends the Rights of the Colonies

When England and the American colonies were at odds, Washington took an early stand in defending the rights of the colonies, although he, together with other American leaders, hoped for reconciliation. He saw the Stamp Act as "a direful attack on the liberties of the colonists."[2] In 1769, he believed that action should be taken "to maintain the liberty which we have derived from our ancestors."[3] As a member of the Virginia Assembly, he presented, and secured, a non-importation agreement.

## Commander of the Continental Army

In 1774-1775, Washington represented Virginia as a delegate to the Continental Congress. In the summer of 1775, it became necessary to send a Continental army to Boston. At this moment of crisis, John Adams had the foresight and wisdom of uniting the South with New England in their common cause for independence, by selecting a Virginian to lead her army. At Adams' recommendation, Colonel George Washington was chosen.[4] In December 1777, Washington was camped in Valley Forge for the winter, his troops of 11,000 suffering great deprivation due to the cold, sickness and lack of food and clothing.

## George Washington's Prayer at Valley Forge

But this godly man knew the source of his strength and provision, calling out to God for His help. Isaac Potts witnessed the following event, as related by Ruth Anna Potts:

In 1777 while the American army lay at Valley Forge, a good old Quaker by the name of Potts had occasion to pass through a thick woods near headquarters. As he traversed the dark brown forest, he heard, at a distance before him, a voice which as he advanced became more fervid and interested. Approaching with slowness and circumspection, whom should he behold in a dark bower, apparently formed for the purpose, but the Commander-in-Chief of the armies of the United Colonies on his knees in the act of devotion to the Ruler of the Universe! At the moment when friend Potts, concealed by the trees, came up, Washington was interceding for his beloved country. With tones of gratitude that labored for adequate expression he adored that exuberant goodness which, from the depth of obscurity, had exalted him to the head of a great nation, and that nation fighting at fearful odds for all the world holds dear... Soon as the General had finished his devotions and had retired, Friend Potts returned to his

The Prayer Window in the
Congressional Prayer Room, U.S. Capitol, Washington, D.C.
In the center, Washington is kneeling in prayer. Above him are the words
"One Nation Under God." Around him are the words from Psalm 16:1
– "Preserve Me O God, for in thee do I place my Trust."
Around the outer border our 50 states in the Union are inscribed.

house, and threw himself into a chair by the side of his wife. "Heigh! Isaac!" said she with tenderness, "thee seems agitated; what's the matter?" "Indeed, my dear," quoth he, "if I appear agitated 'tis no more than what I am. I have seen this day what I shall never forget. Till now I have thought that a Christian and a soldier were characters incompatible; but if George Washington be not a man of God, I am mistaken, and still more shall I be disappointed if God do not through him perform some great thing for this country."[5]

## Washington's Godly Character

Washington's godly character earned him the loyalty and respect of his volunteer army. He faithfully exhorted them about the importance of maintaining the spiritual caliber of their lives, even in the midst of war, as shown below:

> While we are zealously performing the duties of good citizens and soldiers, we certainly ought not to be inattentive to the higher duties of religion. To the distinguished character of patriot, it should be our highest glory to laud the more distinguished character of Christian. The signal instances of Providential goodness which we have experienced and which have now almost crowned our labors with complete success demand from us in a peculiar manner the warmest returns of gratitude and piety to the Supreme Author of all good.[6]

## Thomas Jefferson Describes Washington's Christian Character

Thomas Jefferson's description of the character of George Washington further shows his qualifications for the task to which he was called:

> He was incapable of fear, meeting personal dangers with the calmest unconcern. Perhaps the strongest feature in his character was prudence, never acting until every circumstance, every consideration, was maturely weighed; refraining if he saw a doubt, but, when once decided, going through with his purpose, whatever obstacles opposed. His integrity was most pure, his justice the most flexible I have ever known, no motive of interest or consanguinity, or friendship or hatred, being able to bias his decision. He was in every sense of the words, a wise, a good and a great man.[7]

## God's Hand upon the Nation

Washington knew that the hand of God had been strong in shaping not only his own personal life, but that of the newly formed nation. Note the following letter he wrote on August 20, 1778 to his Virginian friend, Thomas Nelson:

> The hand of Providence has been so conspicuous in all this (the course of the war) that he must be worse than an infidel that lacks faith, and more wicked that has not gratitude to acknowledge his obligations; but it will be time enough for me to turn Preacher when my present appointment ceases.

# Washington Proclaims National Day of Thanksgiving — February 19, 1795

It was not in this man's destiny to become a preacher, but as president of the United States he was able to channel that sense of gratitude to Almighty God, felt by him and his countrymen, into a national tradition, continuous and unbroken to this day. On January 1, 1795, he wrote his famed *National Thanksgiving Proclamation*:

When we review the calamities which afflict so many other nations, the present condition of the United States affords much matter of consolation and satisfaction. Our exemption hitherto from foreign war, an increasing prospect of the continuance of that exemption, the great degree of internal tranquility we have enjoyed, the recent confirmation of that tranquility by the suppression of an insurrection* which so wantonly threatened it, the happy course of our public affairs in general, the unexampled prosperity of all classes of our citizens, are circumstances which peculiarly mark our situation with indications of the divine beneficence toward us. In such a state of things it is in an especial manner our duty as a people, with devout reverence and affectionate gratitude, to acknowledge our many and great obligations to Almighty God, and to implore Him to continue and confirm the blessings we experienced.

Deeply penetrated with this sentiment, I, George Washington, President of the United States, do recommend to all religious societies and denominations, and to all persons whomsoever, within the United States, to set apart and observe Thursday, the 19th day of February next, as a day of public thanksgiving and prayer, and on that day to meet together and render sincere and hearty thanks to the great Ruler of nations for the manifold and signal mercies which distinguish our lot as a nation; particularly for the possession of constitutions of government which unite and, by their union, establish liberty with order; for the preservation of our peace, foreign and domestic; for the reasonable control which has been given to a spirit of disorder in the suppression of the late insurrection, and generally for the prosperous condition of our affairs, public and private, and at the same time humbly and fervently beseech the kind Author of these blessings graciously to prolong them to us; to imprint on our hearts a deep and solemn sense of our obligations to Him for them; to teach us rightly to estimate their immense value; to preserve us from the arrogance of prosperity, and from hazarding the advantages we enjoy by delusive pursuits, to dispose us to merit the continuance of His favors by not abusing them, by our gratitude for them, and by a corresponding conduct as citizens and as men to render this country more and more a safe and propitious asylum for the unfortunate of other countries; to extend among us true and useful knowledge; to diffuse and establish habits of sobriety, order, morality and piety, and finally to impart all the blessings we possess or ask for ourselves to the whole family of mankind. In testimony whereof, I have caused the seal of the United States of America to be affixed to these presents, and signed the same with my hand. Done at the city of Philadelphia the first day of January, 1795.

(signed) George Washington

*The Whiskey Insurrection in Western Pennsylvania*

THE WASHINGTON FAMILY
1796

*After the original painting by Edward Savage*
*in the National Gallery of Art, Washington, D.C.*

WASHINGTON'S TOMB, MOUNT VERNON

## Washington's Last Will and Testament

Washington's last Will and Testament shows where his first allegiance lay: It begins: "In the name of God, Amen." Of primary concern was the liquidation of all personal debt:

> Imprimus — All my debts, of which there are but few, and none of magnitude, are to be punctually and speedily paid, and the legacies, hereinafter bequeathed, are to be discharged as soon as circumstances will permit, and in the manner directed.

Second on his list of importance, was the care and safekeeping of his wife, Martha:

> Item – To my dearly beloved wife, Martha Washington, I give and bequeath the use, profit, and benefit of my whole estate, real and personal, for the term of her natural life... My improved lot in the town of Alexandria, situated on Pitt and Cameron Streets, I give to her and her heirs forever; as I also do my household and kitchen furniture of every sort and kind with the liquors and groceries which may be on hand at the time of my decease, to be used and disposed of as she may think proper.

Thirdly, Washington showed care and concern for his slaves:

> Item — Upon the decease of my wife it is my will and desire that all the slaves whom I hold in my own right shall receive their freedom... And to my mulatto man, William, (calling himself William Lee,) I give immediate freedom, or, if he should prefer it (on account of the accidents which have befallen him, and which have rendered him incapable of walking, or of any active employment), to remain in the situation he now is, it shall be optional in him to do so: In either case, however, I allow him an annuity of thirty dollars during his natural life, which shall be independent of the victuals and clothes he has been accustomed to receive, if he chuses the last alternative; but in full with his freedom if he prefers the first; — and this I give him, as a testimony of my sense of his attachment to me, and for his faithful services during the Revolutionary War.[10]

## Washington's Christian Character Extolled by John Adams

A December 22, 1799 newspaper article published nine days after the death of George Washington gives the personal recollections of our second U.S. President, John Adams, on the life and character of his friend and colleague. The Address, delivered to the U.S. Senate, is as follows:

...the life of our Washington cannot suffer by a comparison with those of other countries, who have been most celebrated and exalted by Fame. The attributes and decorations of Royalty, could only have served to eclipse the majesty of those virtues, which made him, from being a model citizen, a more resplendent luminary. Misfortune, had he lived, could hereafter have sullied his glory only with those superficial minds, who, believing that character and actions are marked by success alone, rarely deserve to enjoy it. Malice could never blast his honor, and envy made him a singular exception to her universal rule. For himself, he had lived enough, to lift and to glory. For his fellow citizens, if their prayers could have been answered he would have been immortal. For me, his departure is at a most unfortunate moment. Trusting, however, in the wise and righteous dominions of Providence over passions of men, and the result of their councils and actions, as well as over their lives, nothing remains for me but humble resignation. His example is now complete, and it will teach wisdom and virtue to magistrates, citizens and men, not only in the present age, but in future generations as long as our history shall be read...[11]

# NATHAN HALE
"I only regret that I have but one life
to lose for my country"
(1755 - 1776)

## The "Martyr Spy"

Hanged by the British in New York on September 22, 1776, Captain Nathan Hale has been called the "martyr spy" of the American War for Independence. He was, indeed, a true patriot in every sense of the word, and a great national hero. He is remembered by the youth of our nation, chiefly by virtue of his last words, prior to laying down his life for God and country:

> I only regret that I have but one life to lose for my country.[1]

## Nathan Hale's Christian Foundations

Hale was born on June 6, 1755, at Coventry, Connecticut. Deacon Richard Hale, Nathan's father, was a farmer and undaunted patriot for the cause of freedom. His mother, Elizabeth Strong, was praised for her virtue and integrity, which she demonstrated both in the home and in her outreach to the community. Nathan Hale's ancestry was comprised of citizens whose hallmarks were excellence in education, manners and character, originating from solid Christian foundations and upbringing. Nathan grew up on a large farm, helping with the work and chores, but also developing sportsmanship as he hunted, fished and swam.[2]

## Nathan is Prepared for Yale College by a Man of God

Reverend Joseph Huntington prepared Nathan and his brother, Enoch, for entry into Yale College. This minister of the Gospel was a man of God and an exceptional scholar.[3]

## Hale Meets Yale's Greatest President

While a student at Yale, Nathan met Reverend Timothy Dwight, Yale's greatest president, who befriended the young man. They had much in common, having both been prepared for studies at that college by two ministers of the Gospel, Rev. Joseph Huntington and Rev. Enoch Huntington, who were brothers. Nathan and Reverend Dwight, both avid readers, worked hand in hand to build up Yale's Linonia Library.[4]

On September 3, 1773, Nathan Hale graduated from Yale. This took place in the Old Brick Meeting House of Center Church, where

NATHAN HALE

CAPTAIN
ARMY OF THE UNITED STATES
BORN AT COVENTRY CONNECTICUT
JUNE 6 1755
IN THE PERFORMANCE OF HIS
DUTY HE RESIGNED HIS LIFE
A SACRIFICE TO HIS COUNTRIES
LIBERTY
AT NEW YORK
SEPTEMBER 22 1776

*After the original bronze statue in front of the Department of Justice,*
*Constitution Avenue, Washington, D.C.*

Nathan participated in a debate entitled: "Whether the Education of Daughters Be Not, Without Any Just Reason, More Neglected Than That of Sons." It has been reported that Hale took the side of the daughters.[5]

## Nathan Hale, the Educator

Immediately after graduation, Hale journeyed to Portsmouth, New Hampshire, to visit his uncle, Major Samuel Hale, a Harvard graduate and educator.[6] It was there that he met his cousin, Samuel Hale, who was a lawyer by profession. He then taught school in both East Haddam and New London, from 1773 to 1775. History records that Nathan Hale displayed graciousness, diplomacy and discipline; and that he was an excellent teacher as well as an accomplished sportsman.[7]

In New London, Nathan made an inspirational speech for the cause of American independence at a town meeting. This took place in April 1775, after receiving news of the "embattled farmers" at Lexington. Once again, he proved himself to be a debater, par excellence, captivating his audience.[8]

## Hale Joins the Continental Army

Hale subsequently joined the Continental Army, participating in the siege of Boston. A solitary entry is seen in the diary he kept on foregoing his customary evening prayers to his heavenly Father. He writes: "Evening prayers omitted for wrestling."[9]

Nathan Hale became a captain on January 1, 1776. Boston being evacuated in March 1776, the colonial army moved to New York. Hale joined the troops a month later. His patriotism, diligence, steadfastness and conscientiousness led to his being chosen by Lieutenant Colonel Thomas Knowlton of Connecticut as one of his four captains.[10]

## George Washington Makes an Urgent Appeal for a Volunteer Spy

At this time of pending disaster during the War for Independence, George Washington made an urgent appeal for a volunteer to obtain for him, the enemy's strategies and plans. A trustworthy and able spy was needed to penetrate enemy lines. Being apprised of the situation, Lieutenant Colonel Knowlton called upon his captains for volunteers. No one volunteered after the first call. Nathan Hale was the sole volunteer after a second call. William Hull, a trusted friend, tried his utmost to dissuade Hale from this dangerous task. Nathan's response, however, was the following:

I wish to be useful, and every kind of service necessary to the public good
becomes honorable by being necessary.[11]

## Nathan is Betrayed by his Tory Cousin Samuel

On September 12, Nathan entered the enemy lines, taking his
college diploma with him, with the intention of playing the part of
schoolmaster. Successfully achieving his goal, he returned from Long
Island to New York. On September 21, 1776, close to his own army

*Bronze relief of bound feet of the "Martyr Spy," Nathan Hale.*

lines, he was stopped, identified as a spy and taken to General Howe.[12]
This God-fearing, patriotic young man was betrayed by his cousin,
Samuel Hale. History tells us that strategic plans and documents were
in his possession. This being the case, General Howe ordered that he
be hanged on the gallows the following morning without a trial.[13]

On Sunday, December 22, just prior to his execution, Nathan met
Captain John Montresor, Chief Engineer of the British Army, and
spent his last hours with this gentleman, in his marquee. Montresor
greatly respected and admired the young American's gallantry and
calmness after being sentenced to death. Montresor records Hale's last
desires and words for us. He requested paper and pen with which to
write to his brother Enoch and to Colonel Knowlton. Montresor's eyewitness account of Nathan Hale is that he went to the gallows with few
people around him.[14] His immortalized, dying words are engraved in
America's historic annals. These were the last words of an inspiring and
moving speech made by the young hero.

At the time of betrayal, Samuel Hale was serving General Howe as Deputy Commissary of Prisoners. He died in 1787 in England, where he had subsequently fled.

## Nathan Hale Immortalized in America's History

A tombstone to the memory of Nathan Hale was erected in 1794 in the graveyard at Coventry. Its immortalized message to future generations states that "he resigned his life a sacrifice to his country's liberty at New York, September 22, 1776."[15]

# Character Sketches of Nathan Hale

## Testimony of Frances Manwaring Caulkins (1796 - 1869)

Born only 20 years after Hale was executed, Frances Caulkins most likely personally knew acquaintances of Hale. She is considered an authority on local traditions of that area:

> Those who knew Capt. Hale in New London, have described him as a man of many agreeable qualities; frank and independent in his bearing; social, animated, ardent; a lover of the society of ladies, and a favorite among them. Many a fair cheek was wet with bitter tears, and gentle voices uttered deep execrations on his barbarous foes, when tidings of his untimely fate were received.
>
> As a teacher, Capt. Hale is said to have been a firm disciplinarian, but happy in his mode of conveying instruction, and highly respected by his pupils. The parting scene made a strong impression on their minds. He addressed them in a style almost parental; gave them earnest counsel, prayed with them, and shaking each by the hand, bade them individually farewell.[16]

## Colonel Samuel Green's Picture of Hale as a School Teacher (January 1847)

> ...Hale a man peculiarly engaging in his manners — scholars old and young exceedingly attached to him — respected highly by all his acquaintances — fine moral character — Was exceedingly active... a vigorous, robust, healthy man — form symmetrical — social, sprightly — steady — in nature and education every way equal — about my height — face full of intelligence and benevolence — manners mild and genteel — a face and appearance that would strike any one anywhere — face indicative of good sense and good feeling — warm and ardent — captivating to all who saw him—
>
> Taught the classics and English — the school owned by the first gentlemen in the city — recommended by the faculty of Yale College probably — children all loved him for his tact and amiability —
>
> Went first from New London to see his parents — then to Cambridge — had been in the school about a year before he left — wonderful control over boys — without severity...
>
> His fate made an indelible impression upon all the boys of his school...[17]

## Mrs. Thomas Poole's Tribute (1837)

In 1837 William Wanton Saltonstall (1793-1862), of New London, secured the following statement about Hale from Mrs. Thomas Poole, also of New London, an aged, long-widowed gentlewoman:

> ...His Capacity as a teacher, and the mildness of his mode of instruction, was highly appreciated by Parents and Pupils; his appearance, manners, and temper secured the purest affection of those to whom he was known. As a Companion in the social, particularly in the domestic circle, his simple unostentatious manner of imparting right views and feelings to less cultivated understandings was unsurpassed by any individual who then, or since has fallen under my observation. He was peculiarly free from the shadow of guile! His remarkably expressive features were an index of the mind and heart that every new emotion lighted with a brilliancy perceptible to even common observers. No species of deception had any lurking-place in his frank, open, meek and pious mind; his soul disdained disguise, however imperious circumstances of personal safety might demand a resort to duplicity and ambiguity. — On the whole I then thought him (and his tremendous fate has not weakened the impression) one of the most perfect human characters recorded in history or exemplified in any age or nation...[18]

The above testimonies summarize Hale's life as an exceptionally good teacher — kind, but firm, and well-liked by both parents and students. He was a man of prayer and was known for his Christian character traits of meekness, godliness, moral excellence and guilelessness. He was refined, well-mannered and highly respected. His courageous and patriotic deed of laying down his life for God and country epitomizes the high price of liberty enjoyed by all Americans today.

# JOHN ADAMS
## Champion of the Declaration of Independence
## on the Floor of Congress
## (1735 - 1826)

John Adams, second U.S. president, was born October 30, 1735, the oldest son of a successful farmer. He married Abigail Smith, who came from a long line of ministers of the Gospel, highly respected for their character and integrity. Her father was the Reverend William Smith, minister of the Congregational Church at Weymouth, Massachusetts, for over 40 years.[1] Her mother, Elizabeth Quincy, was the granddaughter of Reverend John Norton. Her maternal grandfather, John Quincy, was the grandson of Thomas Shepard, a reputed minister of Charlestown.[2]

## John Adams' Consideration of the Ministry; his Career in Law

Encouraged by his parents, he seriously considered becoming a minister of the Gospel. At age 21, after much deliberation, he decided to pursue a career in law, graduating from Harvard in 1755.[3] He taught school for a short time. In those days, education was promoted as an outreach of its primary goal — that is, to study and enact the Scriptures in daily life. The focus of educating youth in intellectual pursuits fell under the prerequisite of sound Christian nurture and development of godly qualities, in order to equip them for a holy calling.[4] Classical studies were a natural, implicit result of mastering the Old and New Testaments, providing an essential understanding of the controversies which raged between biblical freedoms and tyrannical power. Hence, mastery over these subjects gave authority to its possessors.[5] The clergy became fountains of knowledge to their communities, and guardians of their education, as well as their spiritual leaders.

## Christianity, the Foundation of Adams' Life

That Christianity was the foundation of his life, is illustrated from many sources written in his own words, including this diary entry, probably written as a student:

> I am resolved not to waste my time as I did last year. I am resolved to rise with the sun and to study the Scriptures on Thursday, Friday, Saturday and Sunday mornings.[6]

## Also from his Diary:

> The Christian Religion is, above all the religions that previously existed in ancient or modern times, the religion of virtue, equity and humanity... It is resignation to God, it is goodness itself to man.[7]

*After the original portrait of the Founding Father by Charles Willson Peale in the Independence National Historical Park Collection, Philadelphia.*

# In Letters to his Friend, Thomas Jefferson:

I do not know how to prove physically that we shall meet and know each other in a future state... My reasons for believing it, as I do most undoubtedly, are that I cannot conceive such a being could make such a species as the human, merely to live and to die on this earth. If I did not believe in a future state, I should believe in no God... And if there is a future state, why should the Almighty dissolve forever all the tender ties which unite us so delightfully in this world and forbid us to see each other in the next?[8]

April 19, 1817:

...Without religion, this world would be something not fit to be mentioned in polite company...[9]

October 7, 1818:

...Have you ever found in history, one single example of a Nation thoroughly corrupted that was afterwards restored to virtue? ... And without virtue, there can be no political liberty...[10]

# John Adams Describes Sermons and Church Services to his Wife Abigail

Due to his responsibilities to his country, Adams frequently had to be away from his family. However, he and Abigail kept in frequent correspondence by letter. In many of his letters to her, he described sermons or church services he had been a part of. Following is one such example:

Philadelphia, June 11, 1775:

I have been this morning to hear Mr. Duffield, a preacher in this city, whose principles, prayers and sermons more clearly resemble those of our New England clergy than any that I have heard. His discourse was a kind of exposition of the 35th chapter of Isaiah. America was a wilderness, and the solitary place, and he said it would be glad, 'rejoice and blossom as the rose.' He labored 'to strengthen the weak hands and confirm the feeble knees.' He said to them that were of a fearful heart, 'be strong, fear not. Behold, your God will come with vengeance, even God with a recompense; he will come and save you.' 'No lion shall be there, nor any ravenous beast shall go up thereon, but the redeemed shall walk there,' etc. He applied the whole prophecy to this country, and gave us as animating an entertainment as I ever heard. He filled and swelled the bosom of every hearer. I hope you have received a letter, in which I enclosed you a pastoral letter from the synod of New York and Philadelphia; by this you will see, that the clergy this way are but now beginning to engage in politics, and they engage with a fervor that will produce wonderful effects.[11]

# The Founding Fathers' Christian Character Molded by Biblical Truth

The above not only shows the founding fathers' underlying strength; their wisdom and Christian character being molded by these historic sermons, but also the zeal and fervor which emanated from America's pulpits, where God's servants of righteousness preached biblical freedom from an alien power.

## Abigail Adams' Trust in the Lord

Abigail Adams, in her letters to her husband, reveals her trust in the Lord even in the midst of the severe trial of the revolutionary war:

> ...And whether the end will be tragical, Heaven only knows. You cannot be, I know, nor do I wish to see you, an inactive spectator; but if the sword be drawn, I bid adieu to all domestic felicity, and look forward to that country where there are neither wars nor rumours of war, in a firm belief that through the mercy of its King we shall both rejoice there together...[12]

## John Adams and Independence

John Adams was an ardent supporter of independence. He wrote newspaper articles and a pamphlet against the Stamp Act, and was influential in politics in Massachusetts. He was a delegate to the Continental Congress, and present at its first session which began with prayer, as recorded in the *Journals of Congress* at 9 a.m. on September 7, 1774:

> The Congress met according to adjournment. Agreeable to the resolve of yesterday, the meeting opened with prayers by the Reverend Mr. Duché. Noted, that the thanks of Congress be given Mr. Duché by Mr. Cushing and Mr. Ward, for performing divine service, and for the excellent prayer, which he composed and delivered on that occasion.[13]

OPENING PRAYER OF THE CONTINENTAL CONGRESS

*After a reproduction of the event in Harper's New Monthly Magazine, 1876.*

## The First Prayer in Congress

Reverend Jacob Duché, an Episcopal clergyman, officiated, becoming the first of an unbroken chain of Christian chaplains to open each session of both the U.S. House of Representatives and the Senate in prayer, to this day. Following is the text of the *First Prayer in Congress*:

> O Lord, our Heavenly Father, high and mighty King of kings, and Lord of lords, who dost from Thy throne behold all the dwellers of the earth, and reignest with power supreme and uncontrolled over all kingdoms, empires, and governments, look down in mercy, we beseach Thee on these American States, who have fled to Thee from the rod of the oppressor, and thrown themselves on Thy gracious protection, desiring to be henceforth dependent only on Thee. To Thee they have appeared for the righteousness of our cause; to Thee do they now look up for that countenance and support which Thou alone canst give. Take them, therefore, Heavenly Father, under Thy nurturing care. Give them wisdom in council and valor in the field. Defeat the malicious designs of our adversaries; convince them of the righteousness of our cause; and, if they still persist in sanguinary purposes, oh, let the voice of Thine own unerring justice sounding in their hearts, constrain them to drop the weapons of war from their unnerved hands in the day of battle.
>
> Be Thou present, O God of Wisdom, and direct the councils of this honorable assemblage; enable them to settle things on the best and surest foundation, that the scenes of blood may be speedily closed, and order, harmony, and peace may be effectually restored, and truth and justice, religion and piety prevail and flourish amongst Thy people; preserve the health of their bodies and the vigor of their minds; shower down upon them and the millions they here represent, such temporal blessings as Thou seest expedient for them in this world and crown them with everlasting glory in the world to come. All this we ask, in the name and through the merits of Jesus Christ, Thy Son, our Saviour. Amen[14]

## John Adams' Description of the First Prayer in Congress to his Wife Abigail

Not long after, while waiting for Congress to assemble, John Adams wrote excitedly to his wife about that uplifting and moving time of prayer with Reverend Duché:

> ... Accordingly, next morning he appeared with his clerk and in his pontificals, and read several prayers in the established form; and then read the Collect for the seventh day of September, which was the thirty-fifth Psalm. You must remember this was the next morning after we heard the horrible rumor of the cannonade of Boston. I never saw a greater effect upon an audience. It seemed as if Heaven had ordained that Psalm to be read on that morning.
>
> After this Mr. Duché, unexpected to everybody, struck out into an extemporary prayer, which filled the bosom of every man present. I must confess I never heard a better prayer, or one so well pronounced. Episcopalian

KEY TO PAINTING "FIRST PRAYER IN CONGRESS"

## The First Prayer In Congress, September 7, 1774

1. Caesar Rodney, Del.
2. Edward Rutledge, S.C.
3. T. Cushing, Mass.
4. Ephilet Dyer, Conn.
5. Samuel Adams, Mass.
6. John Adams, Mass.
7. Patrick Henry, Va.
8. John Rutledge, S.C.
9. George Washington, Va.
10. Peyton Randolph, Va.
11. Col. N. Folsom, N.H.
12. Robt. Treat Paine, Mass.
13. George Read, Del.
14. Silas Dean, Conn.
15. Richard Smith, N.J.
16. Philip Livingston, N.Y.
17. Thomas Lynch, S.C.
18. *Sthephen Hopkins, R.I.
19. John Dehart, N.J.
20. William Livingston, N.J.
21. Thomas M'Kean, Del.
22. Roger Sherman, Conn.
23. William Paca, Md.
24. Rev. Mr. Duche, Pa.
25. Samuel Rhodes, Pa.
26. Col. William Floyd, N.Y.
27. Stephen Crane, N.J.
28. Samuel Chase, Md.
29. John Morton, Pa.
30. Thomas Mifflin, Pa.
31. Charles Thomson, Pa.
32. Richard Henry Lee, Va.
33. John Jay, N.Y.
34. Isaac Low, N.Y.
35. Benjamin Harrison, Va.
36. Samuel Ward, R.I.

*Spelled as on Library of Congress key

### Taken from the famed T.H. Matteson 1848 painting, "The First Prayer in Congress, September 7, 1774"

as he is, Dr. Cooper himself (Dr. Samuel Cooper, well known as a zealous patriot and pastor of the church in Brattle Square, Boston) never prayed with such fervor, such earnestness and pathos, and in language so elegant and sublime — for America, for the Congress, for the Province of Massachusetts Bay, and especially the town of Boston. It has had an excellent effect upon everybody here. I must beg you to read that Psalm. If there was any faith in the Sortes Biblicae, it would be thought providential...[15]

## The Fourth of July to be Celebrated by Solemn Acts of Devotion to God Almighty

Adams was zealous for independence. He was part of the committee assigned with the task of drafting the Declaration of Independence. When Congress finally voted to take the course of independence, he was ecstatic in a speech to Congress, declaring that forevermore it would be celebrated as the "day of deliverance by solemn acts of devotion to God Almighty..." Following is an excerpt:

> The second day of July, 1776,* will be the most memorable epoch in the history of America, to be celebrated by succeeding generations as the great anniversary festival commemorated as the day of deliverance by solemn acts of devotion to God Almighty from one end of the Continent to the other, from this time forward forevermore. You will think me transported with enthusiasm, but I am not. I am well aware of the toil, the blood, and the treasure that it will cost us to maintain this Declaration and support and defend these states; yet, through all the gloom, I can see the rays of light and glory; that the end is worth all the means; that posterity will triumph in that day's transaction, even though we shall rue it, which I trust in God we shall not.[16]

## John Adams' Inaugural Address Glorifies God

Adams served as the second president of the United States from 1797-1801. His inaugural address acknowledged his need for God in this difficult task:

> ...I shall need, too, the favor of that Being in whose hands we are, who led our fathers, as Israel of old, from their native land and planted them in a country flowing with all the necessities and comforts of life, and who has covered our infancy with His providence and our ripe years with His wisdom and power.[17]

## John Adams' Prayer for Those who Would Dwell in the White House

The night after his arrival in the White House, he wrote to his wife, Abigail, expressing his prayer for all who would dwell in the White House in years to come. Many years later, it was inscribed upon the mantel of the White House State Dining Room, reading thus:

> I pray Heaven to bestow THE BEST OF BLESSINGS ON THIS HOUSE and All that shall hereafter Inhabit it, May none but Honest and Wise Men ever rule under This Roof.

---

* The Declaration of Independence was proclaimed on July 2, 1776, but actually signed on July 4, 1776.

## John Adams' Death

John Adams, Champion of the Declaration of Independence on the floor of Congress, died five short hours after Thomas Jefferson, on July 4th, 1826, exactly 50 years after the signing of this immortal document. His last words were: "Independence forever."

*I Pray* Heaven *To Bestow*
**THE BEST OF BLESSINGS ON**
*This House*

From a Letter of
JOHN ADAMS

November
MDCCC

*And* All *that shall hereafter* Inhabit it
*May none but* Honest *and* Wise Men *everrule under* This Roof.

*After the original engraved Prayer of John Adams upon the mantel of the State Dining Room, the White House.*

# THOMAS JEFFERSON
## Champion of Religious Freedom
### (1743 - 1826)

We hold these truths to be self-evident, that all men are created equal. That
they are endowed by their Creator with certain inalienable rights. Among
these are life, liberty, and the pursuit of happiness, that to secure these rights
governments are instituted among men... and for the support of this
Declaration, with a firm reliance upon the Protection of Divine Providence,
we mutually pledge our lives, our fortunes and our sacred honor.

*Excerpted from the Declaration of Independence, July 4, 1776*

Thomas Jefferson, author of the famous Declaration of Independence, was a member of the Continental Congress. On January 11,
1776, he was appointed to the Committee of five assigned to draft the
Declaration, which, in turn, unanimously selected him to actually
write the document.[1] Before submitting it to the Committee, he sought
out the criticism of two of the Committee members, Benjamin Franklin
and John Adams, whose opinions he deeply respected. Jefferson wrote
that they made only two or three verbal alterations.[2] It was presented
to the Committee and then to Congress on June 28, 1776.[3]

## Attacks on the Declaration of Independence

In the debate which ensued in Congress over it, there were some
who complained that it "contained no new ideas," that it was a
"common-place compilation, its sentiments hackneyed in Congress
for two years before," "its essence contained in Otis' pamphlet," and
that "it was copied from Locke's treatise on government."[4]

## Jefferson Defends His Declaration

In a letter written to James Madison years later in 1823, Jefferson
defended his work as follows:

Otis' pamphlet I never saw, and whether I gathered my ideas from reading
or reflection, I do not know. I know only that I turned to neither book nor
pamphlet while writing it. I did not consider it as any part of my charge to
invent new ideas altogether, and to offer no sentiments which had never been
expressed before...[5]

## John Adams' Valiant Defense of the Declaration

In spite of the hesitation of some to embrace the bold venture, there
were those who stood firmly with Jefferson. He wrote regarding John
Adams:

...I will say for Mr. Adams, that he supported the Declaration with zeal and
ability, fighting fearlessly for every word of it...[6]

THOMAS JEFFERSON

*After the original portrait by Charles Willson Peale.*
*Independence National Historical Park Collection, Philadelphia.*

## John Witherspoon Defends the Declaration

And it was John Witherspoon, a minister of the Gospel and the president of Princeton College, who delivered the galvanizing speech that caused the members of the Continental Congress to rush forward to sign the Declaration of Independence, that historic July 4th in 1776.

Prior to the vote, a member had lamented, "We are not ripe for revolution," to which Witherspoon replied, "Not ripe, Sir, in my judgment, we are not only ripe, but unless some action is taken, we will be rotting." It was followed by a riveting speech, which can be found in the chapter of this book on Witherspoon.[7]

## Celebrated by Succeeding Generations by Solemn Acts of Devotion to God Almighty

John Adams predicted that the event would "be celebrated by succeeding generations as the Great Anniversary festival commemorated as the day of deliverance by solemn acts of devotion to God Almighty from one end of the Continent to the other, from this time forward forevermore."[8]

## Abraham Lincoln on the Declaration of Independence

Years later, and a short time before the Civil War, Abraham Lincoln referred to the significance of the Declaration stating that,

> It was not the mere matter of the separation of the Colonies from the motherland, but that sentiment in the Declaration of Independence which gave liberty, not alone to the people of this country, but hope to all the world, for all future time. It was that which gave promise that in due time the weights would be lifted from the shoulders of all men, and that all should have an equal chance. This is the sentiment embodied in the Declaration of Independence...[9]

## Religious Freedom in America

Thomas Jefferson believed his greatest accomplishments were the writing of the Declaration of Independence and the passage of his *Act for Establishing Religious Freedom* in the state of Virginia in 1786. Jefferson fought against Virginia's state-supported clergy and church, as had been common practice in Europe. He believed that each individual should be free to contribute according to his conscience to a pastor and church of his own choice, and that one's religious beliefs should not in any way determine his suitability for civil government. Following are the introduction and conclusion to the Act:

> ...Well aware that Almighty God hath created the mind free; that all attempts to influence it by temporal punishments and burthens, or by civil

incapacitations tend only to beget habits of hypocrisy and meanness, and are a departure from the plan of the Holy Author of our Religion, who, being Lord both of body and mind, yet chose not to propagate it by coercions on either, as was in his Almighty power to do; that the impious presumption of legislators and rulers civil, as well as ecclesiastical who being themselves but fallible and uninspired men, have assumed dominion over the faith of others, setting up their own opinions and modes of thinking as the only true and infallible, and as such endeavoring to impose them on others, hath established and maintained false religions over the greatest part of the world, and through all time: That to compel a man to furnish contributions of money for the propagation of opinions which he disbelieves, is sinful and tyrannical; that even the forcing him to support this or that teacher of his own religious persuasion, is depriving him of the comfortable liberty of giving his contributions to the *particular pastor whose morals he would like to pattern, and whose powers he feels most persuasive to righteousness*...be it therefore enacted by the General Assembly, That no man shall be compelled to frequent or support any religious worship, place or ministry whatsoever, nor shall be enforced, restrained, molested, or burthened, in body or goods, nor shall otherwise suffer on account of his religious opinions or belief; but that all men shall be free to profess and by argument maintain their opinions in matters of religion, and that the same shall in no wise diminish, enlarge, or affect their civil capacities...[10]

## The First Amendment Clause of the U.S. Constitution

The following year, on September 17, 1787, the U.S. Constitution was written and signed. It included the important First Amendment Clause, that, "Congress shall make no law respecting an establishment of Religion, or prohibiting the free exercise thereof." Jefferson's 1786 *Act for Establishing Religious Freedom* was a forerunner to the *First Amendment of the Constitution*.

## Separation of Church From Interference by the State— Jefferson's Letter to the Danbury Baptists

In recent years, those who would like to interpret the First Amendment in a manner our forefathers never intended, have made use of the term "Separation of Church and State" to mean that there could be no possible impact or influence of Christianity upon civil government — or even upon education.

The true meaning of the Establishment Clause can be stated in these terms — "Separation of Church from interference by the State." The only time the expression "Separation of Church and State" was used by a founding father, is in an off-the-record, non-political letter written by Thomas Jefferson to the Danbury Baptist Association. He wrote this letter on January 1, 1802 replying to their public address which applauded his stance for establishing Religious Freedom.

Jefferson prefaces his statement with an assurance to the Danbury Baptists that he concurs with their belief of man being accountable to God alone for his mode of worship, without the government's coercion or interference:

> …Believing with you that religion is a matter which lies solely between man and his God, that he owes account to none other for his faith or his worship, that the legislative powers of government reach actions only, and not opinions, I contemplate with sovereign reverence that act of the whole American people which declared that their legislature should "make no law respecting an establishment of religion, or prohibiting the free exercise thereof," thus building a wall of separation between Church and State…[11]

## Religious Values Protected From Government Interference

The wall of separation between Church and state of which Jefferson speaks, is clearly in reference to protecting religious worship from the government's interference, and not the government being encroached upon by religious values. Furthermore, the Declaration of Independence itself concludes with an emphasis upon this new nation's dependence upon God's protective care:

> …with a firm reliance upon the protection of Divine Providence, we mutually pledge our lives, our fortunes and our sacred honor.

## Biblical Principles and Christian Values— the Framework for Good Government

It is seen, again and again in the founding fathers' writings, that they stressed the need of biblical principles and Christian values as the framework for good government, as attested to throughout this book. While we do not have evidence of Thomas Jefferson having accepted Jesus Christ as his Lord and Savior, the *only* way to salvation, we can affirm that he governed his life by many Christian values and principles. Following are some examples from his writings to illustrate this.

## Jefferson's Life Governed by Many Christian Principles and Values

A letter to Thomas Jefferson Smith, advising this young man on the course of life:

> *Adore God. Reverence and cherish your parents. Love your neighbor as yourself* and your country more than yourself. Be just. Be true. Murmur not at the ways of Providence. So shall the life, into which you have entered, be the portal to one of eternal and ineffable bliss…[12]

A letter to Peter Carr, dated August 10, 1787:

> ...Above all things, lose no occasion of exercising your dispositions to be grateful; to be generous; to be charitable; to be humane; to be true, just, firm, orderly, courageous, etc. Consider every act of this kind as an exercise which will strengthen your moral faculties, and increase your worth.[13]

A letter to Samuel Adams, dated March 4, 1801:

> ...When I have been told that you were avoided, insulted, frowned on, I could but ejaculate: *"Father forgive them, for they know not what they do."* I confess I felt an indignation for you, which for myself I have been able, under every trial, to keep entirely passive. However, the storm is over, and we are in port...[14]

## Jefferson Writes a Poem Based Upon Psalm 15

Jefferson wrote the following poem, titled, *Portrait of a Good Man*, as an example to follow in life. It is based upon Psalm 15:

> Lord, who's the happy man that may to thy blest courts repair,
> Not stranger like to visit them, but to inhabit there?
> 'Tis he, whose every thought and deed by rules of virtue moves;
> Whose generous tongue disdains to speak the thing his heart disproves.
> Who never did a slander forge, his neighbor's fame to wound;
> Nor hearken to a false report, by malice whispered round.
> Who vice in all its pomp and power, can treat with just neglect;
> And piety, though clothed in rags, religiously respect.
> Who to his plighted vows and trust has ever firmly stood;
> And though he promise to his loss, he makes his promise good.
> Whose soul in usury disdains his treasure to employ;
> Whom no rewards can ever bribe the guiltless to destroy.
> The man who, by his steady course, has happiness insured,
> When earth's foundations shake,
> Shall stand by Providence secured.[15]

In a letter to Miles King, Jefferson stated that Christianity alone, regardless of denominational preferences, was the road to Heaven. However, the distinction not made by Jefferson was that one had to be "born again" into the family of God through faith in Christ Jesus as one's personal Savior, regardless of church attendance. (In Christ's own words — John 3:3; 13-16.)

A letter to Miles King, September 26, 1814:

> ...Nay, we have heard it said that there is not a Quaker or a Baptist, a Presbyterian or Episcopalian, a Catholic or a Protestant in Heaven; that on entering that gate, we leave those badges of schism behind, and find ourselves united in those principles only in which God has united us all. Let us not be uneasy then about the different roads we may pursue, as believing them the shortest to that our last abode; but, following the guidance of a good

conscience, let us be happy in the hope that by those different paths we shall all meet in the end. And that you and I may there meet and embrace, is *my earnest prayer*. And with this assurance I salute you with brotherly esteem and respect.[16]

## Jefferson's Catalogue of Biblical Paintings

Jefferson was the architect for his beautiful home, "Monticello," in Charlottesville, Virginia. As the home is the reflection of those who live in it, Jefferson's parlour or living room contained numerous evidences of the impact of Christianity upon his life and the culture of his day. This founding father drew up his own Catalogue of Paintings, Sculpture and Objets d'Art, replete with Scripture references and explanations on each of the biblical themes, quoting both chapter and verse from the Bible. Among the Scriptures given are: Matt. 21:22; Matt. 26:75; Luke 2:46; Mark 15:16-20; Genesis 22; Matt. 27; Matt. 14:11; Mark 6:28; Luke 3:21-22; Luke 23:44-45; Judges 11; Matt. 27:51-52.[17]

Among the paintings adorning these walls, were the Ascension of Christ into heaven; the Holy Family, the Transfiguration; the Prodigal Son; Jesus among the Doctors of the Law; Jesus driving the money-changers out of the Temple; Peter weeping in repentance; John the Baptist heralding the Messianic Lamb of God; Christ before Pilate; the flagellation of Christ, and His crucifixion on Golgotha's hill. The Old Testament stories of Abraham offering Isaac, with an angel of the Lord stopping his hand; Jephtha offering his daughter and David and Goliath, are also portrayed.

## His Personal Library

Thomas Jefferson catalogued his own personal library of more than 6,000 volumes. Of the 190 entries under the title *Religion* (now in the Jefferson Collection of the Rare Book Division of the Library of Congress), 187 fit into the category of Christianity. A vast array of Old and New Testament Bibles, Concordances, Biblical sermons and writings, (such as John Witherspoon's sermons) were hand-initialled by Jefferson and made part of his collection. The three remaining books under *Religion* were: Boyse's and King's heathen gods, "to understand ancient poetry, coins and medals;" and a Sale's Koran — most probably to understand that philosophy.

## Jefferson's Maxims for Daily Living

Jefferson, being a very disciplined person, developed his own maxims for practical daily living under the title:

**A Decalogue of Canons for Observation in practical life**

1) Never put off till tomorrow what you can do today.
2) Never trouble another for what you can do yourself.
3) Never spend your money before you can have it.
4) Never buy what you do not want because it is cheap; it will be dear to you.
5) Pride costs us more than hunger, thirst and cold.
6) We never repent of having eaten too little.
7) Nothing is troublesome that we do willingly.
8) How much pain have cost us the evils which have never happened.
9) Take things always by their smooth handle.
10) When angry, count 10 before you speak; when very angry, a hundred.[18]

## His Courtesy and Hospitality

A rare Library of Congress history book of Jefferson's day gives us the following account of a visitor who entered Monticello:

> While the visitor was yet lost in the contemplation of these treasures...he was met by the tall, and animated, and stately figure of the patriot himself, his countenance beaming with intelligence and benignity, and his outstretched hand, with its strong and cordial pressure, confirming the courteous welcome of his lips. And then came the charm of manner and conversation that passes all description—so cheerful—so unassuming—so free, and easy, and frank, and kind, and gay—that even the young, and overawed, and embarrassed visitor at once forgot his fears, and felt himself by the side of an old and familiar friend. There was no effort, no ambition in the conversation of the patriot. It was as simple and unpretending as nature itself. And while in this easy manner he was pouring out instruction, like light from an inexhaustible solar fountain, he seemed continually to be asking, instead of giving information. The visitor felt himself lifted by the contact, into a new and nobler region of thought, and became surprised at his own buoyancy and vigor...and all this carried off so lightly, so playfully, so gracefully, so engagingly, that he won every heart that approached him, as certainly as he astonished every mind.[19]

## Jefferson on Slavery: The Abolition of Slavery, the Great Object of Desire in these Colonies

In regard to the issue of slavery at the time of the founding of this nation, the question arises: If the founding fathers were against slavery as a great moral evil, why didn't they free the slaves?

Prior to the revolution, some of the colonial legislatures had attempted to prevent further importation through duties and prohibitions, but interference by the British government prevented them from doing so. Jefferson's sentiments and those of other colonists on the slavery issue are noted in his famous 1774 *A Summary View of the Rights of British America* (set forth in some Resolutions intended for the inspection of the present Delegates of the people of Virginia, now in Convention). It outlines the grievances of the colonies against England, as excerpted below:

> ...*The abolition of domestic slavery is the great object of desire in those colonies, where it was unhappily introduced in their infant state.* But previous to the enfranchisement of the slaves we have, it is necessary to exclude all further importations from Africa; yet our repeated attempts to effect this by prohibitions, and by imposing duties which might amount to a prohibition, have been hitherto defeated by his majesty's negative: Thus preferring the immediate advantages of a few African corfairs (slaves) to the lasting interests of the American states, and to the rights of human nature deeply wounded by this infamous practice...[20]

## Initiation of a Congressional Bill Against Slavery

After the Declaration of Independence, Jefferson was free to initiate a bill in Congress, which he did in 1779, proposing an initial attempt to deal with the slavery issue. In his autobiography, he wrote the following account of it:

> The bill on the subject of slaves was a mere digest of the existing laws respecting them, without any intimation of the plan for a future and general emancipation. It was thought better that this should be kept back, and attempted only by way of amendment, however the bill should be brought on. The principles of the amendment however were agreed on, that is to say, the freedom of all born after a certain day, and deportation at a proper age. But it was found that the public mind would not yet bear the proposition, nor will it bear it even at this day. Yet the day is not distant when it must bear and adopt it, or worse will follow...[21]

Jefferson could foresee the tremendous evil that would befall this country if the young nation did not eradicate this "infamous practice," which had deeply wounded human beings. He said that "commerce between master and slave is despotism," and gave this warning:

> It is still in our power to direct the process of emancipation and deportation peaceably and in such slow degree as that the evil will wear off insensibly and their place be pari passu filled with free white laborers. If on the contrary it is left to force itself on, human nature must shudder at the prospect held up...Commerce between master and slave is despotism.[22]

Unfortunately, Jefferson's admonitions as to what would befall this nation if the slavery issue was not fully resolved, became the reality of a tragic civil war within a century. Abraham Lincoln was God's instrument, raised up to totally eradicate this great moral evil from American soil. This he did with his Emancipation Proclamation, an immortal document, setting the slaves free on a permanent basis in

1863.

## Jefferson's Death: "A Divine Conspiracy of Circumstances"

On the 28th of June, 1826, Jefferson lay at Monticello dying. Although his doctor had pronounced that he could not live through the night, Jefferson prayed that he might survive to celebrate the Jubilee of the Declaration of Independence. Miraculously, he lived on until the 4th of July, his last words to his family and friends being, "I have done for my country, and for all mankind all that I could do, and now I resign my soul, without fear, to my God, my daughter, to my country." And then he uttered distinctly two times like Simeon of old, "Lord, now lettest thou thy servant depart in peace."[23]

That Thomas Jefferson should leave this world at the very hour and day of the great Jubilee celebrating America's biblical freedoms – at ten minutes to one o'clock, the time when the Declaration of Independence had received its final reading – showed the Hand of God so clearly evidenced in the affairs of this nation. While America marveled at what a historian called a "Divine Conspiracy of Circumstances," Jefferson's intimate friend, John Adams, himself champion of the Declaration of Independence on the floor of Congress, left this world five short hours later. His last words were "Independence forever," and "Jefferson survives."[24]

A noted historian of that day tells us that "Heaven itself mingled visibly in the Jubilee celebration of American liberty, hallowing anew this day by a double apotheosis."

And let it be so.

READING OF THE DECLARATION
OF INDEPENDENCE

*Taken from the original painting*
*"Reading of the Declaration of Independence" by Edwin A. Abbey*

*After a portrait of the founding father by Charles Willson Peale.*
*Original in the Independence National Historical Park Collection, Philadelphia.*

# JAMES MADISON
## Father of the U.S. Constitution
### (1751 - 1836)

James Madison, father of the U.S. Constitution, was also the fourth president of the nation.

## Madison's Christian Education

He was born in Port Conway, Virginia in 1751, and received an excellent childhood education; his character being greatly influenced by his tutor, Reverend Thomas Martin, who pastored "the Brick Church," St. Thomas Parish.[1] He graduated from Princeton College in 1771, spending an additional year at the college to study Hebrew under its president, John Witherspoon, Doctor of Divinity, a great educator who later became delegate to the Continental Congress. Witherspoon was the only preacher-signer of the Declaration of Independence.[2]

## Madison Continues Biblical Studies, Along with Law

Returning to his home, Madison continued his biblical studies, along with law. Although he did not select the Christian ministry for his life's work, his study and thorough knowledge of the Bible formulated his views and principles in government.

## Delegate to the Continental Congress

In 1780, he was elected as a delegate to the Continental Congress, working tirelessly to secure a strong central government.[3]

## Madison Opposes the Establishment of Religion by Law

In 1785 he led the opposition to a bill for the establishment of religion by law.

Both Madison and Jefferson, called the "Champions of Religious Freedom," stood against legislation that would require citizens to be taxed for the support of something which they may be opposed to in conscience. In this case, it was the support of the teachers of the Christian religion of one sect, selected by the government. Madison was outraged at this affront to Christianity. He was apparently in the minority. As he states here in his acclaimed *Memorial and Remonstrance*, it appears only the Quakers and Mennonites as a whole could foresee the error of passing such a law:

> ...Who does not see that the same authority, which can establish Christianity in exclusion of all other religions, may establish with the same ease, any particular

sect of Christians, in exclusion of all other sects; that the same authority, which can force a citizen to contribute threepence only of his property, for the support of any one establishment, may force him to conform to any other establishment, in all cases whatsoever....Are the Quakers and the Mennonites the only sects who think a compulsive support of their religions unnecessary and unwarrantable? Can their piety alone be intrusted with the care of publick worship? Ought their religions to be endowed, above all others, with extraordinary privileges, by which proselytes may be enticed from all others....[4]

## Madison: Christianity Does Not Need the Help of the State

Not only was the bill not beneficial to Christianity, but the passage of such a bill was based upon ignorance, rather than faith in God. As he clearly shows, Christianity not only does not need the help of the State for support, but such help would result in a weakening of the church:

...Because the establishment proposed by the bill is not requisite for the support of the Christian Religion. To say that it is, is a contradiction to the Christian Religion itself; for every page of it disavows a dependence on the power of this world; it is a contradiction to fact, for it is known that this religion both existed and flourished, not only without the support of human laws, but in spite of every opposition from them; and not only during the period of miraculous aid, but long after it had been left to its own evidence and the ordinary care of Providence: nay, it is a contradiction in terms; for any religion, not invented by human policy must have pre-existed and been supported, before it was established by human policy; it is, moreover, to weaken in those, who profess this religion, a pious confidence in its innate excellence, and the patronage of its Author; and to foster in those, who still reject it, a suspicion that its friends are too conscious of its fallacies, to trust it to its own merits....[5]

## Separation of Church and (from Interference by) the State

Madison then goes on to explain that this has been proven repeatedly through the 15 centuries of Christianity prior to the Reformation. What have been its fruits, asks Madison?

...pride and indolence in the clergy; ignorance and servility in the laity: in both, superstition, bigotry and persecution. Inquire of the teachers of Christianity for the ages in which it appeared in its greatest lustre; those of every sect point out the ages prior to its incorporation with civil policy...what influence, in fact, have ecclesiastical establishments had on civil society? In some instances, they have been seen to erect a spiritual tyranny on the ruins of the civil authority; in more instances, have they been seen upholding the thrones of political tyranny; in no instance have they been seen the guardians of the liberties of the people....[6]

## Madison: "Christian Forebearance, Love and Charity Mutually Prevailing" Prior to Bill

The adverse effects of this law in the future could be seen by

Madison, even in the initial discord it currently brought to the Christian church, as he writes:

> ...The very appearance of the bill has transformed that "Christian forbearance, love and charity," which of late mutually prevailed, into animosities and jealousies, which may not soon be appeased. What mischiefs may not be dreaded, should this enemy to the publick quiet be armed with the force of law?...Because the policy of the bill is adverse to the diffusion of the light of Christianity. The first wish of those, who ought to enjoy this precious gift, ought to be, that it may be imparted to the whole race of mankind. Compare the number of those who have as yet received it, with the number still remaining under the dominions of false religions, and how small is the former! Does the policy of the bill tend to lesson the disproportion? No; it at once discourages those who are strangers to the light of truth, from coming into the regions of it; and countenances, by example, the nations who continue in darkness in shutting out those who might convey it to them....[7]

## Madison's Leading Role in the Constitutional Convention

Madison took a leading role in the Constitutional Convention of 1787. His clearly defined and outlined views on government formed the basis for the "Virginia Plan" providing a framework for our U.S. Constitution.[8] After the Constitution was adopted, he was instrumental in its acceptance by the states. Along with Alexander Hamilton and John Jay, he wrote a series of articles, called the Federalist, which helped to educate the public in respect to the new form of government.[9] Madison was a member of the Virginia Convention which met to deliberate the ratification of the U.S. Constitution. His brilliant analysis and powerful argument brought about, more than any other delegate, its safe procurement.[10]

Aptly is Madison called the Father of the U.S. Constitution and a great Christian founding father.

## Madison's Stance Against Government Interference in the Mode of Worship of Christian Denominations

John Quincy Adams, sixth president of the United States in his "Eulogy on the Life and Character of James Madison," delivered at the request of the Mayor, Alderman and Common Council of the City of Boston, September 27, 1836, throws further light on his stance against government interference in the mode of worship of all mainline Christian denominations:

> ...After the close of the War, in the year 1784, Mr. Jefferson introduced into the Legislature a Bill for the establishment of Religious Freedom. The principle of the Bill was the abolition of all taxation for the support of Religion, or of its Ministers, and to place the freedom of all religious opinions wholly beyond the control of the Legislature.[11]

# BENJAMIN FRANKLIN
## Signer of The Declaration of Independence
## (1706 - 1790)

### Franklin— Statesman, Author, Inventor

Benjamin Franklin — famous statesman, author, inventor — was born in Boston on January 17, 1706. He was fifteenth of 17 children born to Josiah Franklin.[1] Franklin was baptized at the Old South Meeting House in Boston.

### A Poor Bostonian Arrives in Philadelphia— His Accomplishments

At age 17 he arrived in Philadelphia a poor Bostonian. Franklin rapidly excelled in his early trade, that of a printer. But he developed his skill as a journalist as well, authoring his popular *Poor Richard's Almanac*, which became a household word, and establishing the *Pennsylvania Gazette*.[2] He initiated many civic improvements, such as a police force, fire companies, libraries, to include the Library Company, founded in 1731 "for the advancement of knowledge and literature." This library served as our first Library of Congress, from 1774-1800.[3] He also founded the Philosophical Society of Pennsylvania, and the Pennsylvania Hospital in 1751, composing the inscription for its cornerstone, which reads:

> In the year of Christ, 1755: George the second happily reigning, (for he sought the happiness of the people); Philadelphia flourishing, for its inhabitants were publick-spirited. This building, by the bounty of the Government and of many private persons, was piously founded, for the relief of the sick and miserable. May the God of mercies bless the undertaking!

### Franklin, a Key Figure in the Continental Congress

In politics he was a key figure in the Continental Congress, serving on 10 committees including the one that drew up the Declaration of Independence, to which he placed his signature. He also represented America as a diplomat in England and France, distinguishing himself as a brilliant, tactful, versatile and accomplished statesman.

### Franklin and God's Intervention in the Constitutional Convention

After independence was declared in 1774; the war won in 1781; and the peace treaty signed in 1783, the delegates faced yet another enormous task: to create a strong, yet representative form of govern-

BENJⁿ FRANKLIN

*After the original painting "Benjamin Franklin — History"*
*by Constantino Brumidi, in the ceiling of the President's Room,*
*U.S. Capitol, Washington, D.C. For many years the Presidents used this*
*room as the ceremonial chamber for signing documents.*

ment for the new nation.  In 1787 the 55 delegates met in Philadelphia
with George Washington as president of the Constitutional Convention.   When it seemed   they had come to an impasse, Benjamin
Franklin gave a dramatic address, reminding the delegates how God, in
answer to their earlier prayers, had sovereignly guided them in their
previous efforts.  He recommended that henceforth, each morning's
session commence in prayer, beseeching God's assistance in the enormous task ahead:

Mr. President:

The small progress we have made, after four or five weeks' close attendance,
and continual reasonings with each other, our different sentiments producing
as many noes as ayes, is, methinks, a melancholy proof of the imperfection of
human understanding.  We indeed seem to feel our own want of political
wisdom, since we have been running around in search of it.  We have gone
back to ancient history for models of government, and examined the different
forms of those republics which, having been originally formed with the seeds
of their own dissolution, now no longer exist, and we have viewed modern
states all round Europe, but find none of their constitutions suitable to our
circumstances.

In this situation of this assembly, groping, as it were in the dark, to find
political truth, and scarce able to distinguish it when presented to us, how has
it happened, sir, that we have not hitherto once thought of humbly applying
to the Father of Lights, to illuminate our understandings?  In the beginning
of the contest with Britain, when we were sensible of danger, we had daily
prayers in this room for the Divine protection.  Our prayers, sir, were heard,
and they were graciously answered.  All of us who were engaged in the struggle
must have observed frequent instances of a superintending Providence in our
favor.  To that kind Providence we owe this happy opportunity of consulting
in peace on the means of establishing our future national felicity.  And have
we now forgotten that powerful Friend?  or do we imagine we no longer need
His assistance?  I have lived, sir, a long time, and the longer I live the more
convincing proofs I see of this truth, that God governs the affairs of men.  And
if a sparrow cannot fall to the ground without His notice, is it probable that
an empire can rise without His aid?  We have been assured, sir, in the sacred
writings that "except the Lord build the house, they labor in vain that build
it." (Psalm 127:1)  I firmly believe this, and I also believe that without His
concurring aid we shall succeed in this political building no better than the
builders of Babel; we shall be divided by our little, partial, local interests, our
projects will be confounded, and we ourselves shall become a reproach and a
by-word down to future ages.  And, what is worse, mankind may hereafter,
from this unfortunate instance, despair of establishing government by human
wisdom, and leave it to chance, war, and conquest.

I therefore beg leave to move —

That henceforth prayers, imploring the assistance of Heaven and its
blessings on our deliberations, be held in this assembly every morning before
we proceed to business; and that one or more of the clergy of this city be
requested to officiate in that service.[4]

## Franklin's Application of Psalm 127:1
## to the Framing of the U.S. Constitution

How reassuring for Americans to know that this brilliant and versatile founding father revered and loved God; considering Him "a powerful Friend;" that he had the courage of his convictions, knowing that without God's aid it would be impossible to build an empire; and that he believed human intelligence to be devoid of true, godly wisdom.

## Ben Franklin's Daily Devotions

He recognized his need for God's help, not only in governing the nation, but also in governing his own inner man, as seen in his daily devotions:

> That I may be averse to Tale bearing, Backbiting,
> Detraction, Slander, and Craft, and Overreaching,
> Abhor Extortion and Perjury and every Kind of Wickedness,
> Help me, O Father.

> That I may be honest and open hearted, gentle, merciful
> and good, cheerful in spirit, rejoicing in the Good of others,
> Help me, O Father.

> That I may have a constant Regard to Honor and
> Probity; That I may possess a perfect innocence and
> a good Conscience, and at length become Truly Virtuous
> and Magnanimous,
> Help me, Good God.
> Help me, O Father.[5]

## Franklin's Life Governed by Christian Principles

There are many evidences in Franklin's writings which testify to his life being governed by Christian principles, morals and virtues. Some of these are to be found in his *Yearbook*, as follows:

| | |
|---|---|
| Time | He that idly loses five shillings' worth of time loses five shillings, and might as prudently throw five shillings into the sea. |
| Patience | He that can have patience can have what he will. |
| Covetousness | Covetousness is ever attended with solicitude and anxiety |
| Bear the burdens of others | To bear other people's afflictions, everyone has courage enough to spare. |
| Moderation | Avoid extremes. |
| Honesty | My father convinced me that nothing was useful which was not honest. |

| | |
|---|---|
| The Preservation of History | Happy that nation, fortunate that age, whose history is not diverting |
| Humility | Search others for their virtues, thyself for thy vices. |
| Straight-forwardness | Tricks and treachery are the practice of fools that have not wit enough to be honest. |
| The value of words | Avoid trifling conversation. |
| Forgiveness | Forbear resenting injuries as much as you think they deserve. |
| The Sovereignty of God | Whenever we attempt to amend the scheme of Providence, we had need be circumspect, lest we do more harm than good. |
| Obedience | Let thy child's first lesson be obedience and the second will be what thou wilt. |
| Judge not lest ye be judged (Mt. 7:1) | Don't throw stones at your neighbors, if your own windows are glass. |
| Good stewardship | Talents for the education of youth are the gift of God. |
| Almighty God, the Healer | God heals; the doctor takes the fee. |
| Frugality | He that goes a-borrowing, goes a-sorrowing. |
| Freedom | Freedom is not a gift bestowed upon us by other men, but a right that belongs to us by the law of God and nature. |
| Truth | He always speaks the thing he means, which he is never afraid or ashamed to do, because he knows he always means good. |
| Marriage | She that will eat her breakfast in her bed, and spend the morn in dressing of her head, and sit at dinner like a maiden bride, and talk of nothing all day but of pride; God in his mercy may do much to save her, but what a case is he in that doth have her! |
| Discretion | Be slow in choosing a friend, slower in changing. |
| Contentment | It is no more in a man's power to think than look like another. |
| Self-government | There should be a mutual dependence between governors and governed. |
| Integrity | To receive credit and character as a tradesman, I took care not only to be in reality industrious and frugal, but to avoid all appearance to the contrary. |

| Respect for women | Let the fair sex be assured that I shall always treat them and their affairs with the utmost decency and respect. |
| Happiness | Virtue alone is sufficient to make a man great, glorious and happy. |
| Boast not | What great difference can there be between putting yourself up, or putting your neighbor down? |
| Morality | It was about this time I conceived the bold and arduous project of arriving at moral perfection. |
| Self-control | It is easier to suppress the first desire than to satisfy all that follow it. |
| Godly suffering | Remember Job suffered and was afterwards prosperous. |
| The Omniscience of God | The event only God knows. |
| Guilelessness | Use no hurtful deceit, think innocently and justly; and, if you speak, speak accordingly. |
| Usefulness | Be little burdensome and essentially useful to friends. |
| Health | Virtue is the best preservative of health. |
| Steadfastness | Stick to it steadily. |
| Faith, hope and charity (love) | Hope and faith may be more firmly grounded upon charity, than charity upon hope and faith. |
| God, the Rewarder | God will certainly reward virtue and punish vice, either here or hereafter. |
| Avoid flattery | Foes counteract the mischief flatterers might do us. |
| Keep your mind on eternal things (Colossians 3) | If our desires are to the things of this world, they are never to be satisfied. |
| The goodness of God | The pleasures in this world are, rather from God's goodness than our own merit. |
| A brief span on earth | It is time for an old man, as I am, to be thinking of his great remove.[6] |

With the completion of the U.S. Constitution on September 17, 1787, Franklin retired from official public life, but yet continued in his work to promote the good of mankind.

## Franklin on Slavery

One of the most notable accomplishments in this phase of his life is his work against slavery. He organized and became President of the world's first anti-slavery society, the *Pennsylvania Society for Promoting the Abolition of Slavery*. He wrote the first remonstrance against slavery, which was presented to the Congress of the United States.[7]

## Franklin's Death

The entire nation mourned his death on April 17, 1790. He died at the age of 84, after a full, long and useful life. His mortal remains were laid to rest in the burial grounds of Christ Church, Philadelphia, later called "the Nation's Church" because of the central role played by the founding fathers who established our new government. They worshipped God in this church. Franklin's wife and life-long companion, Deborah, is buried by his side.

There is no evidence that Franklin ever acknowledged Jesus Christ as his personal Lord and Savior, the only way to eternal life. However, there can be no doubt that Franklin's life was deeply influenced by Christianity, and, as he points out, so was the well-being of the nation— as his maxims, and morals, his letters and political writings exude. Of equal importance, his actions and selfless giving of his talents for the good of the new nation, attest to a Christian value system and world view.

# PATRICK HENRY
"Give me Liberty or Give me Death!"
(1736 - 1799)

## The Student who Failed

As a child, Patrick Henry appeared to be one unlikely to succeed in his studies.[1] He loved nature but cared little about school. Born on May 29, 1736, he was the son of John Henry, a successful, well-educated Scotchman and a judge in Hanover County, Virginia. At age 18, he married Sarah Shelton, having neither a career nor funds.[2] By age 23, he had failed as a clerk, a farmer, and a storekeeper. Surprisingly, he was accepted at the Wythe School of Law at the College of William and Mary, and found his life's calling as a lawyer.[3] Later he distinguished himself as Commander-in-Chief of the Virginia troops, (1775) and Governor of Virginia, (1776).[4]

## Patrick Henry "Blessed with Poverty, an Honest Heart and Sound Judgment"

Speaking on the Life and Character of Patrick Henry, William R. Drinkard of Petersburg, Virginia gave this description of him in 1840:

> ...Blessed with poverty, an honest heart, and a sound judgment, he was insensible alike to the smiles and frowns of courtiers and of princes... The advantages of an academic education were denied him, and the limited means which he possessed were but indifferently employed... In the midst of his embarrassments, and in the depth of his poverty... he commenced the study; and soon thereafter the practice of law. Here was opened to him a new field for the exercise of those varied and transcendent powers, which had been dormant for so long a time, and which none ever supposed him to possess. The sleeping energies of his mind were aroused; as it were in the twinkling of an eye a mighty genius was called into existence. The cries of his suffering countrymen pierced his heart, and he nobly resolved to hazard all in their defence...[5]

## Patrick Henry's Genius Comes Alive

In 1763, Henry gained widespread attention for his speech in a celebrated case called the "Parson's Case," in which he denied the right of the king to repeal acts made by the colonial legislature. He was elected to the House of Burgesses, and again gained notice for his fiery and sobering speech against the Stamp Act, which brought him into the ranks of men such as Samuel Adams, who launched the American Revolution.[6]

PATRICK HENRY

*After the original portrait of the Founding Father by Thomas Sully,*
*in the Independence National Historical Park Collection, Philadelphia.*

## Patrick Henry and Thomas Jefferson Draft a National Day of Prayer, Humiliation and Fasting

Patrick Henry had become the popular leader of the House of Burgesses in 1768, when young Thomas Jefferson was elected a member. After the British Parliament closed the port of Boston in 1774, Henry called upon Jefferson to draft a joint resolution for a National Day of Prayer, Humiliation and Fasting. George Washington wrote in his diary for that day, June 1, 1774: "...went to church and fasted all day."[7]

## Henry a Delegate to the Continental Congress

Patrick Henry was a delegate from Virginia to the First Continental Congress which met in Philadelphia on September 7, 1774. Recognizing the great need of God's blessing on the enormous task before them, the delegates invited Jacob Duché, pastor of Christ Church in Philadelphia — the founding fathers' church — to open the meeting in prayer. He read Psalm 35 in its entirety, then broke out into extemporaneous prayer, which John Adams described as "filling the bosom of every man present..." praying with "such fervor, such earnestness and pathos, and in language so elegant and sublime, for America, for Congress, for the Province of Massachusetts Bay, and especially for the town of Boston. It has had an excellent effect upon everybody there."[8]

## Patrick Henry Delivers a Great Oration on the Unity of the Colonies

It was in the midst of that electrifying atmosphere, that Patrick Henry delivered a great oration expressing the oneness of the individual colonies as a nation. The only surviving record of it, is that which follows, comprising notes taken by John Adams, delegate from Massachusetts:

### I am not a Virginian, but an American

Government is dissolved. Fleets and armies and the present state of things show that government is dissolved. Where are your landmarks, your boundaries of colonies? We are in a state of nature, sir I did propose that a scale should be laid down, that part of North America which was once Massachusetts Bay and that part which was once Virginia, ought to be considered as having a weight. Will not people complain? Ten thousand Virginians have not outweighed one thousand others.

I will submit, however: I am determined to submit, if I am overruled.

A worthy gentleman near me seemed to admit the necessity of obtaining a more adequate representation.

I hope future ages will quote our proceedings with applause. It is one of the great duties of the democratical part of the constitution to keep itself pure. It

is known in my province that some other Colonies are not so numerous or rich as they are. I am giving all satisfaction in my power.

The distinctions between Virginians, Pennsylvanians, New Yorkers, and New Englanders are no more. *I am not a Virginian, but an American.*

Slaves are to be thrown out of the question, and if the freeman can be represented according to their numbers, I am satisfied. I agree that authentic accounts cannot be had, if by authenticity is meant attestations of officers of the Crown. I go upon the supposition that government is at an end. All distinctions are thrown down. All America is thrown into one mass. We must aim at the minutiae of rectitude.[9]

## Patrick Henry Denounces Tyranny with a Galvanizing Speech

On March 23, 1775, Henry delivered his most famous oration, as a member of the second Virginia Convention, in which he stressed the time for the colony to take action against the British had arrived. It was given at St. John's Episcopal Church in Henrico Parish, Richmond, Virginia, where the delegates had convened after being barred from the Capitol by the Governor. Following is the complete text:

### Give Me Liberty, or Give Me Death!
*To the Convention of Delegates* (1775)

Mr. President: no man thinks more highly than I do of the patriotism, as well as abilities, of the very worthy gentlemen who have just addressed the House. But different men often see the same subject in different lights; and, therefore, I hope that it will not be thought disrespectful to those gentlemen, if, entertaining as I do, opinions of a character very opposite to theirs, I shall speak forth my sentiments freely and without reserve. This is no time for ceremony. The question before the House is one of awful moment to this country. For my own part I consider it as nothing less than a question of freedom or slavery; and in proportion to the magnitude of the subject ought to be the freedom of the debate. It is only in this way that we can hope to arrive at truth, and fulfill the great responsibility which we hold to God and our country. Should I keep back my opinions at such a time, through fear of giving offense, I should consider myself as guilty of treason toward my country, and of an act of disloyalty toward the majesty of heaven, which I revere above all earthly kings.

Mr. President, it is natural to man to indulge in the illusions of hope. We are apt to shut our eyes against a painful truth, and listen to the song of that siren, till she transforms us into beasts. Is this the part of wise men, engaged in a great and arduous struggle for liberty? Are we disposed to be of the number of those who, having eyes, see not, and having ears, hear not, the things which so nearly concern their temporal salvation? For my part, whatever anguish of spirit it may cost, I am willing to know the whole truth; to know the worst and to provide for it.

I have but one lamp by which my feet are guided; and that is the lamp of experience. I know of no way of judging of the future but by the past. And judging by the past, I wish to know what there has been in the conduct of the British ministry for the last ten years to justify those hopes with which gentlemen have been pleased to solace themselves and the House? Is it that insidious smile with which our petition has been lately received? Trust it not, sir; it will prove a snare to your feet. Suffer not yourselves to be betrayed with a kiss. Ask yourselves how this gracious reception of our petition comports with these warlike preparations which cover our waters and darken our land. Are fleets and armies necessary to a work of love and reconciliation? Have we shown ourselves so unwilling to be reconciled, that force must be called in to win back our love? Let us not deceive ourselves, sir. These are the implements of war and subjugation; the last arguments to which kings resort. I ask gentlemen, sir, what means this martial array, if its purpose be not to force us to submission? Can gentlemen assign any other possible motives for it? Has Great Britain any enemy, in this quarter of the world, to call for all this accumulation of navies and armies? No, sir, she has none. They are meant for us; they can be meant for no other. They are sent over to bind and rivet upon us those chains which the British ministry have been so long forging. And what have we to oppose to them? Shall we try argument? Sir, we have been trying that for the last ten years. Have we anything new to offer on the subject? Nothing. We have held the subject up in every light of which it is capable; but it has been all in vain. Shall we resort to entreaty and humble supplication? What terms shall we find which have not been already exhausted? Let us not, I beseech you, sir, deceive ourselves longer. Sir, we have done everything that could be done to avert the storm which is now coming on. We have petitioned; we have remonstrated; we have supplicated; we have prostrated ourselves before the throne, and have implored its interposition to arrest the tyrannical hands of the ministry and parliament. Our petitions have been slighted; our remonstrances have produced additional violence and insult; our supplications have been disregarded; and we have been spurned, with contempt, from the foot of the throne. In vain, after these things, may we indulge the fond hope of peace and reconciliation. There is no longer any room for hope. If we wish to be free — if we mean to preserve inviolate those inestimable privileges for which we have been so long contending — if we mean not basely to abandon the noble struggle in which we have been so long engaged, and which we have pledged ourselves never to abandon until the glorious object of our contest shall be obtained, we must fight! I repeat it, sir, we must fight! An appeal to arms and to the God of Hosts is all that is left us.

They tell us, sir, that we are weak; unable to cope with so formidable an adversary. But when shall we be stronger? Will it be the next week, or the next year? Will it be when we are totally disarmed, and when a British guard shall be stationed in every house? Shall we gather strength by irresolution and inaction? Shall we acquire the means of effectual resistance by lying supinely on our backs, and hugging the delusive phantom of hope, until our enemies shall have bound us hand and foot? Sir, we are not weak, if we make a proper use of the means which the God of nature hath placed in our power. Three millions of people armed in the holy cause of liberty, and in such a country as that which we possess, are invincible by any force which our enemy can send against us. Besides, sir, we shall not fight our battles alone. There is a just God who presides over the destinies of nations; and who will raise up friends to fight our battles for us. The battle, sir, is not to the strong alone; it is to the vigilant, the active, the brave. Besides, sir, we have no election. If we were base enough to desire it, it is now too late to retire from the contest. There is no retreat but in submission and slavery! Our chains are forged! Their clanking may be heard on the plains of Boston! The war is inevitable — and let it come! I repeat it, sir, let it come!

It is in vain, sir, to extenuate the matter. Gentlemen may cry peace, peace — but there is no peace. The war is actually begun! The next gale that sweeps from the North will bring to our ears the clash of resounding arms! Our brethren are already in the field! Why stand we here idle? What is it that gentlemen wish? What would they have? Is life so dear, or peace so sweet, as to be purchased at the price of chains and slavery? Forbid it, Almighty God! I know not what course others may take; but as for me, give me liberty, or give me death![10]

## Patrick Henry's Key to Success:
## There is a Just God Who Will Fight Our Battles for Us —

From whence came Patrick Henry's boldness and assurance of success? Clearly from his knowledge of the Bible, which tells us that God will fight our battles for us, and that He is on the side of His own. (Psalm 35; II Chronicles 20). Henry affirms that:

...an appeal to arms and to the God of Hosts is all that is left us...; armed in the holy cause of liberty... There is a just God who presides over the destinies of nations; and who will raise up friends to fight our battles for us...

He decries the impending slavery of his countrymen with this galvanizing call to action:

Forbid it, Almighty God! I know not what course others may take; but as for me, give me liberty, or give me death!"

This was the cry that heralded the American Revolution.

# GEORGE MASON
## Author of the Virginia Declaration of Rights
## (1725 - 1792)

George Mason, although perhaps not as well known as the other founding fathers, was a significant figure during the years encompassing the American Revolution. Born in 1725 in northern Virginia, he grew up on a plantation, being tutored at home. He was a close friend and neighbor of George Washington.

## Founder of Our Merchant Marine

As the wealthiest man in Virginia, George Mason owned 15,000 acres of land around his baronial estate, about 80,000 acres of land in Kentucky and a large estate in Ohio. He also owned or chartered a number of ships sailing from ports in Virginia and Maryland and engaged in the carrying trade of the colonies with England, France and the West Indies, and therefore may be said to have been the founder of our Merchant Marine.

## Mason, Statesman, Legislator and Judge

This American son was a member of the Board of Trustees of Alexandria, represented Fairfax County in the Virginia Assembly and was one of the presiding judges of the county.[1]

## Mason, a Fervent Christian

A fervent Christian, Mason was active in church life. For 35 years he was a vestryman of Truro Parish, which consisted of three churches. Along with George Washington, he also served on the building committee of Pohick Church, their own parish church constructed in 1774.

## Mason Takes an Firm Stand Against Slavery

In 1759 he became a member of the Virginia House of Burgesses, at the same time as George Washington. He took an firm stand against slavery, drafting the "Non-importation Association," which George Washington presented in 1769 in Williamsburg; and the "Resolves" adopted at a general meeting of the freeholders of Fairfax County, 18 July, 1774.[2] These resolves are regarded as one of the best expositions regarding the points of issue between the colonies and Great Britain of that period. In regard to slavery, it stated the following:

> ...That during our present difficulties and distress, no slaves ought to be imported into any of the British colonies on this continent; *and we take this*

GEORGE MASON

*After the original painting by John Hesselius (c. 1760).*
*Original in the Virginia State Library and Archives, Richmond.*

*opportunity of declaring our most earnest wishes to see an entire stop forever put to such a wicked, cruel and unnatural trade.*[3]

## James Madison Called Him "The Master Builder of the Constitution"

George Mason was a member of the Virginia Convention, held in Richmond, July 1775. Although he did not accept the appointment offered him as a delegate to the Continental Congress, he was a foremost figure in shaping both state and national political policy with his principles of free government.[4] He wrote the Virginia Declaration of Rights, adopted by the Convention on 12 June, 1776. James Madison called him "the master builder of the Constitution" of Virginia.[5] A noted historian says the following about this American patriot:

> George Mason was the first man in the history of the world to formulate the principles of liberty and justice in a great state paper. His Virginia Constitution was the forerunner and pattern of all the Constitutions subsequently made. The first ten amendments of the Constitution of the United States are practically his and may be found expressed in the Virginia Bill of Rights. The influence of his work is worldwide. His ideals of Liberty, Freedom and Equality constitute the essence of all modern thought on this subject.
>
> His ideals have become a safeguard to human rights all the world over...He was probably the wisest and most disinterested man to whom so great a task has ever been allotted by Divine Providence. He must be considered one of the greatest benefactors of our race.[6]

## Mason's War Cry: "The People Should Control the Government, not the Government the People"

Among those who admired his multi-faceted personality was General Fitzhugh Lee, who said of him:

> He was indeed the people's man in a people's government. The tent of his faith was pitched upon the bedrock of the freedom of the citizen. Great was his belief in the security of a purely Republican form of government. Sublime was his reliance in the power of the people. This life of George Mason is proper and opportune. A period in our history has been selected to which we should more frequently recur, by calling attention to the service of a man with whose career we should become more familiar. "The people should control the government, not the government the people," was his war cry.[7]

## The Virginia Bill of Rights — A Christian Document

The last of the 16 articles in the Virginia Bill of Rights, authored by George Mason, and forerunner to the United States Bill of Rights, reads:

That Religion, or the Duty which we owe to our Creator, and the Manner
of discharging it, can be directed only by Reason and Conviction, not by Force
or Violence; and therefore, all Men are equally entitled to the free exercise of
Religion, according to the Dictates of Conscience; and that it is the mutual
Duty of all to practice Christian Forbearance, Love, and Charity, towards
each other.

Article XVI
The Virginia Declaration of Rights

## Mason on Slavery:
## "Every Master of Slaves is Born a Petty Tyrant"

He took an active part in the Constitutional Convention of 1787,
which met in Philadelphia. Among other issues, he spoke strongly
regarding slavery, believing that Congress should be given the control
of slavery.[8] James Madison wrote the following report concerning
Mason's speech on slavery:

This infernal traffic originated in the avarice of British merchants. The
British government constantly checked the attempts of Virginia to put a stop
to it. The present question concerns not the importing States alone, but the
whole Union...Slavery discourages arts and manufactures. The poor dispise
labor when performed by slaves. They prevent the emigration of whites, who
really enrich and strengthen a country. They produce the most pernicious effect
on manners. Every master of slaves is born a petty tyrant. They bring the
judgment of Heaven on a country. As nations cannot be rewarded or punished
in the next world, they must be in this. By an inevitable chain of causes and
effects, Providence punishes national sins by national calamities. He (George
Mason) lamented that some of our eastern brethren had, from a lust of gain,
embarked in this nefarious traffic...He held it essential in every point of view,
that the General Government should have power to prevent the increase of
slavery.[9]

Shortly before his death, he told Thomas Jefferson that,

the Constitution as agreed to for a fortnight before the Convention rose
was such a one as he would have set his hand and heart to... With respect to
the importation of slaves, it was left to Congress. This disturbed the two
southernmost states, who knew that Congress would immediately suppress
the importation of slaves...[10]

"Under the coalition, the great principles of the Constitution were
changed in the last days of the Convention," wrote George Mason.
This founding father rejected the Constitution, refusing to put his
signature to the document chiefly due to its exclusion of his views on
slavery.[11]

## George Mason's Account of His Godly Wife in His Family Bible

In regard to his personal life, Mason married Ann Eilbeck in 1750. She died at the age of 39, her husband writing the following account of his godly and beloved wife's death in their family Bible:

On Tuesday, the 9th of March, 1773, about three o'clock in the morning, died at Gunston-Hall, of a slow fever, Mrs. Ann Mason, in the thirty-ninth year of her age; after a painful and tedious illness of more than nine months, which she bore with truly Christian patience and resignation, in faithful hope of eternal happiness in the world to come. She, it may be truthfully said, led a blameless and exemplary life. She retained unimpaired her mental faculties to the last; and spending her latest moments in prayer for those around her, seem'd to expire without the usual pangs of dissolution. During the whole course of her illness, she was never heard to utter one peevish or fretful complaint, and constantly, regardless of her own pain and danger, endeavoured to administer hope and comfort to her friends, or inspire them with resignation like her own. For many days before her death she had lost all hopes of recovery, and endeavour'd to wean herself from the affections of this life, saying that tho' it must cost her a hard struggle to reconcile herself to the hopes of parting with her husband and children, she hoped God would enable her to accomplish it; and after this, tho' she had always been the tenderest parent, she took little notice of her children, but still retain'd her usual serenity of mind. She was buried in the new Family-burying-ground at Gunston-Hall; but (at her own request) without the common parade and ceremony of a grand Funeral.

Her funeral sermon was preached in Pohick Church by the Reverend Mr. James Scott, Rector of Dettingen Parish in the County of Prince William, upon a text taken from the 23rd, 24th, and 25th verses of the 73rd Psalm: "Nevertheless, I am continually with Thee; Thou hast taken hold of my right hand. With Thy counsel Thou wilt guide me, And afterward receive me to glory. Whom have I in heaven but Thee? And besides Thee I desire nothing on earth."

In the beauty of her person and the sweetness of her disposition she was equalled by few and excelled by none of her sex. She was something taller than the middle size and elegantly shaped. Her eyes were black, tender and lively; her features regular and delicate; her complexion remarkably fair and fresh. Lilies and roses (almost without a metaphor) were blended there, and a certain inexpressible air of cheerfulness and health. Innocence and sensibility diffused over her countenance formed a face the very reverse of what is generally called masculine. This is not an ideal but a real picture drawn from the life, nor was this beautiful outward form disgraced by an unworthy inhabitant. "Free from her sex's smallest faults, and fair as womankind can be."

She was blessed with a clear and sound judgement, a gentle and benevolent heart, a sincere and an humble mind, with an even, calm and cheerful temper to a very unusual degree; affable to all, but intimate with few. Her modest virtues shunned the public eye; superior to the turbulent passions of pride and envy, a stranger to altercation of any kind, and content with the blessings of a private station, she placed all her happiness here, where only it is to be found, in her own family. Though she despised dress she was always neat; cheerful but not gay; serious but not melancholy. She never met me without a smile! Though an only child she was a remarkably dutiful one. An easy and agreeable companion, a kind neighbor, a steadfast friend, a humane mistress, a prudent and tender mother, a faithful, affectionate and most obliging wife; charitable to the poor and pious to her Maker, her virtue and religion were unmixed with hypocrisy or ostentation. She was formed for domestic happiness, without one jarring atom in her frame! Her irreparable departure I do ever shall deplore, and though time, I hope, will soften my sad impressions and restore me greater serenity of mind than I have lately enjoyed, I shall ever retain the most tender and melancholy remembrance of one so justly dear.[12]

## Eulogy on Mason—
## "Active, Earnest and Influential in the Counsels of Virginia"

On the reverse side of the eulogy on his beloved wife, are found the following lines written shortly after his death by a family member. It gives an accurate account of the founding father's stature and caliber as a patriot.

George Mason of Gunston died at the Seat of Gunston Hall in Fairfax County, Virginia, on the afternoon of Sunday, the seventh day of October, 1792 in the 67th year of his age, and was buried on the family ground at that place. A profound statesman and a pure patriot, he was a man of the first order, among those who acted on the theatre of the Revolution. He was active, earnest and influential in the counsels of Virginia, steering the struggle with Great Britain and took a zealous part, as a member of the Federal Convention in 1787, giving strong reasons, why the proposed Constitution, as it then stood, should not be adopted, and finally refused to sign it; for which he published to the world his reasons. The Virginia Convention of 1788 called to pass on that Constitution, he then opposed its adoption, and advocated another General Convention to revise it.

## George Mason Trusts, "Through the Merits of His Blessed Savior, a Remission of His Sins."

George Mason's last Will and Testament shows forth his love and adherence to the Lord Jesus Christ, during his sojourn upon earth, believing in the remission of his sins, through the merits of his blessed Savior:

I, George Mason, of "Gunston Hall," in the parish of Truro and county of Fairfax, being of perfect and sound mind and memory and in good health, but mindful of the uncertainty of human life and the imprudence of man's leaving his affairs to be settled upon a deathbed, do make and appoint this my last Will and Testament. My soul, I resign into the hands of my Almighty Creator, whose tender mercies are over all His works, who hateth nothing that He hath made and to the Justice and Wisdom of whose dispensation I willingly and cheerfully submit, humbly hoping from His unbounded mercy and benevolence, through the merits of my blessed Savior, a remission of my sins.[13]

# PETER von MUHLENBERG
## "The Fighting Parson"
## (1746 - 1807)

## A Memorial Erected To Honor Peter von Muhlenberg

On Thursday, April 1, 1976, the *Religious News Service* circulated this press release in respect to Peter von Muhlenberg:

> Washington, D.C. — A memorial will be erected here to honor Peter Muhlenberg, remembered in American history as "the fighting parson of the American Revolution" ...A clergyman who dramatically pulled open his clerical vestments at the close of a sermon 200 years ago to reveal the uniform of a colonel in the Continental Army, Muhlenberg went on to serve a total of eight years' military service for the then fledgling country... Ultimately promoted to the rank of Major General, John Peter Gabriel Muhlenberg was the eldest of eleven children of Henry Melchior Muhlenberg, who has been referred to as the "patriarch" of Lutherans in this country. The younger Muhlenberg was ordained by the Lutheran ministerium of Pennsylvania in 1768, serving parishes in New Germantown, Pennsylvania, and Bedminister, New Jersey. Then moving to Woodstock, Virginia, he was asked by the Anglican Church to serve German-speaking settlers there, agreeing to be ordained as Anglican minister in 1772. It was at the close of a four-year ministry at the Anglican Church in Woodstock in 1772 that he threw off his black clerical robe and revealed his Continental Army uniform, quoting the Bible from the Book of Ecclesiastes, Chapter 3, verse 8: 'There is a time for peace and a time for war.'[1]

## Muhlenberg's Farewell Scripture

This Scriptural admonition reads, in its entirety, as follows:

> There is an appointed time for everything
> And there is a time for every event under heaven
> A time to give birth and a time to die;
> A time to plant, and a time to uproot what is planted
> A time to kill and a time to heal;
> A time to tear down, and a time to build up
> A time to weep and a time to laugh;
> A time to mourn and a time to dance.
> A time to throw stones, and a time to gather stones;
> A time to embrace and a time to shun embracing
> A time to search and a time to give up as lost;
> A time to keep and a time to throw away
> A time to tear apart and a time to sew together
> A time to be silent and a time to speak
> A time to love and a time to hate;
> A time for war, and a time for peace.
> Ecclesiastes 3:1-8.

*After the original marble sculpture in the Small House Rotunda,*
*U.S. Capitol, Washington, D.C.*

The original record of this unique epic of American history tells us that the congregation had just sung Martin Luther's beautiful hymn, "A Mighty Fortress Is Our God," praising God's sovereignty and power in the midst of great tribulation.[2]

## Muhlenberg's Parishioners Galvanized to Action

A number of Muhlenberg's parishioners readily enrolled for service in the War for Independence. Thus, the German regiment was complete in March, 1776, its officers and men being for the most part, German settlers from Pennsylvania and New Jersey.[3]

A well-known poem, based upon this exciting saga of America's history, was composed by Thomas Buchanan Read. A favorite among students, it used to be featured in most public school "readers:"

> The pastor rose; the prayer was strong;
> The psalm was warrior David's song;
> The text, a few short words of might
> 'The Lord of Hosts shall arm the right!'
> He spoke of wrongs too long endured,
> Of sacred rights to be secured,
> Then from the patriot tongue of flame
> The startling words for Freedom came.
> The stirring sentences he spake
> Compelled the heart to glow or quake,
> And, rising on his theme's broad wing,
> And grasping in his nervous hand
> The imaginary battle brand,
> In face of death he dared to fling
> Defiance to a tyrant king.
> Even as he spoke, his frame, renewed,
> In eloquence of attitude,
> Rose, as it seemed, a shoulder higher;
> Then swept his kindling glance of fire
> From startled pew to breathless choir;
> When suddenly his mantle wide
> His hands impatient flung aside,
> And lo! he met their wondering eyes
> Complete in all a warrior's guise.
> 'Who dares' this was the patriot's cry,
> As striding from the desk he came
> 'Come out with me in Freedom's name,
> For her to live, for her to die?'
> A hundred voices answered, 'I!'[4]

## Peter von Muhlenberg's Amazing Accomplishments

Peter von Muhlenberg's distinguished career shows these amazing accomplishments:

Chairman of the Committee of Safety and Correspondence of Dunmore County, Virginia, June 16, 1774; Member of the Virginia House of Burgesses, 1774; Delegate to the Virginia Convention, 1774; Colonel, Eighth Regiment, Virginia Line, February 13, 1776; Brigadier-General, Continental Army, February 21, 1777; Brevet Major-General, September 30, 1783; at Brandywine, Germantown, Valley Forge, Monmouth, Stony Point, Green Spring and Yorktown. Member of the Virginia State Society of the Cincinnati, transferred to the Pennsylvania State Society, 1789.[5]

Born at Trappe, Montgomery County, Pennsylvania, Peter was the eldest of 11 children of Henry Melchior Muhlenberg and his wife, Anna Maria Weiser, daughter of the well-known frontiersman and Indian Interpreter, John Conrad Weiser.[6]

He was an intelligent child, with a love of nature. His father noted in his diary at age 13, Peter enjoyed hunting and fishing, but didn't care much for female society.[7]

## Peter Is Trained for the Ministry

When Peter was 15 his family moved from Trappe, Pennsylvania to Philadelphia. He and his two younger brothers entered Philadelphia Academy, forerunner to the University of Pennsylvania. Two and a half years later, the three boys went to a German school in Halle, Germany. At age 22, Peter began his biblical studies to prepare him for his calling as a minister of the Gospel. He did his pastoral internship in Philadelphia under a Lutheran pastor. Muhlenberg attracted great numbers of German Christians, who listened with rapt attention to the Word of God being brought to life through the preaching of powerful messages in their language.[8]

## Pastor-Preacher in Both English and German

Muhlenberg was then called by an Episcopal Church ministering to German settlers in the town of Woodstock, Virginia, as a preacher in both English and German languages, his salary being 250 pounds a year.[9]

## His Christian Character Traits

Peter's disposition was honest, sincere and zealous. His ministry as rector of Woodstock Church, was fruitful and productive in the harvesting and nurturing of souls for Christ's Kingdom.

## Muhlenberg Is Elected to the House of Burgesses

His interest and involvement in community affairs led to his being elected to the House of Burgesses in Williamsburg. He was present at the famous meeting in Raleigh Tavern, Williamsburg, after the patriots were banned from meeting at the Capitol by the British Governor. Patrick Henry made a renowned speech on this occasion, urging action on the part of the patriots. As a result, George Washington stated that he would "raise and subsist one thousand men to go with them to Boston" to counter the British there. The decision was made to no longer export goods to England, nor to use British merchandise.[10]

## The Source of Peter Von Muhlenberg's Strength—the Bible

All these exciting events characterizing the life and deeds of Peter von Muhlenberg during the War for Independence, find their source, once again, in God's Book—the Bible—for it was immediately after his farewell sermon preached from the old log church in Woodstock, followed by the dramatic removal of his pastor's cloak to disclose a soldier's uniform, that "the fighting parson" began defending our freedoms.

CAESAR RODNEY

DELAWARE

*After the original marble statue in the Senate Connecting Corridor,*
*U.S. Capitol, Washington, D.C.*

# CAESAR RODNEY
## Heroic Rider of the Revolution
## (1728 - 1784)

## Delaware's Greatest Statesman

Signer of the Declaration of Independence, Caesar Rodney is represented in the U.S. Capitol as one of Delaware's foremost statesmen. On June 26,1934, at the unveiling of Caesar Rodney's statue in the Hall of Fame of the U.S. Capitol, Dr. George H. Ryden of the University of Delaware stated of him:

> ...Caesar Rodney was one of Delaware's greatest sons, the principal founder of our State as a political entity, independent of Pennsylvania, and one of a galaxy of distinguished men who in a time of great stress and danger were not afraid to think nobly and to act courageously when they severed the tie of the mother country with her colonies.[1]

He was the only member of the Continental Congress who served continuously from its first session in 1774, until after the signing of the treaty of peace with Great Britain. [2]

Rodney was the son of William Rodney, who emigrated to America around 1681, and of Elizabeth (Crawford) Rodney, daughter of the Reverend Thomas Crawford, first missionary sent to Dover, Delaware, and its environs by the Society for the Propagation of the Gospel in Foreign Parts. [3] Most of Caesar's education came from his parents.

## Justice of the Supreme Court

Appointed third justice of the Supreme Court of Delaware for the Three Lower Counties in 1769, he was commissioned second justice of the same court in 1773.

## Delegate to the First Continental Congress

In 1765 he was elected by the House of Assembly as the representative of Kent County in the Stamp Act Congress, which met in New York to protest to the king against the actions of Parliament. This assembly appointed Rodney, Thomas McKean and George Read to attend the First Continental Congress.[4] Rodney had the dramatic distinction of casting the vote which made the colonies unanimous in voting for independence.

## Caesar Rodney's Heroic Ride for Independence

As the day of the vote drew near, Caesar had returned to Dover to fulfill his other responsibilities as speaker of the Delaware Assembly.[5] While McKean was an enthusiastic supporter of independence, Read would not vote in favor of it, thus cancelling one another's votes.

McKean hired a messenger to make the 80-mile trip to Dover on horseback, in order to alert Rodney to the problem.[6] He quickly responded, making the ride in sultry weather, a thunderstorm and a change of horse in mid-course. He arrived at the State House in Philadelphia muddied and weary, but just in time to cast his vote on that historic day. In answer to the roll call vote, he said:

> As I believe the voice of my constituents and of all sensible and honest men, is in favor of independence, my own judgment concurs with them. I vote for independence.[7]

It has been said that had even one of the colonies not voted in favor of independence, it could have been disastrous to the cause.[8]

In June 1776, Rodney presided over the session of the Colonial Assembly at New Castle, which passed a resolution supplanting the authority of the crown of England in the government of the Three Lower Counties, and which issued new instructions to Rodney and his two colleagues from Delaware, authorizing them to cooperate with the other colonies.[9]

## John Adams' Testimony of Rodney's Qualities

Of this great American son, John Adams wrote that

> . . . there is a sense of fire, spirit, wit and humor in his countenance.[10]

## Rodney, Commander of the Delaware Militia

Rodney fought throughout the Revolution. He was in command of the Delaware militia as brigadier-general, when the British invaded the state in September 1777. Shortly thereafter, the acting president of the state, Thomas McKean, commissioned Rodney as major-general of the Delaware Militia.[11]

## Caesar Rodney's Character Traits and Virtues

Frank B. Lord, writing in the *Washington Post* on June 28, 1931, reported the following regarding his character:

> . . . A contemporary wrote of him that he was 'about 5 feet 10 inches high; his person was very elegant and genteel; his manners graceful, easy and polite. He had a good fund of humor, and the happiest talent in the world of making wit agreeable, however sparkling and severe. He was a great statesman, a faithful public officer, just in all his dealings, easy to his family and debtors, sincere to his friends, beneficent to his relatives and kind to his servants, and always given to a generous and social style. . .'[12]

## His Self-sacrifice for Independence

Suffering with a facial cancer, he had been urged to go to England for treatment, but due to his sense of responsibility to the cause of independence, he remained in America. It finally caused his death on June 29, 1784. He had written in a letter about the illness, that it was "truly dangerous, and what will be the event God only knows; I still live in hopes, and still retain my usual spirits."

Rodney, who never married, was buried on his estate in an unmarked grave in Kent County, Delaware. His mortal remains were later moved to Christ Episcopal Church burial ground in Dover.

## Proceedings of the Convention of the Delaware State

Of great interest to Americans wishing to gain insight into the foundational strength of our nation at its inception, are the *Proceedings of the Convention of the Delaware State*, held at New Castle on Tuesday, the 27th of August 1776. It is hereunder excerpted:

> 1. That each member of this convention take the following Oath of Affirmation: I, _____, will to the utmost of my power, support and maintain the Independence of this State as declared by the Honorable Continental Congress, and I will to the utmost of my ability endeavor to form such a system of Government for the people of this state as in my opinion may be best adapted to promote their happiness and secure to them the enjoyment of their natural, civil and religious rights and privileges.
>
> 2. That every member make and subscribe the following Declaration, to wit: I, _____, do profess faith in God the Father and Jesus Christ his only Son, and in the Holy Ghost, one God blessed forevermore.
>
> This the president on the chair, and afterwards, the members present, took the subscribed same.[13]

## A Declaration of Rights and Fundamental Rules of the Delaware State

The same Convention formulated *A Declaration of Rights and Fundamental Rules of the Delaware State*, formerly stiled the *Government of the Counties of New Castle, Kent and Sussex upon Delaware*:

> That all persons professing the Christian Religion ought forever to enjoy equal rights and privileges of this State, unless under colour of Religion any man disturb the Peace, the happiness or safety of society.

To which was added this oath of personal testimony:

> I do profess faith in God the Father, and Jesus Christ his only Son, and in the Holy Ghost, one God forevermore, and I do acknowledge the Holy Scriptures of the Old and New Testament to be given by divine inspiration.[14]

What an incredible witness to the hand of Almighty God, through Jesus Christ His Son, upon Delaware, the first state to ratify the U.S. Constitution! It is little wonder that God's blessings have been showered upon America, from coast to shining coast, from her earliest beginnings — our trust being in God alone, and in none other.

# THOMAS NELSON, JR.
## Yorktown, Virginia
## (1738 - 1789)

Thomas Nelson was born in York County, Virginia, on December 26, 1738, the son of William Nelson, governor of Virginia 1770-71. Thomas was educated in Cambridge, England.[1]

## Nelson Moves for the Declaration of Independence

He returned to Yorktown in 1761, and was a member of the provincial conventions, 1774-76. He introduced the resolution instructing the delegates from Virginia to move for a declaration of independence in the Continental Congress, and later became a delegate himself from 1775-77, and a signer of the Declaration of Independence.[2]

## Thomas Nelson's "Sacred Honor"

His heirs, in testimony to the General Assembly of the Commonwealth of Virginia, reported the following:

> ...He often declared, that he did not consider the assertions made in that sacred instrument, by those who signed it, as the empty menace of excited feeling, but as the heart-felt solemn pledge of honourable men, determined on its redemption and fulfillment, as occasion and the necessities of the country should demand...[3]

## His "Ardent and Generous Spirit"

Due to ill health, he was forced to resign from the Continental Congress, but not for long, as stated in the testimony of his heirs:

> ...His ardent and generous spirit could not long brook the listlessness of retirement, while all around were roused to action by the pressure of a foreign foe. Whilst regaining his health by a short repose, he heard the din of war in the north, and the gallant Washington calling to the tented field, his countrymen to rally around the banner of the Union in squadrons of volunteers... The ancestor of these petitions, heard from afar this pressing call, and ever ready with his aid, when needed by his country, he buckled on his armor, and summoned to the field, a band of the gallant youth of his native state, amounting to 70 in number, and being chosen as their commander, he marched them to Philadelphia, the seat of the Continental Congress, and there made a tender of their services to that venerable body...[4]

## Nelson, Commander of the Virginia Militia

He remained at the head of the Virginia State forces until 1782. In the final battle of the Revolution at Yorktown, Virginia in 1781, he

After the original "Victory Monument" in Colonial Yorktown, Virginia.
Liberty stretches out her arms toward America.
Around the base of the column are 13 figures with a star upon each head,
representing the 13 original states in the union, with the wording:
"One Country, One Constitution, One Destiny."

commanded 3,500 Virginia militia. It was there that Earl Cornwallis, Commander of the British forces at Yorktown, surrendered to George Washington, Commander-in-Chief.[5]

## He Pledged his Fortune for Independence

The war had not only been costly to him in terms of his health, but also his possessions, as again stated in the report of his heirs:

> ...He entered the revolutionary arena, as a champion to maintain the rights of America, possessed of a very large estate, unincumbered with debts, and holding by inheritance from his father's great success in commerce, a capital of 40,000 pounds, in bonds of the most solvent men of the country. All these he may with truth be said to have offered as a sacrifice on the altar of the public weal. For at the close of his life, doubtless shortened by infirmity and sickness, contracted by exposure during the arduous conflict, and which occurred in a very few years after the end of the war, there remained, after the application of his property to the payment of his debts, but a pittance of his immense estate, for the support of a large and numerous family, reduced almost to want, by the generous and disinterested sacrifices of their ancestor, made to promote the freedom and independency of his beloved country...[6]

## Thomas Nelson, Jr., Patriot, Soldier, Christian Gentleman

General Nelson died January 2, 1789, and is buried in the courtyard of Colonial Grace Church of York-Hampton Parish. His epitaph reads:

> General Thomas Nelson, Jr., Patriot, soldier, Christian gentleman. Born December 18, 1738. Died January 2, 1789; mover of the Resolution of May 15, 1776 in the Virginia Convention instructing her delegates in Congress to move that body to declare the colonies free and independent states. Signer of the Declaration of Independence. War Governor of Virginia. Commissioner of Virginia's forces. He gave all for liberty.

From the above testimonies, we see that General Thomas Nelson was not only a fervent patriot and soldier in the great struggle for independence, but that he was a true Christian gentleman, exemplifying self-sacrifice, humility, courage and generosity, to the point of deprivation.

In signing the Declaration of Independence, Thomas Nelson had pledged his life, his fortune and his sacred honor for the cause of liberty. Proudly can Americans affirm that,

"He gave all for liberty."

# JOHN JAY
## First Chief Justice of the U.S. Supreme Court
## (1745 - 1829)

John Jay, first Chief Justice of the U.S. Supreme Court, stood but a little lower than Washington in the estimation of Americans. He was a man whom Washington trusted with perfect confidence, on whose wisdom and efficiency he placed his firmest reliance.[1]

## Jay: Unanimously Confirmed Chief Justice

John Jay accepted the position of Chief Justice of the newly-formed U.S. Supreme Court in 1789.[2] His nomination was unanimously confirmed by the Senate, from whom he received a letter stating their full confidence:

> ...that the love which you bear to our country, and a desire to promote the general happiness, will not suffer you to hesitate for a moment to bring into action the talents, knowledge and integrity which are so necessary to be exercised at the head of that department, which must be considered as the key-stone of our political fabric...[3]

## A Christian Upbringing

Jay was born in the city of New York on December 12, 1745. He came from a Christian Huguenot family, his grandfather, Augustus Jay, being the first to have emigrated to New York.[4] He always considered it an honor being descended from those who feared God and kept His commandments, and so were counted worthy to suffer for the sake of Christ. Jay's education to the age of eight was at his mother's knee. He was then sent to grammar school, taught by the pastor of the French Church at New Rochelle.[5]

## John Jay Goes to College at Age 14, Practicing Virtue.

At age 14, he entered Kings's College (now Columbia College) and in spite of the usual temptations of youth, he proved himself to be morally upright and unblameable in his practise of virtue, as well as a diligent student. Jay became an expert in writing and composition. It is recorded that at night he would have a piece of paper and a pencil next to his bedside, jotting down valuable thoughts and ideas as they came to his mind.[6]

## Jay Elected to the First Continental Congress

On September 5, 1774, Jay took his seat in the First Continental Congress, at Carpenter's Hall, Philadelphia. The fervent prayers of

JOHN JAY - NEW YORK

*After the original painting by Gilbert Stuart
in the National Gallery of Art, Washington, D.C.*

that group of men, led by Jacob Duché, Rector of Christ Church, Philadelphia, and later the first Chaplain to Congress, were memorialized in the painting "the First Prayer in Congress" by T.H. Matteson in 1848.

## Jay Affirms the Declaration of Independence

Mr. Jay was in meetings in New York with the State Convention when the Declaration of Independence was signed on July 4, 1776.[7] Five days later, he received a copy of it, and drafted the following resolution which was unanimously adopted by New York:

> Resolved, unanimously, that the reasons assigned by the Continental Congress, for declaring these united colonies free and independent states, are cogent and conclusive; and that, while we lament the cruel necessity which has rendered this measure unavoidable, we approve the same, and will, at the risk of our lives and fortunes, join with the other colonies in supporting it.[8]

## John Jay's Christian Character

Mr. Jay took part in guiding the councils of the friends of liberty in New York until he left the country in 1779 for Spain, having been appointed Minister Plenipotentiary to the court of Spain.[9] By his prudence, courage, steadfastness and perseverance, he rendered invaluable services to our nation, sacrificing his — and his family's comfort to do this:[10]

> ...I believe firmly the old adage, "that nothing is profitable that is not honest;" and therefore before politicians and others deviate from integrity, they should well consider the consequences... I have done nothing but serve my country for these six years past, and that most faithfully. I confess I did it, and am still doing it, as much or more for my own sake as for theirs; that is, because I thought, and think it my duty, without which I know I cannot please my Maker and get to heaven. Provided He is satisfied with my conduct, the mistaken opinions of others cannot deprive me of happiness...[11]

Here we see Jay's desire to please God, and the honesty and integrity with which he governed his life. John Jay was a true patriot.

## On Eternal Life

At the death of his beloved father, John Jay expressed his Christian belief in the immortality of the soul, and the importance of nurturing it for the life hereafter. To this effect, he writes to a friend:

> ...His affection for me was unbounded, and he knew I was conscious of it... Thank God, there is another world in which we may meet and be happy. His being there is a new motive to my following his footsteps. I assure you I know the value of Christian resignation: it has been friendly to me on several

occasions, which may, perhaps, one day furnish us with matter for conversation. I thank you most sincerely for reminding me of the great business and purpose of my life. Such admonitions, so given, are never unreasonable, and always kind. I am persuaded that they who have no regard for their own souls, will seldom have much for the interest and happiness of others...[12]

## On Slavery

Jay's view on slavery was a reflection of the Word of God, which tells us that men and women are made in His image (Genesis 1:26). This firm conviction, he expresses in another letter:

As to my sentiments and conduct relative to the abolition of slavery, the fact is this: In my opinion, every man, of every color and description, has a natural right to freedom, and I shall advocate for the manumission* of slaves, in such a way as shall be consistent with the justice due to them, with the justice due to their masters, and with the regard due to the actual state of society. These considerations unite in convincing me that the abolition of slavery must necessarily be gradual...[13]

## John Jay and Benjamin Franklin Good Friends

John Jay and Benjamin Franklin were generous in expressing their mutual admiration as good friends. This fact is even more significant when we realize that Jay was a reserved man, seldom showing enthusiasm.[14] From Madrid, he writes to his trusted friend, Dr. Franklin, in this vein:

...I have often congratulated my country and myself on your being at present in France. I once expected to have seen you there, and to have profited by the lessons which time and much experience have taught you. Miracles have ceased, and my constitution does not promise length of days, or I should probably desire you, when you ascend, to drop me your mantle. That you may long retain it is one of the prayers of your friend and servant.[15]

The friendship between Jay and Franklin remained steadfast. Twenty years after Franklin's death, Jay's loyalty remained firm even after Franklin was maligned by one of Jay's close associates.[16]

## Jay: "God has Brought About our Political Salvation"

John Jay's address to the people of the state of New York, on the subject of the Constitution, gives insight into this brilliant statesman's full support of it; and his assertion that God has blessed the Union of these States, thus bringing about "our political salvation":

...When the King of Great Britain, misguided by men who did not merit his confidence, asserted the unjust claim of binding us in all cases whatsoever, and

*Emancipation

prepared to obtain our submission by force, the object which engrossed our attention, however important, was nevertheless plain and simple. 'What shall we do?' was the question. The people answered, let us unite our councils and our arms. They sent delegates to Congress and soldiers to the field... Union was then considered as the most essential of human means... That union was the child of wisdom. Heaven blessed it, and it wrought out our political salvation...[17]

He concludes his address by exhorting the citizens of New York
> to receive it with the same candor with which it was written, and may the spirit of wisdom and patriotism direct and distinguish your counsels and your conduct.

*A citizen of New York*[18]

## John Jay Reads First Corinthians 15 to His Children at Their Mother's Death

In May, 1801, Jay and his family moved to Bedford, in Westchester County, to a farm which he had inherited from his ancestors. His beloved wife died shortly thereafter of a serious illness. Mr. Jay, calm and resigned, watched by her bedside as she died. Immediately after her Spirit had left her body to be with her Saviour, Jesus Christ, he took his children, who were with him, into the next room.

As tears filled his eyes, he read to them Chapter 15 of the Apostle Paul's first letter to the Corinthians, which, excerpted, reads as follows:

> Now I make known to you, brethren, the gospel which I preached to you, which also you received, in which also you stand, by which also you are saved, if you hold fast the word which I preached to you, unless you believed in vain. For I delivered to you as of first importance what I also received, that Christ died for our sins according to the Scriptures, and that He was buried, and that He was raised on the third day according to the Scriptures, and that He appeared to Cephas, then to the twelve. After that He appeared to more than five hundred brethren at one time, most of whom remain until now, but some have fallen asleep; then He appeared to James, then to all the apostles; and last of all, as it were to one untimely born, He appeared to me also. For I am the least of the apostles, who am not fit to be called an apostle because I persecuted the church of God. But by the grace of God I am what I am, and His grace toward me did not prove vain; but I labored even more than all of them, yet not I, but the grace of God with me. Whether then it was I or they, so we preach and so you believed.
>
> Now if Christ is preached, that He has been raised from the dead, how do some among you say that there is no resurrection of the dead? But if there is no resurrection of the dead, not even Christ has been raised; and if Christ has not been raised, then our preaching is vain, your faith also is vain. Moreover we are even found to be false witnesses of God, because we witnessed against God that He raised Christ, whom He did not raise, if in fact the dead are not raised. For if the dead are not raised, not even Christ has been raised, and if

Christ has not been raised, your faith is worthless; you are still in your sins. Then those also who have fallen asleep in Christ have perished. If we have hoped in Christ in this life only, we are of all men most to be pitied...

Now I say this, brethren, that flesh and blood cannot inherit the kingdom of God; nor does the perishable inherit the imperishable. Behold, I tell you a mystery; we shall not all sleep, but we shall all be changed, in a moment, in the twinkling of an eye, at the last trumpet; for the trumpet will sound, and the dead will be raised imperishable, and we shall be changed. For this perishable must put on the imperishable, and this mortal must put on immortality. But when this perishable will have put on the imperishable, and this mortal will have put on immortality, then will come about the saying that is written, "Death is swallowed up in victory. O Death, where is your victory? O death, where is your sting? The sting of death is sin, and the power of sin is the law; but thanks be to God, who gives us the victory through our Lord Jesus Christ. Therefore, my beloved brethren, be steadfast, immovable, always abounding in the work of the Lord, knowing that your toil is not in vain in the Lord.

I Corinthians 15:1-19; 50-58

Thus, he pointed them to their mother's future glory and immortality with Christ Jesus.[19]

## Jay Founded a Church

Jay subsequently established the first Episcopal Church in Bedford. His Christian life was rich and constant. Every morning, prior to breakfast, the family and servants would gather for prayer, Bible reading and devotions. This American Christian observance was repeated every evening at nine o'clock, prior to retiring for the night.[20] Loving the Word of God, John Jay would read one chapter of the Bible to them, morning and evening.

## John Jay, President of the American Bible Society

In 1821, Mr. Jay was elected president of the American Bible Society, being reelected each year until his death.[21]

## John Jay's Death

On May 14, 1829, he contracted palsy, losing his speech. He died on May 17, 1829, at the age of 84.

## John Jay's Prayer of Faith in Christ Jesus, His Redeemer

This great American statesman, first U.S. Supreme Court Chief Justice, left us a deathbed testimony to the sustaining power of his Christian faith. The consistent witness of his life and actions make such a testimony unnecessary. The following prayer, penned in his own handwriting, was found among his papers. It provides further evidence of his faith in Jesus Christ, Son of God, Savior, who shed His blood for the forgiveness of His child's sins. It is excerpted below:

> Merciful Father, who desirest not the death of the sinner, but will have all men to be saved and to come to the knowledge of the truth, give me grace so to draw nigh unto thee as that thou wilt condescend to draw nigh unto me; and enable me to offer unto Thee, through thy beloved Son, supplication and thanksgiving acceptably... Above all, I thank Thee for Thy mercy to our fallen race, as declared in Thy Holy Gospel, by Thy beloved Son, 'who gave Himself a ransom for all.' I thank Thee for the hope of the remission of sins, of regeneration, and of life and happiness everlasting, through the merits and intercession of our Saviour... Let Thy Holy Spirit purify and unite me to my Saviour forever, and enable me to cling unto Him as my very life, as indeed He is. Perfect and confirm my faith, my trust, and hope of salvation in Him and in Him only.[22]

Such was the inner life and motivating force behind John Jay, illustrious first Chief Justice of the U.S. Supreme Court — a biblical character par excellence. Of all the men whom history has made known to us, no one more fully deserves the title of "the model statesman."[23]

NOAH WEBSTER L.L.D.

*Noah Webster, after the original 1823 painting by Samuel F.B. Morse.*

# NOAH WEBSTER
## Webster's International Dictionary
## (1758 - 1843)

Noah Webster is world renowned for his famous dictionary, *An American Dictionary of the English Language*, published in 1828. In addition to his work as a lexicographer, he was also an educator of the highest caliber.[1]

Born in Hartford, Connecticut on October 16, 1758, he was the son of a respectable farmer and Justice of the Peace. He was a descendant of John Webster, one of the first settlers of Hartford, his mother's ancestor being the godly William Bradford, second governor of the 1620 Pilgrim colony at Plymouth.[2]

## Noah's Christian Background

Noah was tutored by Reverend Nathan Perkins, Doctor of Divinity, pastor of the parish. In 1774 he entered Yale College. He interrupted his studies, however, to volunteer his services in the American Revolution, serving under his father. Not having the means to attend law school, Webster pursued studies on his own while regularly employed, and was admitted to the bar in 1781.[3]

## A Foremost Educator

As a teacher in Goshen, New York, in the 1780's, he began to write textbooks for children. Christian values, virtues and morals, together with patriotism, permeate his texts. His books were instrumental in teaching correct spelling and pronunciation in this country. Webster believed that it was essential that the newly-formed nation set its own high goals in education, rather than rely on standards set by England.[4]

Webster was not only a schoolmaster, lecturer, pamphleteer and publisher of schoolbooks, but he was also the author of a pamphlet entitled: "Sketches of American Policy." The following initialed notation in Webster's handwriting shows his intricate involvement with founding fathers George Washington and James Madison in establishing a unique form of government. All three men were American Christian statesmen of the highest caliber:

> The following sketches were written in the month of February, 1785, before any proposal had even been made to remodel the government of the States. In May I carried one copy of them to Virginia and presented it to General Washington. Mr. Madison saw and read it at the General's soon after, and in November the same year, he, in conversation with me, expressed a

warm approbation of the sentiments it contains. At the next session of the Legislature, which indeed began the same month, a proposition was made in the Assembly, for appointing the commissioners, who afterward met at Annapolis and whose recommendations originated the convention at Philadelphia in 1787.[5]

## A Man of Steadfastness and Purpose

Webster devoted many years to the collection of new words and the preparation of more detailed and exact definitions. The results of his enquiries into the origin and filiation of languages were comprised in a work about the size of *An American Dictionary* entitled: *A Synopsis of Words in Twenty Languages.*

During these labors, Mr. Webster found his resources inadequate to support his family at New Haven. He thus moved, in 1812, to Amherst, a country town eight miles from Northampton, Massachusetts. In 1824, after spending two months in Paris consulting rare books at La Bibliotéque du Roi, and a subsequent eight months at Cambridge University in England, his most famous work, *An American Dictionary*, was finally completed in May of 1825.[6]

## Webster's Trust in Christ Jesus

Webster expressed his entire resignation to the will of God, and his unshaken trust in the atoning blood of his Redeemer, the Lord Jesus Christ.[7]

In his "Memoir of the Author" the Editor concludes:

> It may be said that the name Noah Webster, from the wide circulation of some of his works, is known familiarly to a greater number of the inhabitants of the United States, than the name, probably, of any other individual except the father of the Country. Whatever influence he thus acquired was used at all times to promote the best interests of his fellowmen. His books, though read by millions, have made no man worse. To multitudes they have been of lasting benefit not by the course of early training they have furnished, but by those precepts of wisdom and virtue with which almost every page is stored.
>
> August, 1847.[8]

## An American Dictionary of the English Language

In 1828, Webster's greatest work, *An American Dictionary of the English Language—with pronouncing vocabularies of Scripture, classical and geographical names,* was published.

There were 2,500 copies printed, followed by an edition of 3,000 copies in England. It contained 12,000 words and 40,000 definitions not found in any similar publication. In 1840-41 he published a second edition in two volumes with extensive additions to the vocabulary and corrections of definitions.[9]

# An Instrument for the Propagation
## of Science, Arts, Civilization and Christianity

The preface from Webster's 1848 Dictionary includes the following excerpts explaining his work:

> In the year 1783, just at the close of the Revolution, I published an elementary book for facilitating the acquisition of our vernacular tongue, and for correcting a vicious pronunciation, which prevailed extensively among the common people of this country. Soon after the publication of that work, I believe in the following year, that learned and respectable scholar the Rev. Dr. Goodrich of Durham, one of the trustees of Yale College, suggested to me the propriety and expediency of my compiling a dictionary, which would complete a system for the instruction of the citizens of this country in the language... About 35 years ago, I began to think of attempting the compilation of a dictionary... I published my compendious dictionary in 1806; and soon after made preparation for undertaking a larger work... It is not only important, but in a degree necessary, that the people of the country should have an "American Dictionary of the English Language;" for, although the body of the language is the same as in England, and it is desirable to perpetuate the sameness, yet some differences must exist. Language is the expression of ideas; and if the people of one country cannot preserve an identity of ideas, they cannot retain an identity of language. Now, an identity of ideas depends materially upon a sameness of things or objects with which the people of the two countries are conversant. But in no two portions of the earth, remote from each other, can such identity be found. Even physical objects must be different. But the principal differences between the people of this country and of all others, arise from different forms of government, different laws, institutions and customs... If the language can be improved in regularity, so as to be more easily acquired by our own citizens and by foreigners, and thus be rendered a more useful instrument for the propagation of science, arts, civilization and Christianity... and if, in short, our vernacular language can be redeemed from corruptions and our philology and literature from degradation; it would be a source of great satisfaction to me to be one among the instruments of promoting these valuable objects....

## A Great Masterpiece Completed

Webster penned these words as he neared completion of his work:

> I was seized with trembling, which made it somewhat difficult to hold my pen steady for writing. The cause seems to have been the thought that I might not then live to finish the work... But I summoned strength to finish the last work, then, walking about the room a few minutes, I recovered.

## Webster's Self-Sacrifice and Good-Stewardship of God's Bounty

An 1828 newspaper clipping announced the completion of Webster's famous dictionary, in these terms, showing forth his sacrifice, and the good stewardship of his God-given talents and abilities:

Noah Webster, Esq., author of the Spelling Book, has given notice in the Eastern newspapers, that he has completed a Dictionary of our language, "at the expense of 20 years of labor, and thirty thousand dollars in money." He mentions that he made a visit to England, partly with a view to ascertain the real state of the language, and there discovered that no book whatever was considered a rule in that country as a standard of orthoepy. He observes, incidentally, that not less than 7 millions of copies of his Spelling Book have been sold. He thinks that the English dictionaries, are all, half a century behind the state of science, and hopes that his fellow citizens will be furnished with something better in the one which he is about to publish.

## Webster's Love of the Word of God

Noah Webster knew and loved the Word of God with such intensity, being thoroughly convinced of its eternal and inerrant value, that he used Scripture verses throughout his dictionary, describing and explaining the meanings and import of much vocabulary and syntax. The title page of his original dictionaries bears this out with the wording: "...with pronouncing vocabularies of Scripture, Classical, and Geographical Names." For example, his descriptions for the verb "to follow," include:

To pursue as an object of desire; to endeavor to obtain. "Follow peace with all men." Hebrews 12

To adhere to; to side with. "The House of Judah followed David." II Samuel 2.

To adhere to; to honor; to worship; to serve. "If the Lord be God, follow Him." I Kings 18.

To be led or guided by. "Woe to the foolish prophets who follow their own spirit and have seen nothing." Ezekiel 13.

And then, the noun "country," is described in the following manner:

The kingdom, state or territory, in which one is born; the land of nativity; or the particular district indefinitely in which one is born. America is my country, or England is my country. "Laban said, it must not be so done in our country." Genesis 29

The region in which one resides. "He sojourned in the land of promise, as in a foreign country." Hebrews 11.

Land, as opposed to water; or inhabited territory. "The shipmen deemed that they drew near to some country." Acts 27. The inhabitants of a region. "All the country wept with a loud voice." 2 Samuel 15.

A place of residence; a region of permanent habitation. "They declare plainly that they seek a country." "They desire a better country, that is a heavenly one." Hebrews 11.

He defined "generation" as follows:

1. The act of begetting, procreation, as of animals.

2. Production, formation; as, the generation of sounds, or of curves or equations.

3. A single succession of natural descent, as the children of the same parents; hence, an age. Thus we say, the 3rd, the 4th or the 10th generation. Genesis XV:16.

4. The people of the same period or living at the same time.

O faithless and perverse generation! Luke IX

5. Genealogy; a series of children or descendants from the same stock. This is the book of the generation of Adam.

Genesis V.

## Webster's Works Among the Greatest American Best-Sellers

Among the greatest American best sellers, after the Bible, are: *Webster's Dictionary of the English Language, Webster's Biographical Dictionary* and *Webster's Dictionary of Synonyms*.

Webster's 1886 *Unabridged Dictionary*, with Scripture quotations throughout, was "warmly recommended by State Superintendents of Public Schools of Maine, New Hampshire, Vermont, Massachusetts, Rhode Island, Connecticut, New York, Pennsylvania, New Jersey, Delaware, Ohio, Virginia, Indiana, Illinois, Wisconsin, Minnesota, Kansas, Nebraska, Arkansas, Texas, Mississippi, Kentucky, California, Colorado, West Virginia, Oregon and ten other States of the Union.[10]

## His Blue-Back Speller Sells More Than 70 Million Copies

By 1947, the year during which Webster's publishers, the G. & C. Merriam Company, celebrated a centennial of Webster's magnificent dictionary, Noah Webster's famous *Blue-Back Speller* published in 1783, had sold more than 70,000,000 copies.[11]

## Webster's International Dictionary

Further to this, an early advertisement for the 1890 edition of Webster's International Dictionary, describes this great book as being invaluable in office, school and home, standard of the United States Government Printing Office, the Supreme Court and of nearly all the schoolbooks; warmly recommended by educators almost without number, The One Great Standard Authority. Hon. D.J. Brewer, Justice of the U.S. Supreme Court, writes: "The International Dictionary is the perfection of dictionaries. I commend it to all as the one great standard authority."[12]

## His Academic and Professional Accomplishments

Webster's academic and professional credentials are quite extensive, ranging from: Member of the American Philosophical Society in Philadelphia; Fellow of the American Academy of Arts and Sciences in Massachusetts; Member of the Connecticut Academy of Arts and Sciences; Fellow of the Royal Society of Northern Antiquaries in Copenhagen; Member of the Connecticut Historical Society; Corresponding Member of the Historical Societies in Massachusetts, New York and Georgia; of the Academy of Medicine in Philadelphia; and of the Columbian Institute in Washington; and Honorary Member of the Michigan Historical Society.[13]

## Webster's Translation of the Bible

One of Webster's greatest contributions was his Common Version translation of the Bible, published in 1833 at the age of 75. Using the original Hebrew and Greek manuscripts of the Old and New Testaments respectively, he translated God's Word into the vernacular. In his Preface to his Common Version translation of *The Holy Bible, containing the Old and New Testaments, with Amendments of the Language*, Webster states:

> The English version of the sacred Scriptures, now in general use, was first published in the year 1611, in the reign of James I. Although the translators made many alterations in the language of the former versions, yet no small part of the language is the same, as that of the versions made in the reign of Queen Elizabeth... The Bible is the Chief moral cause of all that is good, and the best corrector of all that is evil, in human society; the best book for regulating the temporal concerns of men, and the only book that can serve as an infallible guide to future felicity. With this estimate of its value, I have attempted to render the English version more useful, by correcting a few obvious errors and removing some obscurities with objectionable words and phrases; and my earnest prayer is that my labors may not be wholly unsuccessful.
>
> Noah Webster<br>New Haven, 1833.[14]

## Two Great Masterpieces of Our American Christian Heritage

It was thus that Noah Webster used his God-given talents fruitfully and diligently during his span of life on earth, distinguishing himself in the production of two of the greatest masterpieces of our national Christian heritage: Webster's original *Dictionary of the English Language—replete with Scripture verses;* and *The Holy Bible containing the Old and New Testaments, in the Common Version, with Amendments of the Language,* 1833.

## Noah Webster Gives All Praise and Glory to Almighty God

From whence came his strength and the source of his accomplishments? In Webster's own words, penned within the Preface of his 1828 dictionary, he gives all praise and glory to Almighty God:

To that great and benevolent Being, who, during the preparation of this work, has sustained a feeble constitution amidst obstacles and toils, disappointments, infirmities and depression; who has borne me and my manuscripts in safety across the Atlantic, and given me strength and resolution to bring the work to a close, I would present the tribute of my most grateful acknowledgments. And if the talent which He entrusted to my care, has not been put to the most profitable use in His service, I hope it has not been "kept laid up in a napkin" and that any misapplication of it may be graciously forgiven.

New Haven.
Noah Webster.

# CHAPTER IV
Development

# DANIEL WEBSTER
## New Hampshire's Greatest Hero
## (1782 - 1852)

Among the life-size statues in Statuary Hall of the United States Capitol is that of Daniel Webster of New Hampshire. Born in Salisbury, New Hampshire, he was the fourth child of Ebenezer Webster, who was of Puritan ancestry, and the former Abigail Eastman, who was described as "a woman of vigorous understanding, yet tender and self-sacrificing."[1]

## The Bible, Webster's Guide to Life

From the early years of childhood through old age, Webster acknowledged that his Bible had been the foundation of strength and guidance in his life:

> I do not remember when or by whom I was taught to read, because I cannot, and never could recollect a time when I could not read the Bible. I suppose I was taught by my mother, or by my elder sisters. My father seemed to have no higher object in the world than to educate his children to the full extent of his very limited ability...[2]

> I have read through the entire Bible many times. I now make it a practice to go through it once a year. It is the book of all others for lawyers as well as for divines; and I pity the man that cannot find in it a rich supply of thought, and of rules for his conduct. It fits man for life — it prepares him for death![3]

## A Country Boy at College

In 1796, Daniel attended Phillips Exeter Academy, where 90 boys were enrolled. He came from a country home background, while many of his peers were descended from rich, genteel families. Sometimes they would make fun of his different clothes and personality. Little did they know of the renown which awaited Webster, and the honor they would gain, simply by having been in the same class with this country boy! The world passes judgment according to outward appearances, while God reflects upon the character and motives of the inner man.

The following year, Daniel began to study with Reverend Samuel Wood, a minister of the Gospel in the town of Boscawen, six miles from Salisbury. In August 1797, at the age of 15, Webster entered Dartmouth College, proving himself to be a good-natured friend and an excellent student.[4] He was alone in his struggle with poverty, however, but he was happy and grateful in the knowledge that his father had made such great financial sacrifices to send him to college. This remarkable youth began earning money not only for himself, but for his brother, Ezekiel.

*After the original marble statue in Statuary Hall,*
*U.S. Capitol, Washington, D.C.*

He supervised the *Dartmouth Gazette*, a small weekly newspaper, and taught school in the winter to help Ezekiel through college.

## The College Student Becomes an Orator

His ability as a speaker became evident as a college student. One of his classmates testified to this:

> In his movements he was rather slow and deliberate, except when his feelings were aroused; then his whole soul would kindle into a flame. We used to listen to him with deepest respect and interest, and no one ever thought of equalling the vigor and flow of his eloquence.[5]

On July 4, 1800, Webster delivered his first public speech, at the request of the people of Hanover, tracing the history of our country from pioneer days to the revolution.[6]

## Webster's Famed 1820 Oration Commemorates Landing of the 1620 Pilgrims

On December 22, 1820, Webster delivered an inspiring oration at Plymouth commemorating the 200th anniversary of the landing of the Pilgrims. He proved himself a true master of the art of oratory, capturing his audience, who listened with rapt attention:

> Let us rejoice that we hold this day. Let us be thankful that we have lived to see the bright and happy breaking of the auspicious morn which commences the third century of the history of New England... Forever honored be this, the place of our fathers' refuge! Forever remembered the day which saw them, weary and distressed, broken in everything but spirit, poor in all but faith and courage, at last secure from the danger of wintry seas, and impressing this shore with the first footsteps of civilized man!...[7]

In this speech, Webster did not hesitate to emphasize the Christian religion upon which this unique 1620 band of Pilgrim Fathers based their government. People heard his eloquent words as though entranced. John Adams wrote to him, stating:

> If there be an American who can read it without tears, I am not that American... Mr. Burke is no longer entitled to the praise — the most consummate orator of modern times... this oration will be read 500 years hence with as much rapture as it was heard. It ought to be read at the end of every century, and indeed at the end of every year, forever and ever.[8]

In 1825, Webster again delivered a magnificent oration at the laying of the cornerstone of the Bunker Hill Monument. It sealed his place in the front rank of American orators of his day.

## Webster, the Lawyer, Congressman and Secretary of State

As a a leading constitutional lawyer, he had a private law practice and also served in both the U.S. House of Representatives and the Senate, in addition to being appointed Secretary of State in 1840.

## Webster's Beautiful Christian Wife

He was happily married to Grace Fletcher in 1808. Describing her godly character, Judge Story wrote about her

> ...kindness of heart, her generous feelings, her mild and conciliatory temper, her warm and elevated affections, her constancy, purity and piety, her noble disinterestedness, and her excellent sense.[9]

A letter received from his wife, written in the winter of 1824, tells of her deep faith and trust in Christ, at their two-year-old son, Charles' death:

> I have dreaded the hour which should destroy your hopes, but trust you will not let this event afflict you too much, and that we both shall be able to resign him without a murmur, happy in the reflection that he has returned to his Heavenly Father pure as I received him...[10]

Four years after his son's death, his "blessed wife," as he called her, went to be with her Lord and Savior Jesus Christ, forever, in heaven.

Upon returning to Washington to resume his duties as senator, it is recorded for us that Webster was broken-hearted, expressing to a friend how much he longed to have her at his side again:

> Like an angel of God, indeed, I hope she is in purity, in happiness and in immortality; but I would fain hope that, in kind remembrance of those she has left, in a lingering human sympathy and human love, she may yet be, as God originally created her "a little lower than the angels.[11]

And again, he wrote:

> I feel a vacuum, an indifference, a want of motive, which I cannot describe. I hope my children, and the society of my best friends, may rouse me; but I can never see such days as I have seen. Yet I should not repine; I have enjoyed much, very much; and, if I were to die to-night, I should bless God most fervently that I have lived.[12]

With all the fame, applause and renown as America's dynamic orator on the floor of Congress, Webster's marriage, his exemplary family life as a Christian husband and father, give credence to his accomplishments:

## His Christian Character Traits

Once again in the annals of America's history, we see Christian character traits and virtues praised, and held up high for all to follow—that is, the inner life of kindness, generosity, self-control, goodness, gentleness, steadfastness, other-centeredness, self-sacrifice, godliness, purity and wisdom. Without a doubt, this is the basis for our nation's greatness — biblical qualities demonstrated in the lives of our forbears.

## Daniel Webster on Slavery

Webster saw slavery as a great evil, as pointed out in his famed Plymouth oration, as that which ought "...to be set aside from the Christian world; let it be put out of the circle of human sympathies and human regards..."[13] He did not live to see the abolishment of slavery in this nation.

## Daniel Webster: "The Gospel of Jesus Christ a Divine Reality"

In the spring of 1852, Webster fell from his carriage and never entirely recovered. He subsequently made out his will, writing these words of unshakeable faith in the Gospel of Jesus Christ, Son of God, Savior of the world, for his epitaph:

> Lord, I believe; help thou mine unbelief. Philosophical argument, especially that drawn from the vastness of the universe in comparison with the apparent insignificance of this globe, has sometimes shaken my reason for the faith that is in me; but my heart has assured and reassured me that the Gospel of Jesus Christ must be a Divine reality. The Sermon on the Mount cannot be a merely human production. This belief enters into the very depth of my conscience. The whole history of man proves it.[14]

Webster's last words, a few hours prior to his death, reflect his subjection to God's will and purpose for his life during his short pilgrimage upon this earth:

> My general wish on earth has been to do my Maker's will.[15]

Such was the life and legacy of Daniel Webster, New Hampshire's greatest statesman. He has rightly been chosen by the citizens of New Hampshire to represent them as their foremost hero in our United States Capitol—an honor well bestowed.

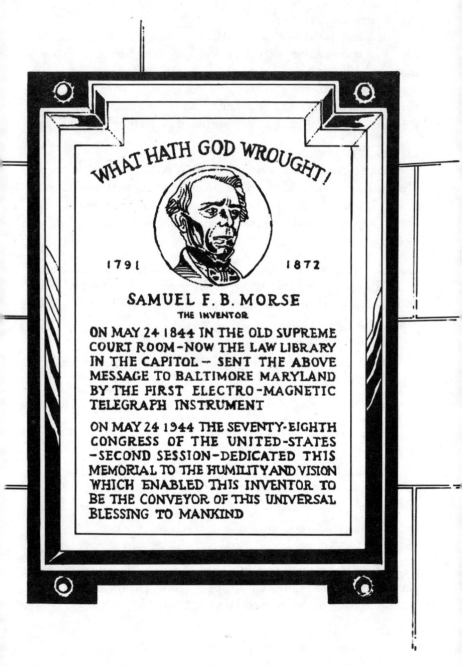

*After the original bronze plaque upon the inner wall of the Small Senate Rotunda, U.S. Capitol, Washington, D.C.*

# SAMUEL F. B. MORSE
## "What Hath God Wrought!"
## (1791 - 1872)

### Samuel Morse - A Universal Blessing to Mankind

Samuel F.B. Morse was born in Charlestown, Massachusetts on April 17, 1791. The telegraph, his great invention, has been described by our United States Congress as "a universal blessing to mankind." This great breakthrough took place from our Capitol building in Washington, D.C. and was received in Baltimore, Maryland on May 24, 1844. The famous first telegraph message, "What Hath God Wrought!" was taken from the Old Testament Scriptures, Numbers 23:23.

### The First Telegraph Message Is Sent, May 24,1844

Early in the morning of May 24, 1844, a small group of dignitaries gathered in the U.S. Supreme Court, at that time located in the Capitol building. Dolly Madison, wife of our fourth United States President, James Madison, was also present. The Baltimore and Ohio Railroad's little Pratt Street Station in Baltimore, Maryland, saw a different audience awaiting this historic communication.[1]

At 8 a.m., Samuel Finley Breese Morse, the artist whose vision it was to "transmit intelligence instantaneously by electricity," tested his new invention. Annie Ellsworth, daughter of the U.S. Commissioner of Patents, entered the room shortly thereafter, handing him a note, upon which was written the choice of Scripture verse which she and her mother had the honor of selecting.[2] At 8:45 a.m. Morse began slowly tapping out the message from a little room on the West side of the ground floor in the center part of the building.[3] Instantly, in Baltimore, Alfred Vail, Morse's colleague and friend joyfully recorded the words, "What Hath God Wrought!" The entire Bible verse comes

*Annie Ellsworth*

from the Book of Numbers, Chapter 23, Verse 23:

> Surely there is no enchantment against Jacob, neither is there any divination against Israel; according to this time it shall be said of Jacob and Israel, "What Hath God Wrought!"[4]

Applause was heard from everyone present, as Vail immediately returned the message to Washington. Great excitement and jubilant cheering followed Morse's invention. Morse and Vail, building upon their success, continued conversing via telegraph. Dolly Madison then asked permission to extend personal greetings to her friend in Baltimore. It was thus that the telegraph was born.[5]

Samuel F.B. Morse, however, prior to his invention, had undergone hardships, ridicule and disappointments, which is often the case with men and women of exceptional talent and ability.[6]

## Samuel Morse's Christian Background

He was the son of the Reverend Jedidiah Morse, well-known preacher of the Gospel of Jesus Christ, and a crusader for lost souls. As author and publisher, Jedidiah Morse was also known as " the father of American geography" because he authored the first geography textbook printed in this country. Reverend Morse was also a great American Christian patriot and close friend of both George Washington and Daniel Webster. Morse's mother was the granddaughter of Dr. Samuel Finley, one of the early Presidents of Princeton University.[7]

## Morse, the Artist

At an early age Samuel displayed great artistic talent. He commenced his studies at Yale University at age 14, helping to pay his expenses by painting portraits of faculty members and students. His studies in art took him to London, after his graduation from Yale in 1810. Morse was widely known and acclaimed for his outstanding paintings and drawings. He gained the reputation of one of the foremost portrait painters in America. In 1819, the artist received a commission from the City of New York to paint a portrait of the Marquis de Lafayette, which he undertook in the White House.

## Morse, the Inventor

Electricity, however, both interested and intrigued him. In 1832, while returning from Europe on the ship "Sully," Morse had the brilliant idea of inventing the electro-magnetic telegraph.[8] One of the passengers, Dr. Charles T. Jackson, of Boston, began speaking about electricity, remarking that "electricity passes instantly over any known length of wire. Benjamin Franklin passed current many miles and noticed no difference of time between the touch at one end and the spark at the other." "If this be so," said Morse, "and the presence of electricity can be made visible in any desired part of the circuit, I see no reason why intelligence might not be instantaneously transmitted by electricity to any distance."[9]

## Morse, the Educator

In 1835 Morse became professor of the Literature of Arts and Design at New York University. Although his board was provided for by the University, he was not recompensed for his work. It was in the fall of 1835, at this university, that he constructed his telegraph instruments carrying on experiments on his invention. He continued to paint, teach, write and live in one solitary chamber.[10]

Finally, our United States Congress agreed to pass an appropriation which resulted in building a telegraph line from Baltimore to Washington. Thus it was, that on May 24, 1844 the famous message "What hath God wrought!" was tapped out, instantly transmitted and received – an accomplished fact.[11]

Although poverty and difficulties dogged Morse during many years, prosperity and honors crowned his closing years. His Christian faith, passed down to him from a godly father – nurtured, sustained and upheld him throughout his entire life.[12]

## Congress Memorializes Morse's "Humility and Vision"

This inventor has left a great legacy to our nation, giving God all the glory for enabling him to make his invention of the first telegraph message, which our 78th Congress appropriately memorialized a hundred years later, on a handsome bronze plaque. It is found near the spot from where this historic event took place in the U.S. Capitol, and reads:

> Samuel F. B. Morse — The Inventor – On May 24, 1844 in the Old Supreme Court Room — now the Law Library in the Capitol — sent the above message to Baltimore, Maryland by the first electro-magnetic telegraph instrument. On May 24, 1944 the seventy-eighth Congress of the United States — Second Session — dedicated this memorial to the humility and vision which enabled this inventor to be the conveyor of this universal blessing to mankind.[13]

From the above, we see the Christian value system of our nation still in operation at that time, by the wording which the U.S. Congress chose to glorify God – not man – in this great invention. In 1944, Congress still recognized that all gifts, talents, creativity, vision and imagination come directly from the hand of God to be employed for His ultimate glory. Samuel F. B. Morse was but God's instrument – "a channel of universal blessing to mankind," affirmed our 78th Congress.

This, indeed, is the hallmark of a truly great statesman.

WILLIAM HOLMES McGUFFEY

*Portrait of William Holmes McGuffey,*
*"Schoolmaster of the Nation"*

# WILLIAM HOLMES McGUFFEY
"Schoolmaster of the Nation"
(1800 - 1873)

## McGuffey Readers Shape American Education and Morals—120 Million Copies Sold

William Holmes McGuffey was an educator and a clergyman whose textbook series, written for the first six grades of elementary school, helped to shape American education and morals for nearly a century. It is estimated that his Eclectic Readers sold over 120 million copies.[1]

## McGuffey's Background—A Presbyterian Minister

McGuffey was born in 1800 in Washington County, Pennsylvania, and in 1826 he graduated from Washington College.[2]

He became a Presbyterian minister in 1829, and though he never actually pastored a church, his biblical morals, virtues, values and principles emanate from the books he authored.[3]

*House in which William Holmes McGuffey was born.*

## Active in Higher Education

From 1826 until his death in 1873, he was active in higher education, as a professor in three different colleges and as president of Cincinnati College in 1836, and Ohio College from 1839 to 1843. Later he became professor of Moral Philosophy at the University of Virginia.[4]

## The Truths of the Bible Applied to Everyday Life in America

In the era in which McGuffey lived, the Bible was revered and respected by American society; its truths applied to everyday life. The primary object of education was to produce upright, godly citizens. It is therefore not surprising that his Readers are filled with stories from the Bible, together with selections that emphasize morality and character development. In addition, many of these selections, particularly in the latter volumes, include the classics of American literature and political life, as well as English literature.

## McGuffey's Eclectic Readers

The first two volumes of McGuffey's Eclectic Readers were published in 1836. Following are excerpts from his *Eclectic First Reader*.

## Small Children Taught to Pray at Night
### Lesson 37 - "Evening Prayer"

At the close of the day, before you go to sleep, you should not fail to pray to God to keep you from sin and from harm. You ask your friends for food, and drink, and books, and clothes; and when they give you these things, you thank them, and love them for the good they do you. So you should ask your God for those things which he can give you, and which no one else can give you. You should ask him for life, and health, and strength; and you should pray to him to keep your feet from the ways of sin and shame.

You should thank him for all his good gifts; and learn, while young, to put your trust in him; and the kind care of God will be with you, both in your youth and in your old age.

| close | before | sleep | would |
|-------|--------|-------|-------|
| fail | pray | from | harm |
| friends | food | drink | books |
| clothes | these | things | them |
| good | should | those | which |
| strength | learn | young | youth |

## Small Children Taught Not to Take Strong Drink
### Lesson 62 - "Don't Take Strong Drink"

No little boy or girl should ever drink rum or whiskey, unless they want to become drunkards. Men who drink strong drink are glad to have any excuse for doing it. So, one will drink it because he is so hot. Another will drink it because he is cold. One will drink it when he is wet, and another because he is dry—one will drink it because he is in company, and another, because he is alone, and another will put it into his glass of water to kill the insects! Thus the pure water from the brook is poisoned with the "drunkard's drink," and the man who uses it, becomes a sot. Then he is seen tottering through the streets, a shame to himself and to all his family. And oh, how dreadful to die a drunkard. The Bible says that no drunkard shall inherit the kingdom of heaven. Whiskey makes the happy miserable, and it causes the rich to become poor.

## Small Children Are Taught "More About the Bible"

In 1837 the third and fourth volumes were published. They included questions, plain rules for reading, and directions for avoiding common errors. Following are several selections from his 1837 **Eclectic Third Reader: "More about the Bible:"**

1. The design of the Bible is evidently to give us correct information concerning the creation of all things, by the omnipotent Word of God; to make known to us the state of holiness and happiness of our first parents in paradise, and their dreadful fall from that condition by transgression against God, which is the original cause of all our sin and misery.

3. The Scriptures are especially designed to make us wise unto salvation through faith in Christ Jesus; to reveal to us the mercy of the Lord in him; to form our minds after the likeness of God our Savior; to build up our souls in wisdom and faith, in love and holiness; to make us thoroughly furnished unto good works, enabling us to glorify God on earth; and, to lead us to an imperishable inheritance among the spirits of just men made perfect, and finally to be glorified with Christ in heaven.

5. We have the most ample and satisfactory proofs that the books of the Bible are Authentic and Genuine; that is, that they were written by the persons to whom they are ascribed. The Scriptures of the Old Testament were collected and completed under the scrupulous care of inspired apostles. The singular providence of God is evident in the translation of the Old Testament into Greek, nearly three hundred years before the birth of Christ, for the benefit of the Jews who were living in countries where that language was used.

7. This will appear in a much stronger point of view when we consider the Jews as the keepers of the Old Testament. It was their own sacred volume, which contained the most extraordinary predictions concerning the infidelity of their nation, and the rise, progress, and extensive prevalence of Christianity.

8. That all the books which convey to us the history of the events of the New Testament, were written and immediately published, by persons living at the time of the occurrence of the things mentioned, and whose names they bear, is most fully proved. 1. By an unbroken series of Christian authors, reaching from the days of the apostles down to the present time. 2. By the concurrent and well-informed belief of all denominations of Christians. 3. By the acknowledgement of the most learned and intelligent enemies of Christianity.

10. Matthew and John were two of our Lord's apostles; his constant attendants throughout the whole of his ministry; eye-witnesses of the facts,

and ear-witnesses of the discourses which they relate. Mark and Luke were not of the twelve apostles; but they were contemporaries and associates with the apostles, and living in habits of friendship and intercourse with those who had been present at the transactions which they record....

13. The manuscripts of the sacred books are found in every ancient library in all parts of the Christian world; and amount in number to several thousands. About five hundred have been actually examined and compared by learned men with extraordinary care. Many of them were evidently transcribed as early as the eighth, seventh, sixth, and even the fourth centuries.

*Questions:* 1. What is the evident design of the Bible? 2. Have we proofs of the authenticity of the Bible? 3. When was the Old Testament translated into Greek? 4. For whose immediate benefit was the translation made? 5. What is confirmed by the quotations of Christians from the Old Testament? 6. How do you prove the authenticity of the New Testament? 7. How could alterations in the Sacred Scriptures have been detected? 8. Where are ancient manuscripts of the Bible now to be found? 9. Do you think a person could now alter the Bible without being detected? 10. If God has condescended to give us His Word to guide us in the way of eternal life, do you not think that he would extend his protective hand for its preservation?

*Errors:* Glo-rous for Glo-ri-ous; sper-ets for spir-its; vol-lum for vol-ume; fust for first; a-pos-sles for a-pos-tles.

*Spell and Define:* 1. Omnipotent; 2. everlasting; 3. salvation; 5. translation; 6. quotation; 7. predictions; 8. acknowledgements; 9. contemporaries; 11. manuscripts; 12. evangelical; 13. promulgation; 14. authenticity.

## Small Children Taught About the Character of Jesus Christ

Lesson 21, in the same McGuffey *Eclectic Third Reader*, speaks about *The Character of Jesus Christ.* Here again we see that, at a tender young age, American children were taught to follow the example of the Son of God, thus producing virtue in their adult lives, as opposed to modern-day vice.

(Rule: In many words the sound of "h" is suppressed where it should be sounded distinctly; and great caution must be used to avoid this fault.)

*Examples:* harm, heel, head, hot, hoarse, who, are pronounced improperly, arm, eel, ead, ot, orse, oo.

1. The morality taught by Jesus Christ was purer, sounder, sublimer and more perfect than had ever before entered into the imagination, or proceeded from the lips of man. And this he delivered in a manner the most striking and impressive; in short, sententious, solemn, important, ponderous rules or maxims; or in familiar, natural, affecting similitudes and parables.

2. He showed also a most consummate knowledge of the human heart, and dragged to light all its artifices, subtleties, and evasions. He discovered every irregular desire before it ripened into action.

3. He manifested, at the same time, the most perfect impartiality. He had no respect of persons. He reproved vice in every situation, with the same freedom and boldness, wherever he found it; and he added to the whole, the weight, the irresistible weight, of his own example.

4. He, and he only, of all the sons of men, acted up, in every minute instance, to what he taught; and his life exhibited a perfect portrait of his religion. But what completed the whole was, that he taught as the evangelist expresses it, with authority, with the authority of a divine teacher.

5. The ancient philosophers could do nothing more than give good advice to their followers; they had no means of enforcing that advice; but our great lawgiver's precepts are all divine commands.

6. He spoke in the name of God: he called himself the Son of God. He spoke in a tone of superiority, and authority, which no one before him had the courage or the right to assume; and finally, he enforced every thing he taught by the most solemn and awful sanctions, by a promise of eternal felicity to those who obeyed him, and a denunciation of the most tremendous punishments to those who rejected him.

7. These were the circumstances which gave our blessed Lord the authority with which he spake. No wonder then, that the people "were astonished at His doctrines," and that they all declared "He spake as never man spake."

*Questions:* 1. Whose character is here portrayed? 2. What was the character of his instructions? 3. How did the life of Christ correspond with his teachings? 4. Wherein did he differ from the ancient philosophers?

*Errors:* Per-fict for per-fect; ir-reg-lur for ir-reg-u-lar; es-press-es for express-es; flos-phers for phi-los-o-phers.

*Spell and Define:* 1. morality; sententious; 2. consummate; irresistible; 6. denunciation; 7. doctrines.

## "Except the Bible, No Other Book or Set of Books Has Influenced the American Mind So Much"

William Earnest Smith, in his work entitled: *About the McGuffeys*, stated: "Except the Bible, no other book or set of books has influenced the American mind so much."[5]

"The readers were used in the public schools longer than any other textbooks. The keen intellectual and literary sense of the composer and the high moral values which were taught, must have been the largest factor in the long tenure of these school books," said Dr. Benjamin Franklin Crawford, in his *Life of William Holmes McGuffey*, published in 1963. McGuffey has been given the title of "Great Schoolmaster of the Nation."

## The National Education Association's Eulogy on McGuffey: "His Christian Character an Example and Model to American Teachers"

The National Education Association (NEA) honored McGuffey with the following resolution at his death:

In the death of William H. McGuffey, late Professor of Moral Philosophy in the University of Virginia, this Association feels that they have lost one of the great lights of the profession whose life was a lesson full of instruction; an example and model to American teachers. His labors in the cause of education, extending over a period of half a century, in several offices as teacher of common schools, college professor and college president, and as author of text books; his almost unequalled industry; his power in the lecture room; his influence upon his pupils and community; his care for the public interests of education; his lofty devotion to duty; his conscientious Christian character—all these have made him one of the noblest ornaments of our profession in this age, and entitle him to the grateful remembrance of this Association and of the teachers of America.

Elmira, New York, August 7, 1873.[6]

# MARCUS WHITMAN
## "The Preacher Who Rode for an Empire"
## (1802 - 1847)

Few Americans are familiar with the story of Marcus and Narcissa Whitman, two great American heroes, and their pioneering missionary work in the Northwest. Marcus made a valiant cross-country ride to save Oregon from falling into the hands of the Hudson Bay Company—and hence the British.

## Marcus and Narcissa Whitman
## Marry for the Cause of the Gospel

Born in Rushville, New York in 1802, Marcus studied medicine in Massachusetts and practiced for several years in Canada. The great spiritual revival which reached many souls for Christ at that time, touched both their lives. Each had planned to remain single in order to better serve the Lord. However, due to Divine Providence and a mutual friend, they married and dedicated their lives to bringing the lifesaving gospel of Jesus Christ to the Indians west of the Rockies. They offered their services to the American Board of Commissioners for Foreign Missions.

## The First Wagon to Cross the Rockies

In 1836, when Marcus and Narcissa Whitman crossed the Mountains into old Oregon as missionaries of the American Board of Commissioners for Foreign Missions, they were but an extension of the Great Revival which broke out at the beginning of the century. Theirs was the first wagon to cross the Rocky Mountains, their means of transportation including sleigh, steamboat, stage, wagon, ox cart, horseback and on foot. They were followed by other settlers who established themselves in what was then called Oregon, but now comprises the states of Washington, Oregon and Idaho.

## Narcissa Whitman—
## "Will the Lord Give Me Patience to Endure It?"

No woman ever made such a journey as that made by Narcissa Whitman. In her fascinating journal for July 27, Narcissa, after speaking of some of her hardships, writes: "Do not think I regret coming. No, far from it. I would not go back for the world. I am contented and happy. Notwithstanding, I sometimes get very hungry and weary. Have six weeks' steady journey before us. Will the Lord give me patience to endure it?"

MARCUS WHITMAN
WASHINGTON

*After the original bronze statue in Statuary Hall,*
*U.S. Capitol, Washington, D.C.*
*He holds a Bible in his right hand; his medical equipment in the left.*

## The Lord Jesus Said: "Lo, I Am With You Always"

On August 29, when from the summit of the Blue Mountains, Narcissa saw the Columbia River and Mount Hood, the goal of their journey, far off in the distance, two biblical promises came to her mind: "As thy days, so shall thy strength be," and "Lo, I am with you alway."

The Whitmans established themselves at Waiilatpu, among the Cayuse Indians. In a rude cabin at Waiilatpu, Alice Clarissa Whitman was born March 14, 1837, the first child of American white parents to be born west of the Rocky Mountains. When the child was two years of age, she drowned in the stream which ran behind their cabin.

## What Was the Gospel of the Oregon Trail?

What was the gospel of the Oregon Trail? What was the gospel that compelled Marcus and Narcissa Whitman to thrust on through the dangers and hazards of the great Northwest? What made them faithful unto martyrdom, perishing at the hands of those to whom they brought the good news of eternal life? What was the gospel which erected the first Protestant church west of the Rockies? What was the gospel that transformed the Indians, causing them to discard their tomahawks and scalping knives; replacing them with the resounding hymns of redemption each morning and evening—filling the mission with praises to Jehovah God? It was the magnificent gospel of Christ the Redeemer, the gospel of salvation from sin through the shed blood of the Lamb of God who takes away the sin of the world. This was the gospel of the Oregon Trail.

## A Providential Answer to the Indians' Search for God

Unbeknownst to the Whitmans, they were the providential answer to a search by a declining Indian tribe in Oregon to find the one, true, triune God. In 1831, four Nez Perce and Flathead Indians came to St. Louis seeking to learn the secret of the white man's success, convinced that the white man's God was more potent than their own. These Indians were: Black Eagle, Rabbit Skin Leggings, No Horns on His Head and Man of the Morning. Their request was that missionaries be sent among them to tell them of the white man's God. The portraits of Rabbit Skin Leggings and No Horns on His Head are in the National Gallery of Art in Washington, D.C., painted by the Indian authority and painter, George Catlin.

## The Indians' Search for "the White Man's Book to Heaven"

In 1866 there appeared in a lecture by missionary Henry Spalding an account of the sorrowful appeal of one of these Indians to General Clark when they were leaving to go back to their own people. Said the Indian:

> I come to you over a trail of many moons from the setting sun. I came with one eye partly open, for more light for my people who sit in darkness. I go back with both eyes closed. How can I go back blind to my people? I made my way to you with strong arms through many enemies and strange lands. I go back with both arms broken and empty. My people sent me to get the white man's Book from Heaven. You took me where you allow your women to dance, as we do not ours, and the Book was not there. You took me where they worship the great Spirit with candles, and the Book was not there. You showed me the images of good spirits and pictures of the good land beyond. But the Book was not among them. I am going back the long, sad trail to my people of the dark land. You make my feet heavy with burdens of gifts, and my moccasins will grow old in carrying them. But the Book is not among them. When I tell my poor, blind people after one more snow in the big Council that I did not bring the Book, no word will be spoken by our old men or by our young braves. One by one they will rise up and go out in silence. My people will die in darkness, and they will go on the long path to other hunting grounds. No white man will go with them, and no white man's Book, to make the way plain. I have no more words.[1]

## The Good News of Salvation Through Christ in "The White Man's Book to Heaven"

The mission established by the Whitmans brought the good news of salvation through Jesus Christ to the Indian people.

## Marcus Whitman's Ride Cross-Country to Save Oregon

The British who had established posts in Oregon through the Hudson Bay Company's fur trading, had intended to colonize the territory. Marcus Whitman undertook the arduous journey to Washington, D.C. to make his appeal for this vast country.

## President Warren Gamaliel Harding's Speech on "the Oregon Trail"

The fascinating story that follows was related by none other than President Warren G. Harding in 1923, in a speech on "The Oregon Trail" at Meacham, Oregon:

> Living history records many indissoluble links, to one of which it seems fitting that I should direct your attention today. Of the many rooms in the White House, which possess the peculiar charm of association with epochal happenings, the one most fascinating to me is that which formerly comprised the Cabinet Room and the President's study... Before my mind's eye as I stood

in that heroic chamber a few days ago appeared the vivid picture. I beheld seated at his desk, immaculately attired, the embodiment of dignity and courtliness, John Tyler, 10th President of the United States. Facing him, from a chair constructed for a massive frame, his powerful spirit gleaming through his cavernous eyes, was the lion-visaged Daniel Webster, Secretary of State. The door opened and there appeared before the amazed statesmen a strange and astonishing figure. It was that of a man of medium height and sturdy build, deep chested, broad shouldered, yet lithe in movement and soft in step. He was clad in a coarse fur coat, buckskin breeches, fur leggings, and boot moccasins, looking much the worse for wear. But it was the countenance of the visitor, as he stood for an instant in the doorway, that riveted the perception of the two Chiefs of State. It was that of a religious enthusiast, tenaciously earnest yet revealing no suggestion of fanaticism, bronzed from exposure to pitiless elements and seamed with deep lines of physical suffering, a rare combination of determination and gentleness—obviously a man of God, but no less a man among men.

Such was Marcus Whitman, the pioneer missionary hero of the vast, unsettled, unexplored Oregon country, who had come out of the West to plead that the State should acquire for civilization the Empire that the churches were gaining for Christianity....

It was more than a desperate and perilous trip that Marcus Whitman undertook. It was a race against time. Public opinion was rapidly crystallizing into a judgment that the Oregon country was not worth claiming, much less worth fighting for; that even though it could be acquired against the insistence of Great Britain, it would prove to be a liability rather than an asset....

And he did not hesitate to speak plainly as one who knew, even like the prophet Daniel. "Mr. Secretary," he declared, "you would better give all New England for the cod and mackerel fisheries of Newfoundland than to barter away Oregon."

Then, turning to the President in conclusion, he added quietly but beseechingly:

"All I ask is that you will not barter away Oregon or allow English interference until I can lead a band of stalwart American settlers across the plains. For this I shall try to do!"

The manly appeal was irresistible. He sought only the privilege of proving his faith. The just and considerate Tyler could not refuse.

"Dr. Whitman," he rejoined sympathetically, "your long ride and frozen limbs testify to your courage and your patriotism. Your credentials establish your character. Your request is granted!"

...Never in the history of the world has there been a finer example of civilization following Christianity. The missionaries led under the banner of the cross, and the settlers moved close behind under the star-spangled symbol of the Nation. Among all the records of the evangelizing effort as the forerunner of human advancement, there is none so impressive as this of the early Oregon mission and its marvelous consequences. To the men and women of that early day whose first thought was to carry the gospel to the Indians—to the Lees, the Spauldings, the Grays, the Walkers, the Leslies, to Fathers DeSmet and Blanchet and DeMars, and to all the others of that glorious company who found that in serving God they were also serving their country and their fellowmen—to them we pay today our tribute; to them we owe a debt of gratitude, which we can never pay, save partially through recognition such as you have accorded it today... I rejoice particularly in the opportunity afforded me of voicing my appreciation both as President of the United States and as one who honestly tries to be a Christian soldier, of the signal service of the martyred Whitman. And finally, as just a human being, I wish I could find words to tell you how glad I am to see you all, and reflecting as you do, from untroubled eyes, and happiness of spirit breathed by your own best song:

There are no new worlds to conquer,
Gone is the last frontier,
And the steady grind of the wagon-train,
Of the sturdy pioneer.
But their memories live like a thing divine,
Treasured in Heaven above,
For the Trail that led to the storied West,
Was the wonderful trail of Love.

Warren Gamaliel Harding
President of the United States
(1865-1923)[2]

## "The Preacher that Rode to Save an Empire" Secures the Oregon Treaty of 1846

Marcus returned to Oregon, taking a large band of settlers with him. By his heroic ride, he was instrumental in securing the vast area of the unsettled Oregon country for the United States. It was secured by treaty in 1846.

## Marcus and Narcissa Whitman's Death

Tragically, Whitman, his wife and 12 others were massacred in a sudden uprising of the Indians. They had been incited to violence by a half-breed from Maine named Jo Lewis, who had circulated the tale that Dr. Whitman was poisoning the Indians.

The tragedy put an end to the organized work of the American Board of Missions among the Indians in Oregon. But the seed that these devoted missionaries had sown did not return unto God void (Isaiah 55:10-11). It still bears fruit in the Christian churches and Christian faith of the Nez Perce and Cayuse Indians. One of the Indians said at their departure:

You are leaving us forever, and my people, O my people will see no more light. My children will live only in a night that will have no morning. When we reach Walla Walla I shall look upon your face for the last time in this world. But this Book in which your hands have written and caused me to write the words of God, I shall carry in my bosom 'til I lie down in the grave.[3]

## The Extraordinary Christian Lives and Witness of Marcus and Narcissa Whitman

Of the extraordinary lives, saga and events which characterize Marcus and Narcissa Whitman's Christian witness among the Indians, Chester Collins Maxey, a former president of Whitman College, writes:

> There has been no other couple like the Whitmans in American history—no wooing more strange, no wedding more extraordinary, no marriage more proof against stress and storm, no union of purpose or effort more perfect, no failure more pathetic, no ending more terrible, no immortality more sublime than theirs. Forces they did not control or understand brought their lives together in a noble enterprise that failed; forces they did not control or understand brought their lives to a dire and agonizing close; yet so greatly did they live, so magnificently did they labor and serve that forces they set in motion will forever enrich the civilization they helped to plant on the Western slopes of the Continental Divide.[4]

## Marcus Whitman Chosen as Washington State's Greatest Hero

Americans owe a great debt of gratitude to pioneers as selfless and as dedicated as Marcus and Narcissa Whitman. They brought "the Book that tells about Heaven" to the Indians, and Marcus Whitman's valiant ride cross-country helped to preserve Oregon for the Union. This undaunted medical missionary left his indelible footprints throughout Washington State, mapping out a great episode in the identity of America's developing era as *a nation under God*. It is little wonder that the citizens of Washington state have chosen him to represent them as their greatest hero in the U.S. Capitol's Hall of Fame.

JASON LEE
FIRST MISSIONARY
TO OREGON

*After the original bronze sculpture in Statuary Hall*
*of the U.S. Capitol, Washington, D.C.*
*He holds a Bible in his left hand.*

# JASON LEE
## Oregon's Greatest Hero
## (1803 - 1845)

Jason Lee came from sturdy New England ancestry. His grandfather, John Lee, left England for America in 1734, becoming one of the early settlers near Cambridge, Massachusetts. Jason's father, Daniel Lee, enlisted in the Wadsworth Brigade, reinforcing General Washington in and around New York City, and taking part in the battle of White Plains in 1776.[1]

## Orphaned at Age 3, Self-supporting at Age 13

Daniel and Sarah Lee's log house in Stanstead, Vermont, saw the birth of their son, Jason, on June 28, 1803. He was the youngest of 15 children — nine boys and six girls. Jason's father died when he was only 3 years old, and the boy had to become self-supporting at the age of 13. Having received his early education in the village school of Stanstead, Lee expressed himself thus: "I was brought up to hard work and have seen the day when I could chop a cord of sugar maple in two hours."[2]

## Jason Accepts Jesus Christ as His Lord and Savior

Lee accepted Jesus Christ as his Lord and Savior through a Wesleyan missionary in 1826, relating his conversion in his diary with this entry, "I saw, I believed, I repented."[3]

## A Classmate Describes Lee's Life of Prayer, His Dependence upon God's Holy Spirit and the Bible

Lee continued working with his hands until 1829, when he entered Wilbraham Academy, a Methodist institution in Wilbraham, Massachusetts. The following is a character sketch left for us by one of his classmates, Bishop Osman C. Baker. It shows his moral excellence, righteousness, and compassion as well as his perseverance in prayer, and sensitivity to the leading of the Holy Spirit:

> Jason Lee was a large, athletic young man, six feet and three inches in height, with a fully developed frame and a constitution like iron. His piety was deep and uniform, and his life, in a very uncommon degree, pure and exemplary. In those days of extensive and powerful revivals, I used to observe, with what confidence and satisfaction, seekers of religion would place themselves under his instruction. They regarded him as a righteous man whose prayers availed much; and when there were indications that the Holy Spirit was moving in the heart of the sinner within the circle of his acquaintance, his warm Christian heart would incite him to constant labor until deliverance would be proclaimed to the captive.[4]

## Lee the Educator and Preacher

After graduation at Wilbraham in 1830, Jason served as a teacher in the Stanstead Academy, preaching in the neighboring towns until time came for him to go to Oregon. He planned to join a certain Captain Nathaniel Wyeth, of Cambridge, Massachusetts, leaving Independence, Missouri in April of 1834. Lee, accompanied by two Indian boys from Oregon, preached throughout New England until his departure. Great crowds listened to him deliver the gospel of Jesus Christ, Son of God and Savior.[5] One of these meetings was held at Lynn, Massachusetts. The *Zion Herald* published the following excerpted account of this meeting:

> Last Sabbath evening there was... an address by Reverend Jason Lee, missionary to the Flat Heads. It was one of the most pleasant meetings ever held in Lynn, of a missionary character. Long before the time appointed to commence, the house was thronged to overflowing, and the audience hung upon the lips of the speaker with such an interest that it could not be mistaken. The collection did honor to Lynn; it amounted to $100.00[6]

## Jason Lee's Missionary Expedition Sets Out to Oregon

On Monday, April 28, 1834, the missionary expedition to Oregon, led by Nathaniel Wyeth, set out from St. Louis, Missouri. Lee was accompanied by four missionaries. He preached "the first formal Protestant religious observance to be held in the vast interior west of the Rocky Mountains at Fort Hill, on July 27, 1834."[7] Lee and his companions continued to Fort Boise, escorted by Thomas McKay and his Hudson's Bay Brigade. From there they continued alone to Fort Walla Walla, where they arrived on September 15, 1834, being warmly welcomed by Dr. John McLoughlin. With the latter's help, they established their mission on the east bank of the Willamette River, just north of Salem.

## Jason Lee's Concern and Burden for Oregon

Lee's concern for more settlers to come to Oregon led him back to New York on March 26, 1838. Thirty-six Americans, including the missionaries, had signed the petition he bore with him. This paper, dated March 16, 1838, urged "the United States to take formal and speedy possession," of Oregon. It was presented to the Senate on January 28, 1839 by Senator Linn, showing Lee's profound interest in the future welfare of Oregon.[8]

On this journey, Jason Lee preached the powerful gospel message in these cities: Alton, Illinois; St. Louis; Carlinville; Jacksonville; Springfield; Peoria and Chicago. In New York, he impressed the Board of Managers of the Methodist Church Missionary Society of the dire need for more missionaries to Oregon. Sent out by the Board, Lee spoke to crowded houses on the East Coast and Canada. In Hartford, Connecticut, "hundreds went away unable to gain admittance into the church," thousands being informed about the importance of Oregon joining the union.[9] As a result of his preaching, 51 missionaries sent out by the Missionary Society, arrived in Vancouver on June 1, 1840.

As is the case with many great missionaries, preachers and evangelists of the past, false charges were made against this man of God. Many of these charges came from those who were dissatisfied with the settlement in Oregon. Consequently, Lee traveled to New York, appearing before his board from July 1-10, 1844, and was cleared of all charges. However, the Board having already appointed his successor, it was too late for Jason Lee to return to the Oregon mission field.[10]

## Jason Lee's Death

On March 12, 1845, Jason relinquished his soul into the hands of his Maker.

## An Oil Painting of Jason Lee Memorializes His Life and Deeds

The life and noble deeds of Jason Lee, Oregon's greatest hero, live on today in the hearts and minds of her citizens. On October 26, 1920, an oil painting of Lee was presented to the state of Oregon. It was painted by Mr. Vesper George of Boston, Massachusetts, the funds having been given by the Methodist Episcopal Church. This lifelike portrait hung behind the Speaker of the House of Representatives' chair in the State Capitol, in Salem, Oregon, until 1935, when the building was destroyed by fire. Thomas A. McBride, Justice of the Oregon State Supreme Court, gave this eulogy at its unveiling, stating that the life and work of Jason Lee, founder of American civilization in Oregon, represented "the fervor of a missionary, the foresight of a seer and the patriotism of a loyal citizen."

> The precious jewel of a Commonwealth; the one thing above all others which it would treasure, and the memory of those grand and self-sacrificing men and women who laid the foundations of its greatness and prosperity. One of these treasured memories, is the life and work of Jason Lee, the founder of American civilization in Oregon... Lee combined the fervor of a missionary, the foresight of a seer, and the patriotism of a loyal citizen.[11]

## Jason Lee, Oregon's Most Heroic Figure

Governor of Oregon, Ben Olcott, accepted the portrait for the people of his state, with these stirring words:

> Unhesitatingly I say that Jason Lee was Oregon's most heroic figure. By every right of achievement, by every right of peaceful conquest, this portrait of Jason Lee should adorn the halls of the Capitol Building in our state, as long as those capitol buildings stand.[12]

## Jason Lee's Blueprint to Life—the Bible

The United States House Joint Resolution No.1, agreed to by the Senate on February 16, 1921, accepted Oregon's choice of Rev. Jason Lee as that state's greatest hero, giving him a place in the Hall of Fame of our United States Capitol.[13]

Interestingly enough, Jason's blueprint to life is in his left hand. It is none other than the Bible, God's Holy Word—the source of his greatness.

# JUNIPERO SERRA
## (1713 - 1784)
### California's Greatest Hero

Junipero Serra, "The Apostle to California," was the first person to bring Christianity to the West coast of America. Serra founded nine missionary outposts, all of which later became major West Coast cities. They range over a 555-mile stretch from San Diego in the south to San Francisco in the north, and between them are San Juan Capistrano, San Gabriel, San Carlos, San Luis Obispo, Santa Clara, Santa Barbara, and Carmel.[1]

## Junipero Serra Dedicated by his Parents to Full-time Service for the Lord

At his birth in 1713 on the island of Majorca, he was all but given up for dead. Nevertheless, his parents dedicated their child to full-time service for the Lord, should his life be spared—and in answer to their prayer, God miraculously saved his life.[2]

In 1750 Serra went to Mexico City, working for nine years as a missionary to the Indians in Sierra Gorda, and then returned to Mexico City. Father Junipero Serra founded Mission San Diego de Alcala, California's first mission, in the year 1769. By 1823, 21 missions had been built, each one being about a day's walk from the next.

## Junipero Serra's Mission—"To Win Souls for Heaven"

The following quotation is taken from the introduction to the *Writings of Junipero Serra*:

> In 1769, Junipero Serra first set foot in the wilderness that was then California. In the face of incredible difficulties he laid the foundations of the mission system. Secular-minded historians may trace the system's progress by plotting year-by-year the increase in livestock and farm produce, the rise of permanent buildings with their distinctive architecture, improvements in highways and means of transportation, the growth of local industries, the availability of consumer goods, and the emergence of the intangibles that contribute to a more diversified form of social living. All this they will admire, and this they will call the great achievement of Serra. To all this, of course, Serra did contribute and to a greater extent than any of his contemporaries. But Serra never regarded it as his legacy to the West. Judged by his personal standard, all these things were mere incidentals. The motives which inspired his missionary labors must be sought much deeper. His standard was a supernatural one. He did not come to California to extract wealth from the soil, but to win souls for Heaven. He came to expand, not the empire of Spain, but the Kingdom of God. The registers of Baptisms and Confirmations were

*After the original bronze statue in Statuary Hall,*
*U.S. Capitol, Washington, D.C.*
*He holds the cross of Christ up high – a model mission in his left hand.*

the balance sheet he consulted. Death might wreak havoc among his hard-won neophytes, but he found consolation in his sorrow for he had prepared them for a future life which, his religious convictions assured him, was worth infinitely more than the life they were leaving and the pain of parting...

Finbar Kenneally, O.F.M.<br>Mattias C. Kieman, O.F.M.[3]

## Ronald Reagan Sworn into Office as Governor of California Upon Junipero Serra's Holy Bible

Junipero Serra's Latin Bible, now in the safekeeping of the Carmel Mission, was printed at Lyons, France, in 1568. Its title page translation reads as follows:

> The Holy Bible
> Very carefully corrected to
> accord with the Hebrew and
> with the testimony of the most reliable manuscripts:
> With figures and geographical
> descriptions in which the structures
> and various buildings and works,
> and regions as well, are placed
> before the eyes of everyone.
> There are in addition interpretations
> of Hebrew, Chaldean and Greek names, as
> well as very full indices.[4]

Ronald Reagan was sworn into office as governor of California on January 2, 1967, using Serra's Bible. This priceless gem of America's Christian heritage was described thus at that time:

> A Bible brought to California by famed Spanish missionary Father Junipero Serra...published in Lyons, France, in 1568 and now...housed permanently in the Archives of the Carmel Mission.... "It is, to my knowledge, the oldest Mission Bible in California," said Harry Downie, curator at the Carmel Mission.[5]

## Abraham Lincoln's Godly Role in the Mission Story

In 1862, President Abraham Lincoln restored the mission lands to the churches in California, after the Mexican Secularization Act of 1833 had taken them from the hands of the church, dispersing the Indian converts and confiscating their property. A copy of this Act of Congress is to be found upon a wall in the Museum of San Diego de Alcala Mission:

> Now know ye, that the United States of America, pursuant to the provisions of the Act of Congress aforesaid of third March, 1851, have given and granted and by these presents I give and grant unto the said Joseph G. Alemony, Bishop of Monterrey, and to his successors, "in trust for the religious purposes and uses to which the same have been respectively appropriated" the

tracts of land embraced and described in the foregoing survey; but with the stipulation that in virtue of the 15th section of the said act, the confirmation of the said claim and this patent, "shall not affect the interests of third persons." To have and to hold the said tracts of land with the appurtenances and with the stipulation aforesaid, unto the said Joseph G. Alemony, Bishop of Monterrey and his successors, in trust for the uses and purposes as aforesaid.

In testimony whereof, I, Abraham Lincoln, President of the United States, have caused these letters to be made patent, and the seal of the General Land Office to be hereunto affixed. Given under my hand at the city of Washington, this 23rd day of May, in the year of our Lord one thousand eight hundred and 62, and of the Independence of the United States the eighty sixth.

By the President, Abraham Lincoln. By N.O. Stoddard, Secretary. Recorded: Vol. 4; pages 94 to 101, inclusive. G.N. Granger, Recorder of the General Land Office.

It has been attested that Junipero Serra's greatest legacy is California itself.[6]

## Junipero Serra's Death—
## After Praying, He "Fell Asleep in Christ"

Those present at his death on August 28, 1784 said that after he had prayed, he "fell asleep in Christ." His funeral service was attended by officers and the crew of the San Carlos, Monterrey Presidio Commandant and soldiers, mission guards, and 600 Indians. Among them was Bernardino de Jesus, the first person baptized by Serra in Upper California (who lived until February 27, 1792). "Melting the hearts of all," the bells continued their mournful double stroke tolling throughout the day.[7]

The following excerpted letter, written on November 25, 1784, by San Fernando College guardian Juan Sancho to the Franciscan Provincial of Mallorca, is a testimony of Junipero Serra's example and ministry:

> I have just received the news from our missions in Monterrey of the death of our beloved countryman, the Reverend Father, Lector, Junipero Serra, who was the president, at San Carlos. I have been informed that he died the death of the just and in such circumstances that besides bringing tender tears to the eyes of all of those present, they all were of the opinion that his happy soul went directly to heaven to enjoy the reward for 34 years of great and continuous labors, undergone for our beloved Jesus, whom he ever kept in mind, suffering them in an inexplicable manner for our redemption. So great was his charity which he always manifested towards those poor Indians that not only the ordinary people, but likewise persons of higher condition were struck with admiration. All men said openly that that man was a saint and that his actions were those of an apostle. It has been the opinion concerning him ever since he arrived in this kingdom. This opinion has been constant and without interruption.[8]

## A Brick Cross Marks the Spot Where Junipero Serra Established First Mission in California

A beautiful brick cross marks the spot where Father Junipero Serra first established civilization on the West Coast of America. A plaque commemorates the event as follows:

> In this ancient Indian village of Cosay discovered and named San Miguel by Cabrillo in 1542, visited and christened San Diego de Alcala by Vizcimo in 1602. Here the first citizen, Fray Junipero Serra, planted civilization in California. Here he first raised the cross. Here began the first mission. Here was founded the first town, San Diego on July 16, 1769. In memory of him and his works. The order of Panama, 1913.

## California Chooses Serra as Its Greatest Hero in the U.S. Capitol

The State of California itself has recognized the contributions of Serra by selecting him as their representative in Statuary Hall, the old legislative chamber of the U.S. Capitol. The life-size bronze statue stands prominently with other great statesmen and heroes of caliber representing all 50 states in the Union. Such was the life and testimony of *Junipero Serra—man of God*.

HENRY OPUKAHAIA
FIRST HAWAIIAN
CHRISTIAN

*After the original drawing in the "Memoirs of Henry Obookiah,*
*a native of Owyhee, and a member of the Foreign Mission School,*
*who died at Cornwall, Connecticut, February 17, 1818, aged 26 years."*

# HENRY OPUKAHAIA
## First Hawaiian Christian
## (1793 - 1819)

### Henry Orphaned at a Young Age

Henry Opukahaia lived only 26 years, but in that brief span of time, his life was the vessel used of God to bring Christianity to countless people in Hawaii. He was orphaned at a young age when his parents were killed in a tribal contest "to see which should be the greatest."[1] Seeking adventure, he and a friend named Hopu boarded the whaler of Captain Brintnel, bound for New York in 1808. Befriended by Brintnel, they followed him home to New Haven, Connecticut.[2]

### Opukahaia Meets New Christian Friends, and Accepts Jesus Christ as His Savior

There they met new Christian friends, who, together with students of the college, began teaching them about the Bible. Within a few years, Opukahaia had met and received Jesus Christ as his Lord and Savior. Soon others began coming from Hawaii, and again displayed a willingness to avail themselves of Christian education.

### A Mission School Established in Connecticut

As a result, the American Board of Commissioners for Foreign Missions, established a school at Cornwall, Connecticut in 1816 for the sons of various tribes.[3]

There the basics of academics and the doctrines and duties of the Christian religion were taught them, dispelling their fears and superstitions. The aim of the school, as found in its Constitution, was as follows:

> The education, in our country, of heathen youths, in such a manner, as with subsequent professional instruction, will qualify them to become useful missionaries, physicians, surgeons, schoolmasters or interpreters and to communicate to the heathen nations such knowledge in agriculture and the arts, as may prove the means of promoting Christianity and civilization.[4]

### Henry is Burdened for His Lost Hawaiian People

Opukahaia, who was nurtured at the school, was filled with thanksgiving to Almighty God and His people. He was moved to compassion, and burdened for his Hawaiian people, who remained in the gross darkness of a heathen and superstitious society. In his new and unpolished English, he verbalized the deep sentiments of his heart in his inimitable, guileless manner:

God will carry through his work for us I do not know what will God do for my poor soul. I shall go before God and also before Christ. I hope the Lord will send the Gospel to the heathen land, where the words of the Savior never yet had been. Poor people! Worship the wood and stone, and shark and almost everything their god. The Bible is not there, and heaven and hell, they do not know about it... O what a wonderful thing is that the hand of the Divine Providence has brought me from the heathenish darkness where the light of Divine truth never had been. And here I have found the name of the Lord Jesus in the Holy Scriptures, and have read that His blood was shed for many. O what a happy time I have now, while my poor friends and relations at home, are perishing with hunger and thirsty, wanting of the Divine mercy and water out of the wells of salvation. My poor countrymen who are yet living in the region and shadow of death, without knowledge of the true God, and ignorant of the future world, have no Bible to read, no Sabbath. I often feel for them in the night season, concerning the loss of their souls. May the Lord Jesus dwell in my heart, and prepare me to go and spend the remaining part of my life with them. But not my will, O Lord, but thy will be done.[5]

## God Hears Opukahaia's Prayers for the Salvation of His People

That God heard the intercession of his heartfelt cries into the night became evident, though not as one might expect. In 1819 the Lord saw fit to take Henry home: he died of typhoid fever in Connecticut, having never seen the fulfillment of his desires to witness his people Christianized.

## A Mission Team Prepares for Hawaii

But that very year, a missionary team, composed of both Americans and Hawaiians, was to be dispatched to Hawaii to begin the work Opukahaia had longed to do. On the occasion of the ordination of the two missionaries, Reverend Hiram Bingham and Reverend Asa Thurston, to the Sandwich Islands (Hawaii), the sermon preached was based on the text Joshua 13:1: "And there remaineth yet very much land to be possessed."

## The Ordination Farewell Sermon Preached

Following is an excerpt from that sermon which shows the zeal Henry Opukahaia had imparted to the Christians in Connecticut:

...But I cannot do less than advert to some of the prominent indications, that the time, even the set time to favor the Sandwich Islands is come. Whence originated the design of sending them the Gospel? Why are we assembled here today? "It is the Lord's doing, and marvellous in our eyes." To him it belongs to bring good out of evil and light out of darkness... But where is your elder brother? Ah! Opukahaia cannot go with you to Owhyhee. He will not, however, forget you. Perhaps, if you should prove steadfast in the faith, he may look down and smile upon you from heaven. Possibly, he may even be permitted to visit you, though unseen; to strengthen you in the hour of temptation, and to whisper consolation to your souls in seasons of despondence. From a land of Bibles and Sabbaths and churches, where you have been nurtured and instructed in Christian charity; where you have enjoyed the prayers and counsels of the wise and good; and where some of you hope that you have been made savingly acquainted with the Lord Jesus Christ, you are going back to that land of idols and darkness, from whence you came...[6]

The following comprises the mission team dispatched to Opukahaia's people in Hawaii:

## Mission to the Sandwich Islands
*Brig Thaddeus*, Boston, Capt. Andrew Blanchard
### Missionaries
Rev. Hiram Bingham, A.M. *Mid. Coll.* of Bennington, Vt.
Rev. Asa Thurston, A.M. *Yale Coll.* of Fitchburg, Mass.
### Assistants
Mr. Daniel Chamberlain, *Agriculturalist*, Brookfield, Mass.
Dr. Thomas Holman, *Physician*, Cooperstown, N.Y.
Mr. Samuel Whitney, *Mechanic & Schoolmaster*, Branford, Con.
Mr. Samuel Ruggles, *Catechist & Schoolmaster*, Brookfield, Con.
Mr. Elisha Loomis, *Printer & Schoolmaster*, Middlesex, N.Y.
### Native Teachers
John Honooree, Native of Owhyhee
Thomas Hopoo, Native of Owhyhee
William Tennooe, native of Atooi
### Females
Mrs. Bingham, (late Miss Sybil Moseley,) Westfield, Mass.
Mrs.Thurston, (Miss Lucy Goodale,) Marlborough, Mass.
Mrs. Jerusha Chamberlain, Mother of 3 sons and 2 daughters, eldest, 13, who go with her
Mrs. Holman, (Miss Lucy Ruggles,) Brookfield, Con.
Mrs. Whitney, (Miss Mercy Partridge,) Pittsfield, Mass.
Mrs.. Ruggles, (Miss Nancy Welles,) East-Windsor, Con.
Mrs. Loomis, (Miss Maria T. Sartwell,) Utica, N.Y.
George Tamoree — son of Tamoree, king of Atooi and Oneeheow, two of the Sandwich Islands, — who has been educated with the other Native Youths, at the Foreign Mission School, Cornwall, Con. returns with the Mission to his Father.[7]

## The Missionaries Arrive in Hawaii
Arriving on March 30, 1820, they first sighted the beautiful Mauna Kea mountains summit above the clouds. Opukahaia's two friends, Hopu and Honolii, together with one of the missionaries, were sent by boat to find out from the natives about the state of the islands, and the whereabouts of their king. How wonderful it was to hear, from these scouts, the exhilarating  news:

Kamehameha is dead — His son Liholiho is king — the tabus are abolished — the images are destroyed, the heiaus of idolatrous worship are burned, and the party that attempted to restore them by force of arms has recently been vanquished![8]

## Kamehameha I's Death Paves the Way for Christianity

Kamehameha's death brought great changes to the island. Once Hawaii's powerful ruler, he enforced tabus and the worship of heathen gods. Head of the Maui nobility, Kaahumanu exercised sovereignty over many of the chiefs of the islands. Kamehameha had instructed his son, Liholiho, to reinforce the idolatry and tabus of Hawaii. However, upon his father's death, Liholiho chose to abolish all tabus and religious laws, in order to promote life free from restraints. The worship of idols was forbidden, but the personal beliefs of the Hawaiians and their superstitious fear of the volcano, the spirits of the dead, the bones of their monarchy, and their kini of gods, that is, the 40,000 deities to whom they were fruitlessly appealing, were expected to be slowly extinguished. Far removed from Liholiho's mind was any conception of God's perfect plan for Hawaii, but his actions were the answers to Opukahaia's fervent prayers for the salvation of his people! Liholiho was but preparing the way for Christianity to be introduced, embraced and readily accepted by the islanders, whose eyes were subsequently opened to the truth of the gospel message.[9]

## A Letter From Kaumualii Shows
## His Belief in the Value of Christianity

In this regard, Hiram Bingham quotes a moving letter from the King of Kauai. After three months of instruction, he wrote to him as leader of the missionary band, expressing his delight and gratitude to the missionaries who had "come to do him good," and his recognition of what had been done for his son, George:

Dear friend, I feel glad that your good people come to my islands to do me good. I thank you. I love them. I give them eat, drink, and land to work on. I thank all American folks, they give my son learning. He know how to read, write all America books. I feel glad he come home. He long time in America. I think he dead. But some man speak "no." I very glad you good people. I love them. I do them good. I hope you do good Hawaii, Oahu and all the islands.

Accept this from your friend, Tamoree

Kaumualii[10]

The openness of the monarchy in allowing the people to be instructed in reading and Christian education was a direct result of the confidence and respect they maintained for the missionaries. That summer, King Kaumualii wrote this simple letter in his limited English to the secretary of the American Board, expressing his belief in the value of Christianity and its educational impact upon his people:

July 28th, 1820

Dear Friend: I wish to write a few lines to you to thank you for the good book you was so kind as to send my son. I think it is a good book, one that God gave us to read. I hope all my people will soon read this, and all other good books. I believe that my idols are good for nothing, and that your God is the only true God — the one that made all things. My idols I have hove away — they are no good — they fool me — they do me no good. I gave them cocoanuts, plantains, hogs, and good many things, and they fool me at last. Now I throw them all away. I have done now. When your good people learn me, I worship your God. I feel glad your good people come here to help us. We know nothing. I thank you for giving my son learning. I thank all America people.

Accept this from your friend, King Tamoree.

Kaumualii[11]

## A Christian School Established in Honolulu

Mrs. Bingham established a Christian school in Honolulu. After three months, it had an enrollment of 40 students, who attended a five- to six-hour school day. A very exciting aspect of this school was the zealous recitation of these majestic truths by 40 little Hawaiian students each morning, in their own language, in one accord:

In the beginning, God created the heavens and the earth.
Jehovah is in heaven, and He is everywhere.
Jesus Christ, the good Son of God, died for our sins.
We must pray to Jehovah, and love His Word.
God loves good men, and good men love God.[12]

## The Prayers of Henry Opukahaia Answered

The agility and talent displayed by the Hawaiians, their ability to understand and rapidly master lessons in Christian education were further proofs of God's providential answer to the prayers of Henry Opukahaia and his Hawaiian fellow-believers.

Sabbath school instruction grew by leaps and bounds. One of the lessons consisted of reading and interpreting the moving Memoirs of Henry Opukahaia, which caused many of the students to weep with conviction and repentance[13]

## The Bible, the Ten Commandments, and Prayer Taught to the Students

The students also learned the Ten Commandments, Catechism for children, and other priceless gems through oral recitation and memorization, prior to the Bible and other books being prepared in their language. They often practised these lessons, rehearsing them to others. Thus they were enlightened about God, the soul, heaven and eternal rewards — the great pivotal doctrines of our faith upon which moral excellence and Christian civilization is based. These, in turn, produced positive, abiding results in the lives of the people and their society.[14]

## A Hawaiian Citizen Praises the Character and Work of the Missionaries

An interesting rare book in the Library of Congress Collection, written by a citizen of Hawaii, C.V. Sturdevant, and published in 1898, provides insight into the true identity and worth of the 1820 missionaries to Hawaii. Under the sub-title *Missionaries*, he states:

> ...As to the early missionaries, it is admitted that they were honest, God-fearing men and women and that they made the Islands what they are religiously. Every person who pays his quarterly bills and behaves himself is styled "a missionary" in Honolulu, whether he attends any church or not and it is for this reason that the real missionaries are blamed for nearly every evil which exists.
>
> The *Advertiser* (newspaper) described the missionary as "one who is never in distress when he sees good government and who has a weakness for the reign of law." The first missionaries landed at Kailua from the brig "Thaddeus" on March 30, 1820, and found more than the native superstition to overcome as "Botany Bay convicts had introduced the art of distilling liquor before the year 1800 and drunkenness had become very prevalent" while all manner of disease and vice was introduced by whalers and others. The missionaries succeeded in abolishing idolatry (the natives were worshippers of stone images), in getting them to accept Christianity and to adopt the dress and customs of civilization in place of those of barbarians.
>
> Not all Hawaiians are Christians any more than all Americans, except nominally.
>
> The missionaries are frequently charged with "trading Bibles for lands." This claim is not well founded as nearly all died poor. The charge is doubtless based on the fact that many "missionary children" are today rich men. This is perfectly natural and would not reflect credit on their business ability if they were not wealthy. Hawaii is one of if not the richest country in the world and to have remained poor when riches could be honestly gained is quite contrary to human nature. Their fortunes were made by themselves, not left to them by their missionary fathers. It is frequently asked "why did not these children follow in the footsteps of their fathers?" Being a Yankee we reply by asking why do not the sons of American ministers do the same? It is believed that a much larger proportion of these missionary children have become active in missionary work than is the case in the United States. The writer can name some thirty

or forty. Moreover, those other sons who have entered the business world are the main financial support of the missionary work not only in Hawaii, but in the South Sea Islands as well.[15]

As it was in 1898, so it is today. Missionaries are blamed for almost every conceivable ill which has befallen Hawaii, when in reality, they brought the Gospel of Jesus Christ, Christian education, medical expertise and a free form of government to Hawaii, along with its incumbent blessings.

## Princess Kapiolani, a Christian, Defies Pele, False Goddess of Volcanoes

One of the fascinating evidences of the monarchy's conversion to Christianity, is that of Princess Kapiolani, daughter of the Great Chief Keawe-mauhili. She was one of the noblest Christians of her time. As an example to her people of the Sovereign power of Jehovah God and His Son Jesus Christ, she defied the dreaded goddess of all volcanoes, Pele, who was said to inhabit the living crater of Kilauea, on Hawaii island.[16] In December 1824, she set about the task of breaking the spell of false worship in Pele, greatly feared by the Hawaiians, thus giving her people an object lesson on the powerlessness of their gods. With 80 persons following her, she journeyed 150 miles to the crater of Kilauea, most of the way on foot. Approaching the crater, she was met by the priestess of Pele who threatened her with death if she broke the tabus.[17]

## Jehovah God the True God of the Universe

"Who are you?" demanded Kapiolani. "One in whom the goddess dwells," she replied. In answer to a letter supposedly received from Pele, Kapiolani cited Scripture passages, showing forth the attributes and sovereignty of the true God, until the priestess was subdued, and confessed that KE AKUA, the deity, had left her. The next morning she and 80 followers climbed down to the black ledge, a distance of about five hundred feet below. There, confronting the eruptions of the inner crater, she ate the "sacred" berries, throwing stones into the fiery lake, with the words:

> Jehovah is my God. He kindled these fires. I fear not Pele. If I perish in her anger, then you may fear Pele; but if I trust in Jehovah, then you must fear and serve Him alone.

They then united in singing a hymn of praise to the true God, and knelt in adoration to the Creator and Governor of the Universe.[18]

## Hawaiian History Revolutionized by Christianity

Hawaiian history, pertaining to the people and their monarchs, was revolutionized by Christianity. Is it little wonder then, that the official seal of the state of Hawaii bears an imprint to this truth. Hawaii's motto, translated, reads:

"The Life of the Land is Preserved in Righteousness."[19]

This beautiful island state has much to be proud of. The soul-rending prayers and petitions of Henry Opukahaia, first Hawaiian Christian, who was burdened for the salvation of his own people, literally changed the course of Hawaii's history; the 1820 missionaries consequently carrying the life-changing Gospel of Jesus Christ to these distant shores.

# CRAWFORD W. LONG, M.D.
## "My Profession Is to Me a Ministry from God"
## (1815 - 1878)

### The Doctor who Served God

A relatively unknown American hero, whose accomplishments in medicine revolutionized medical surgery, is a doctor by the name of Crawford W. Long. His achievements stemmed from the belief that his work was a ministry from God. A native of Georgia, this man was selected to represent his state in Statuary Hall in the United States Capitol. The inscription on the base of the statue reads:

> Georgia's Tribute
> Crawford W. Long, M.D.
> Discoverer of the use of
> Sulphuric Ether as an anaesthetic in surgery
> on March 30, 1842 at
> Jefferson, Jackson County,
> Georgia U.S.A.
> "My profession is to me a Ministry from God."

In the modern world of medicine, few have had to experience having a tooth filled, getting a shot, or having surgery without the use of something to deaden the pain. However, such was not always the case.

### Surgery "A Horror" Before Anesthesia Invented

The following speech given by Dr. Hugh H. Young is found in the Congressional Record of April 23, 1926. It gives insight into the awful reality of the operating table prior to Dr. Long's invention of this "blessing to humanity."

> ...In comparison with *surgical anesthesia*, all other contributions to medical science are trivial... Before anesthesia, surgery was a horror... The awful experiences of operative surgery and the attendant high mortality caused the best minds of medicine to avoid operations... In a letter to the famous surgeon, Sir James Y. Simpson, a patient who had recently lost a leg by amputation, thus described his tortures:

> > 'The blank whirlwind of emotion, the horror of great despair, and the sense of desertion by God and man, bordering closely upon despair, which swept through my mind and overwhelmed my heart, I can never forget. I watched all that the surgeon did with a fascinated intensity. I still recall with unwelcome vividness the spreading out of the instruments, the twisting of the tourniquet, the first incision, the fingering of the sawed bone, the sponge pressed on the flap, the tying of blood vessels, the stitching of the skin, and the bloody, dismembered limb lying on the floor. Their memory still haunts me...'[1]

*After the original marble statue in the Senate Connecting Corridor,*
*U.S. Capitol, Washington, D.C.*

So we see that a compassionate Georgian physician yielded to God's will for his life, putting into practise Christ's great admonition to his own: "Do unto others as you would have them do unto you."

## Fourteen-Year-Old Crawford Goes to College

Crawford Long was admitted, at the age of 14, to Franklin College, now the University of Georgia. He graduated in 1835, second in his class with an A.M. degree, after which he attended medical school at the University of Kentucky. Graduating in 1839 from the University of Pennsylvania, he went to a New York hospital to perfect himself in surgery, remaining there until August, 1841. Long subsequently moved to Jefferson, Georgia, having received the best literary and medical training in our nation. On March 30, 1842, he performed his first surgical operation on a patient, utilizing his new invention of anesthesia through the inhalation of sulphuric ether; a few years later establishing practise at Athens, Georgia.[2] His life was a fruitful one, lived out in the service of others.

## Crawford Long Dies in the Discharge of His Duty

This selfless American son died in the discharge of his duty, on June 16, 1878, at the bedside of a mother who had just given birth to a child. Regaining consciousness for a few moments, his last words were: "How is she?" He then gave instructions for her well-being and breathed his last.[3]

## Senate Chaplain Praises God for "This Humble Country Doctor"

Following are excerpts from the Congressional unveiling and presentation of the marble statue of Dr. Crawford W. Long by the state of Georgia, on April 23, 1926. Senate Chaplain Sam W. Small gave the following moving prayer, glorifying our God and Father:

> Our Heavenly Father, we are gathered to-day in this great national capital, and in a historic chamber of this great building whose atmosphere has thrilled to the eloquence of some of the greatest men of our generation and of generations gone by. We are assembled to represent the citizens of one of the great States of this immutable Union of ours, for the purpose of unveiling to the eyes of the living and to those of the coming generations the marble effigy of one of Thy humble and noble souls, who, inspired by Thy spirit of compassion to humanity, discovered the remedy and the soothing for the acute pains which formerly accompanied the incisions or the excisions of surgery upon the human body. This discovery and application by this faithful and honored son of Georgia has gone around the globe, to assuage the pains of humanity, to bring relief to millions who are suffering from that which to

them seems incurable; and may the Spirit which animated this humble
country doctor of Georgia become the universal spirit of all of us who would
serve Thee in faithfulness, and our brethren with the spirit of helpfulness. We
ask it all for Christ's sake. Amen.[4]

## Crawford's "Love and Sympathy for Suffering Humanity"

Another address, this time given by Dr. Frank K. Boland, followed,
providing insights into Crawford Long's "love and sympathy for suffering humanity; his deep power of observation and his supreme courage,"
all of which form admirable character traits.

...Eighty-four years ago, March 30, 1842, at the age of 27, his sympathy and
love for suffering humanity, his deep power of observation and his supreme
courage, led him to be the first to do, finally, what physicians and scientists
have tried in vain to accomplish for all the centuries — to perform a surgical
operation without producing pain. By this achievement, in that remote,
isolated Georgia village, the young physician gave to mankind a blessing for
which no praise, no expression of gratitude can be too great...

## Testimony of a Pharmacist Friend

Next came an address by Joseph Jacobs, friend and former employee
of Crawford Long and representative of the pharmaceutical profession:

As a pharmacist it was my great good fortune in my early days to be an
apprentice and student in the drug store in the town of Athens, Georgia,
owned and operated by the man whom we commemorate to-day, and I was the
recipient of many kindnesses at his hands, and I am here to testify to the
greatness of this man in every respect; as a physician, kind and gentle; and as
a friend, loyal and true; as a citizen, brave, wise and patriotic. All the nations
of the earth commemorate this man, whose discovery lessened pain, and the
danger and the terror of the surgeon's knife. The skilled and gentle ministrations
of the learned physician were his; the tender love for family and for friends he
ever exhibited in acts of kindness; the poor and distressed found in him ever
a ready and helpful sympathy; his city and State knew him as patriotic, brave
and wise...[5]

## Dr. Long's Christian Character Traits

From these testimonies regarding Dr. Long we see the highly-valued
Christian qualities of kindness, tenderness, gentleness, loyalty, cour-
age, wisdom and patriotism exemplified in this Georgian hero's life.
The greatest of these, however, is godliness, that is, putting God first
in all things. Dr. Long's own witness to his servitude and obedience to
Almighty God gives evidence to this: "My Profession is to Me a
Ministry from God."

May there likewise be those from this generation of young Americans who will boldly declare, "As for me, my profession is to me a
ministry from God."

# FRANCES WILLARD
## Crusader for Temperance
## (1839 - 1898)

## A Woman Honored in the Capitol's Hall of Fame

Frances Willard was the first woman chosen for the honor of being represented in Statuary Hall of the United States Capitol. She was selected by the state of Illinois. The white marble statue of her bears her poignant words inscribed upon its base:

> Ah, it is women who have given the costliest hostages to fortune. Out into the battle of life they have sent their best beloved with fearful odds against them. Oh by the dangers they have dared by the hours of patient watching over beds where helpless children lay by the incense of ten thousand prayers wafted from their gentle lips to heaven. I charge you, give them power to protect along life's treacherous highway those whom they have so loved.

On the pedestal upon which she leans, is a shield bearing the inscription:

> "For God and Home and every Land."

## Her Christian Character

A letter written to Senator Otis F. Glen by Ernest Fremont Tittle, of the First Methodist Episcopal Church, Evanston, Illinois, is dated January 13, 1933. It gives further insight into Frances Willard's Christian life and character:

> Dear Sir:
>
> My attention has been called to the fact that some of the statues now in the Rotunda of the Capitol Building are to be removed. As a citizen of Evanston, Illinois, the home of Frances Willard, and minister of the church from which she was buried, and, further, as one who believes that she was one of the most truly distinguished women America has ever produced, I am earnestly hoping that her statue will be allowed to remain.
> Sincerely yours,<br>(signed) Ernest Fremont Tittle.[1]

## Founder of the Women's Christian Temperance Union: "Christ Shall Be the World's King"

Frances Willard was the founder of the Women's Christian Temperance Union. At a national convention of that organization she delivered a beautiful message which can be summed up as the essence of her life:

> One vital organic thought, one absorbing purpose, one undying ambition. It is that Christ shall be the world's King... King of its courts, its camps, its

*After the original marble statue in Statuary Hall*
*of the U.S. Capitol, Washington, D.C.*

commerce; King of its colleges and cloisters; King of its customs and constitutions... Christ and His law, the true basis of government and the Supreme authority in national and individual life.[2]

## Frances' Portrait Displayed in the White House

In 1873, Frances Willard's portrait, together with portraits of eight U.S. presidents (including George Washington), hung in the East Room of the White House. President Garfield is reported as having said to the donors of Willard's portrait: "I shall be glad to have this picture on these walls."[3] Let us look to the words spoken in her memory to understand President Garfield's sentiments.

## Congress Calls Her "One of the Most Eminent Women of the United States"

In the February 17, 1905 Joint Resolution of both the U.S. House of Representatives and the Senate, Frances Willard is called "one of the most eminent women of the United States." On February 17, 1939, the Centennial of her birth, the Honorable Stephen Bolles of Wisconsin gave this moving speech to the House in her honor:

> Mr. Speaker, on this the centennial of the birth of Frances Willard, one of America's greatest women and first to be honored with a statue in the American Hall of Fame, we have heard a number of eulogistic speeches. Gentlemen from New York and Illinois have paid tribute to Frances Willard, one because she was born in the state of New York, others because she went to college there and became a resident of Illinois. But, Mr. Speaker and my colleagues, the real life of Frances Willard was not formed in New York, nor in Illinois; the plan and outline of her future greatness was the product of Wisconsin. There into the Rock River Valley, three miles from the village of Janesville, came her father, to be like other pioneers — called by the western sun out of Ohio along the trail of homeseekers. Frances Willard was eight years old — a rhyming, romping, roaming girl seeking adventure among the simplicities of the pioneer world. Josiah Willard, her father, was a citizen of value. He helped to build. His home, still standing, is a good house now... There was no schoolhouse; he helped build one. It was in the successor to that schoolhouse, the first and oldest shrine to Frances, that she taught school. That little white building, still stands, preserved with its grove of trees and yard sloping to Rock River's banks... In the building will be preserved many souvenirs of the life of our great American woman — *Pioneer and preacher, evangelist of a new life* for posterity.
>
> The girlhood life of Frances Willard was a part of this great epic of America written by the men and women who, persecuted, whose horizon was narrowed by incompetent authority, and hungry for some mystic breath of life... This epic begins with the explorer. He found America. He mapped its shores. He threaded its rivers and crossed its lakes. The priest, and preacher, and the teacher came; and then the pioneer with Bible and rifle, with ax and plow... Beauty was all around the settler in the Rock River Valley... It was of this that

Frances Willard often wrote in her diary. These beauties which God had planted for her had a marked influence on her life. Her music was the wind in the forest, the summer rain ... the beating snow against the windows. Josiah Willard's farm was a way of living. His home was his castle, his farm his landed domain, his retainers were all members of his own family...[4]

## Congress Calls Her
## "The Uncrowned Queen of Purity and Temperance"

Another moving tribute on the centennial of her birth this time given by Mr. Sheppard to the United States Senate, gives insight into her distinguished life and accomplishments for God's glory and the good of mankind:

*A great woman*  Mr. President, exactly 34 years ago today, the United States Senate and also the United States House of Representatives suspended ordinary business to pay tribute to the memory of a great woman. On that day, the Congress of the United States accepted from the Commonwealth of Illinois a statue of Frances E. Willard to be placed in Statuary Hall in the Nation's Capitol. By law, each State is permitted to have two statues in this Congress of the great. The statue of Frances E. Willard is the only one of a woman to be found in this Hall. But as we study the life and work of this eminent woman, we no longer wonder why the great Commonwealth of Illinois should choose a woman as one of its two representatives in so distinguished a setting... Even as a child, she exhibited those principles and philosophies which were to make her known throughout the world as the 'uncrowned queen of purity and temperance.' Miss Willard attended college at Evanston, Illinois and was graduated with honors. She rounded out her education by travel and study in Europe and then returned to Evanston and became president of the Evanston College of Ladies, the first female college entirely under the control and direction of women. This college was later to become the woman's department of Northwestern University, and Miss Willard became its dean and professor of aesthetics.

*President of the Illinois Women's Christian Temperance Union*  It was in 1874 that Miss Willard resigned her connection with Northwestern University, and the same year marked her active entry into the work which claimed the major portion of the rest of her life — temperance. She became president of the Illinois Woman's Christian Temperance Union and her executive ability and faculty for organization permitted her to organize thousands of women throughout the United States in a Nation-wide crusade. Her influence and the fame of her deeds spread like magic and during her active life she probably addressed a larger number of public audiences than any woman or man of her time.

Miss Willard's work in the cause of temperance seems to overshadow, in the public mind, her history-making accomplishments in other fields. Miss Willard was not only an advocate and untiring worker in behalf of temperance, but she was an ardent campaigner for purity in politics, equal rights for women, and, as a means to secure political reform, woman suffrage.

It was in 1888 that Miss Willard realized the need for a clearing house of women's activities in the United States and the world. She brought 5,000 women together in Washington, D.C., where the National Council of Women was formed, with Miss Willard as president.

*She initiates the honor system*

One of Miss Willard's preeminent faculties was her ability to anticipate the future. Think of it! Sixty years ago hers was a lone voice in the wilderness pleading for an 8-hour day, for courts of conciliation and arbitration, and for justice as opposed to oppression and greed. While with the Evanston College for Ladies she initiated the honor system in the school government, thus anticipating by an entire generation the self-government now popular in all leading American educational institutions.

This year the Nation and the world join in celebrating the centenary of Miss Willard's birth. And it is most fitting and proper that we should pause in our everyday endeavors at this time and try to take stock of the good which Miss Willard's life and career brought to this world.

*woman of culture, an educator – she made purer the moral atmosphere of the United States"*

We consider her life as a woman of culture, an educator, and the fountainhead of one of the greatest movements in all history, we realize that there really is no method by which we can measure all the good Miss Willard did. The hundreds of thousands of women organized in the cause of temperance are but a suggestion of the real results of her activities. Probably the highest benefits of her life must remain intangible. No one dares argue but that she made purer the moral atmosphere of the United States and the world. She made people cleaner minded and saner; millions of wives and children bless her name, and as long as this world shall exist the name of France E. Willard will shine with an ever-increasing brightness...

Womankind has never had a more staunch supporter than Miss Willard. She was the first to organize women into a united front. It was her poet friend John Greenleaf Whittier who wrote of her:

> 'She knew the power of banded ill,
> but felt that love was stronger still,
> And organized for doing good
> The World's united womanhood...'

Thirty-four years ago today, Mr. Littlefield of Maine joining, as a member of Congress, in the acceptance of Miss Willard's statue in Statuary Hall, declared:

*the home the basic unit of our Christian civilization*

The home is the basic unit of our Christian civilization. It is the foundation upon which our free institutions rest. Upon its integrity, purity and character the quality of our civilization depend. It is a holy shrine. Whatever profanes it pollutes the sacred temple of liberty itself. Whoever defends and enobles it insures to our children and our children's children the blessings of freedom and the enduring of a government of the people, for the people, and by the people. A civilization based upon a lecherous and debauched home is rotten to the core.

*Congress calls her "a divinely gifted woman"*

Statesmen, warriors, and patriots may strive and build and achieve, but all their striving, building and achieving is in vain, even as "sounding brass or a tinkling cymbal" if it disregards the eternal moral verities and does not conserve the true happiness and the highest welfare of mankind. This divinely gifted woman bent every energy, shaped every purpose, and devoted every aspiration of a godly life to the consummation of this happiness and welfare. It is fitting that her work should be thus recognized.

*Congress states: "In every land women rise and call her blessed"*

When Illinois decided to place another statue in the Capitol Hall of Fame, many outstanding names came to mind. Probably no State in the Union has been more fortunate in this respect than Illinois. There were Lincoln, Douglas, Grant, Logan and a host of others... I repeat that it is not surprising that the people of Illinois should choose Miss Willard for a distinction like this. She was a dreamer, but she was also a doer. In every land women rise and call her blessed...[5]

## Frances Willard's Christian Character Traits

Frances Willard exemplified morality, purity, temperance, courage, self-sacrifice, perseverance, intelligence; and the love, protection and nurture of the American Christian home, as well as patriotism.

## The Crowning Glory of Her Life—a Biblical Foundation

The crowning glory of her life however, is the biblical foundation upon which it was built — in her own inimitable words:

> ...Christ shall be the world's King... King of its courts, its camps, its commerce; King of its colleges and cloisters; King of its customs and constitutions... Christ and His law, the true basis of government and the Supreme authority in national and individual life.[6]

And let it be so.

# ANDREW JACKSON
## Tennessee's Greatest Hero
## (1767 - 1845)

Andrew Jackson, the seventh president of the United States, was born March 15, 1767 in the Waxhaw settlement, a remote area of South Carolina.[1] His father was an Irish emigrant of Scottish origin who had come to America in search of a better life. [2]

### Andrew Jackson Motivated by Independence

In an oration delivered on June 27, 1845 in commemoration of his death, his entire life and accomplishments were reviewed. The following excerpts from that address are given:

> ...His birth was in 1767, at a time when the people of our land were but a body of dependent colonists, scarcely more than two millions in number, scattered along an immense coast, with no army, or navy, or union; and exposed to the attempts of England to control America by the aid of military force. His boyhood grew up in the midst of the contest with great Britain. The first great political truth that reached his heart, was that all men are free and equal; the first great fact that beamed on his understanding was his country's independence.
>
> The strife, as it increased, came near the shades of his own upland residence. As a boy of 13, he witnessed the scenes of horror that accompany civil war; and when but a year older, with an elder brother, he shouldered his musket, and went forth to strike a blow for his country...[3]

### Andrew Finds Himself Alone in the World

Following the war, he found himself alone in the world, his father having died, his brother killed in the war and his mother also having passed away.

### Jackson Admitted to the Bar—a State Constitution Formed

Settling the wilderness areas to the West became a new challenge for the nation after the war. In November, 1787, he was admitted to the bar.[4] At age 21, Jackson was made a public prosecutor for a wild and remote frontier area in the Cumberland region. The Commemoration speech described those efforts to form a State Constitution:

> ...These adventurers in the wilderness longed to come together in organized society. The overshadowing genius of their time inspired them with good designs, and filled them with the counsels of wisdom. Dwellers in the forest, freest of the free, bound in the spirit, they came up by their representatives, on foot, on horseback, through the forest, along the streams, by the buffalo traces, by the Indian paths, by the blazed forest avenues, to meet in convention among the mountains at Knoxville, and frame for themselves a Constitution.

*After the original bronze statue in the Main Rotunda of the U.S. Capitol, Washington, D.C.*

Andrew Jackson was there, the greatest man of them all—modest, bold, determined, demanding nothing for himself, and shrinking from nothing that his heart approved.

The Convention came together on the 11th day of January, 1796, and finished its work on the sixth day of February. How had the wisdom of the Old World vainly tasked itself to frame constitutions, that could, at least, be the subject of experiment; the man of Tennessee, in less than 25 days, perfected a fabric, which in its essential forms, was to last forever. They came together, full of faith and reverence, of love to humanity, of confidence in truth. In the simplicity of wisdom, they framed their Constitution, acting under higher influences than they were conscious of.

> They wrought in sad sincerity
> Themselves from God they could not free
> They builded better than they knew
> The conscious stones to beauty grew.

In the instrument which they framed, they embodied their faith in God, and in the immortal nature of man. They gave the right of suffrage to every freeman; they vindicated the sanctity of reason, by giving freedom of speech and of the press; they reverenced the voice of God, as it speaks in the soul of man, by asserting the indefeasible right of man to worship the Infinite according to his conscience; they established the freedom and equality of elections; and they demanded from every future legislator a solemn oath 'never to consent to any act or thing whatever that shall have even a tendency to lessen the rights of the people...' The men of Tennessee were now a people, and they were to send forth a man to stand for them in the Congress of the United States... And with one consent, they united in selecting the foremost man among their law-givers—Andrew Jackson.

The love of the people of Tennessee followed him to the American Congress; and he had served but a single term, when the State of Tennessee made him one of its representatives in the American Senate, where he sat under the auspices of Jefferson...[5]

## Major-General Jackson Takes Command

Jackson distinguished himself in the military, leading the Tennessee Militia to victory over hostile Indians in Alabama; as major general of the U.S. Army, soundly defeating the British in the Battle of New Orleans in 1815; and winning in the Seminole Indian uprising in Florida.[6]

The Commemoration Oration gives further insight into his life as follows:

> ...His hospitable roof sheltered the emigrant and the pioneer; and, as they made their way to their new homes, they filled the mountain sides and the valleys with his praise...
>
> None equaled him in the power of endurance; and the private soldiers, as they found him passing them on the march, exclaimed, "he is as tough as hickory." "Yes," they cried to one another. "There goes Old Hickory!..."[7]

## Andrew Jackson, Seventh U.S. President

Jackson served two terms as president of the United States from 1829-1837. It was shortly before the beginning of his second term as president, that Jackson issued his famous "Nullification Proclamation," directed at the people of South Carolina, which a state paper described as "clear in statement, forcible in argument, vigorous in style and glowing with the fire of a genuine and enlightened patriotism."[8] The following year, he took the bold step of withdrawing the government's deposits from the Bank of the United States, causing consternation in the financial world, and bringing upon himself criticism from the Senate. However, by 1835, the national debt was paid off, an occurrence unique in the history of our nation.[9] At the conclusion of his second term as president, Jackson left a surplus in the Federal Treasury.[10]

## Jackson Studied the Bible Faithfully

Again, the Commemoration Oration reported on the events, as his life drew to a close:

> ...Age had whitened his locks, and dimmed his eye, and spread around him the infirmities and venerable emblems of many years of toilsome service; but his heart beat as warmly as in his youth, and his courage was as firm as it had ever been in the day of battle. But while his affections were still for his friends and his country, his thoughts were already in a better world. That exalted mind, which in active life had always had unity of perception and will, which in action had never faltered from doubt, and which in council had always reverted to first principles and general laws, now gave itself up to communication with the Infinite. He was a believer: from feeling, from experience, from conviction. Not a shadow of skepticism ever dimmed the lustre of his mind. Proud philosopher! Will you smile to know that Andrew Jackson perused reverently his Psalter and Prayer-book and Bible? Know that Andrew Jackson had faith in the eternity of Truth, in the imperishable power of popular freedom, in the destinies of humanity, in the virtues and capacity of the people in his country's institutions, in the being and overruling Providence of a merciful and ever-living God...[11]

## Jackson Said "My Sufferings Less
## Than Those of Christ on the Cross"

From a famed Eulogy given in the U.S. Senate on June 8, 1845, we glean further poignant truths pertaining to Andrew Jackson's true Christian identity. From his own words, we have irrefutable evidence of his salvation through dependence upon Christ Jesus and His shed blood on Calvary's cross:

> The last moment of his life on earth is at hand. It is the Sabbath of the Lord: When he first felt the hand of death upon him, 'may my enemies,' he cried, 'find peace; may the liberties of my country endure forever.'

When his exhausted system, under the excess of pain, sunk, for a moment from debility, 'Do not weep,' said he to his adopted daughter; 'my sufferings are less than those of Christ upon the cross;' for he, too, as a disciple of the cross, could have devoted himself, in sorrow, for mankind…His two little grandchildren were absent at Sunday School. He asked for them; and as they came, he prayed for them, and kissed them and blessed them…And that dying man, thus surrendered, in a gush of fervid eloquence, spoke with inspiration of God, of the Redeemer, of salvation, through the atonement, of immortality, of heaven. For he ever thought that pure and undefiled religion was the foundation of private happiness, and the bulwark of republican institutions.

Having spoken of immortality in perfect consciousness of his own approaching end, he bade them all farewell. 'Dear children,' such were his final words, 'dear children, servants and friends, I trust to meet you all in heaven, both white and black—all, both white and black.' And having borne his testimony to immortality, he bowed his mighty head, and without a groan, the spirit of the greatest man of his age, escaped to the bosom of His God. In life, his career had been like the blaze of the sun in the fierceness of its noon-day glory; his death was lonely as the mildest sunset of the summer's evening, when the sun goes down in tranquil beauty without a cloud…[12]

## Jackson's Testimony to His Faith in Christ Jesus, "His Glorious Redeemer"

In a letter written to Commodore Jesse D. Elliott, USN on March 27, 1845, 73 short days prior to his death, Andrew Jackson gives great insight into his vibrant Christian faith and his trust in Jesus Christ, "his glorious Redeemer," whose sacrifice on the cross of Calvary purchased eternal life for him. Elliott had returned from the Middle East with a Roman sarcophagus which he wished to present to Jackson. Andrew Jackson responded thus:

> …I cannot consent that my mortal body shall be lain in a repository prepared for an Emperor or King—my republican feelings and principles forbid it—the simplicity of our system of government forbids it. Every monument erected to perpetuate the memory of our heroes and statesmen ought to bear evidence of the economy and simplicity of our republican institutions and the plainness of our republican citizens, who are the sovereigns of our glorious Union, and whose virtue is to perpetuate it. True virtue cannot exist where pomp and parade are the governing passions. It can only dwell with the people, the great laboring and producing classes, that form the bone and sinew of our confederacy.
>
> I have prepared a humble depository for my mortal body beside that wherein lies my beloved wife, where, without any pomp or parade, I have requested, when my God calls me to sleep with my fathers, to be laid, for both of us there to remain until the last trumpet sounds to call the dead to judgment, when we, I hope, shall rise together, clothed with that heavenly body promised to all who believe in our glorious Redeemer, who died for us that we might live, and by whose atonement I hope for a blessed immortality…[13]

ABRAHAM
LINCOLN
ILLINOIS

*After the marble statue by Vinnie Ream in the Main Rotunda,*
*U.S. Capitol, Washington, D.C.*

# ABRAHAM LINCOLN
## Emancipator of the Slaves
## (1809 - 1865)

Abraham Lincoln, 16th president of the United States, was born in a lowly farm cabin near Hodgensville, Kentucky, on February 12, 1809. He was the first son and second child of Thomas Lincoln and Nancy Hanks, both of the Rockingham County, Virginia.[1]

### Lincoln's Mother's Only Book—the Bible

Nancy Hanks' only book had been the Bible, from which Lincoln was taught and nurtured each day. She taught him to base his entire life upon the contents of that book. At his mother's untimely death when the boy was 10 years old, Lincoln knew much of the Word of God almost by heart. Many years later, as president of the United States, Lincoln is quoted as having said: "All that I am or hope to be, I owe to my angel mother. Blessings on her memory!"[2]

### Young Lincoln Devours Good Books, Especially the Bible

In 1819, Lincoln's father married Sarah Johnston of Kentucky. She brought cheer and kindness into the family, encouraging Abraham in his love for reading, which his father considered idleness. Lincoln had less than a year of formal school attendance, but learned to read, and write and "cipher the rule of three," nonetheless. He devoured books, beginning with the Bible. He worked at home, on neighboring farms, and became a clerk at Gentry's Store.[3]

### 19-Year-Old Abraham Lincoln Witnesses a Slave Market

At age 19 he accompanied the son of his employer to New Orleans on a flatboat trip.[4] It was there that he first saw an auction of slaves, and is reported to have said:

> By the grace of God I'll make the ground of this country too hot for the feet of slaves.[5]

### Lincoln the Captain, Legislator and Lawyer

In 1830, Lincoln moved with his family to Decatur, Illinois, serving the community of New Salem near Springfield as a mill-hand, clerk in village stores, postmaster and deputy surveyor.[6] He quickly gained public respect and appreciation, and was selected Captain in the military force raised to curb Indian disturbances. After becoming a candidate for the legislature in New Salem, he was elected to this body in 1834, and reelected three times thereafter. In the Fall of 1836 he gained admission to the bar with the aid of borrowed books, and little else. The following April he moved to Springfield, commencing his law practice. Abraham Lincoln was elected to Congress from 1846-1849.[7]

## Lincoln's Marriage to Mary Todd

On November 4, 1842 he married Mary Todd, daughter of Robert S. Todd of Louisville, Kentucky. It is recorded that Mrs. Lincoln was "of high social rank, brilliant and cultured" and that she was a devoted wife and mother.[8] During the five years which ensued, Lincoln took his place amongst the prominent lawyers of the Illinois bar. This remarkable American son appreciated the handicap of a defective education and strove valiantly to overcome it.[9]

## The 16th U.S. President Takes Office

On March 4, 1861, Lincoln became the 16th president of the United States.

## Lincoln's February 22, 1861 Independence Hall Address

Shortly before taking office for his first term, Lincoln gave an address at Independence Hall in Philadelphia, affirming the inalienable rights of every American, based on that great document, the Declaration of Independence, and expressing his hope that civil war could be avoided.

Lincoln's address is here reprinted:

Philadelphia, February 22, 1861

I am filled with deep emotion at finding myself standing in this place, where were collected together the wisdom, the patriotism, the devotion to principle, from which sprang the institutions under which we live.

You have kindly suggested to me that in my hands is the task of restoring peace to our distracted country. I can say in return, sir, that all the political sentiments I entertain have been drawn, so far as I have been able to draw them, from the sentiments which originated in and were given to the world from this hall. I have never had a feeling, politically, that did not spring from the sentiments embodied in the Declaration of Independence.

I have often pioneered over the dangers which were incurred by the men who assembled here and framed and adopted that Declaration. I have pondered over the toils that were endured by the officers and soldiers of the army who achieved that independence. I have often inquired of myself what great principle or idea it was that kept this Confederacy so long together. It was not the mere matter of the separation of the colonies from the motherland, but that sentiment in the Declaration of Independence which gave liberty, not alone to the people of this country, but hope to all the world, for all future time. It was that which gave promise that in due time the weights would be lifted from the shoulders of all men, and that all should have an equal chance. This is the sentiment embodied in the Declaration of Independence.

Now, my friend, can this country be saved on this basis? If it can, I will consider myself one of the happiest men in the world if I can help to save it. If it cannot be saved upon that principle, it will be truly awful. But if this country cannot be saved without giving up that principle, I was about to say I would rather be assassinated on this spot than surrender it.

Now, in my view of the present aspect of affairs there is no need of bloodshed and war. There is no necessity for it. I am not in favor of such a course and I may say in advance that there will be no bloodshed unless it is forced upon the government. The government will not use force, unless force is used against it.

My friends, this is wholly an unprepared speech. I did not expect to be called on to say a word when I came here. I supposed I was merely to do something toward raising a flag. I may, therefore, have said something indiscreet. But I have said nothing but what I am willing to live by, and, if it be the pleasure of Almighty God, to die by.

A. Lincoln.[10]

## Lincoln's Famed Gettysburg Address

Unfortunately, that war which Lincoln hoped would never take place, became reality within two months, dominating his terms as president. His well-known Gettysburg Address, delivered on November 19, 1863, best describes his sentiment on that tragic war and his determination to preserve the young nation:

Fourscore and seven years ago our fathers brought forth on this continent a new nation, conceived in liberty, and dedicated to the proposition that all men are created equal. Now we are engaged in a great civil war, testing whether that nation, or any nation so conceived and so dedicated can long endure. We are met on a great battlefield of that war. We have come to dedicate a portion of that field as a final resting-place for those who here gave their lives that that nation might live. It is altogether fitting and proper that we should do this. But in a larger sense, we cannot dedicate, we cannot consecrate, we cannot hallow this ground. The brave men, living and dead, who struggled here, have consecrated it far above our poor power to add or detract. The world will little note, nor long remember, what we say here, but it can never forget what they did here. It is for us, the living, rather to be dedicated here to the unfinished work which they who fought here have thus far so nobly advanced. It is rather for us to be here dedicated to the great task remaining before us, that from these honored dead we take increased devotion to that cause for which they gave the last full measure of devotion; that we here highly resolve that these dead shall not have died in vain; that this nation, under God, shall have a new birth of freedom, and that this government of the people, by the people, for the people shall not perish from the earth.[11]

Lincoln was the first United States president to use the term: "This nation under God" in reference to our country. After his death, in

1865, on each succeeding February 12, a "Lincoln Day Observance Service" is held at the New York Avenue Presbyterian Church, his parish church, situated just two blocks from the White House. In 1954, Dwight Eisenhower was in attendance with his wife at this service. He was so moved by George Docherty's sermon entitled "Under God," taken from Lincoln's words, that he initiated action in Congress to have it permanently made a part of the Pledge of Allegiance: "I pledge allegiance to the Flag of the United States of America and to the Republic for which it stands, *One Nation Under God*, indivisible, with liberty and justice for all."[12]

## His Second Presidential Inaugural Address

Reelected to a second term, Lincoln's second inaugural address summarized the state of the nation, the eradication of slavery being the reason and cause for the Civil War:

> At this second appearing to take the oath of the Presidential office there is less occasion for an extended address than there was at the first. Then a statement somewhat in detail of a course to be pursued seemed fitting and proper. Now, at the expiration of four years, during which public declarations have been constantly called forth on every point and phase of the great contest which still absorbs the attention and engrosses the energies of the nation, little that is new could be presented. The progress of our arms, upon which all else chiefly depends, is as well known to the public as to myself, and it is, I trust, reasonably satisfactory and encouraging to all. With high hope for the future, no prediction in regard to it is ventured.
>
> On the occasion corresponding to this four years ago all thoughts were anxiously directed to an impending civil war. All dreaded it, all sought to avert it. While the inaugural address was being delivered from this place, devoted altogether to saving the Union without war, insurgent agents were in the city seeking to destroy it without war—seeking to dissolve the Union and divide effects by negotiation. Both parties deprecated war, but one of them would make war rather than let the nation survive, and the other would accept war rather than let it perish, and the war came.
>
> One-eighth of the whole population were colored slaves, not distributed generally over the Union, but localized in the southern part of it. These slaves constituted a peculiar and powerful interest. All knew that this interest was somehow the cause of the war. To strengthen, perpetuate, and extend this interest was the object for which the insurgents would rend the Union, even by war; while the Government claimed no right to do more than to restrict the territorial enlargement of it. Neither party expected for the war the magnitude or the duration which it has already attained. Neither anticipated that the cause of the conflict might cease with, or even before, the conflict itself should cease. Each looked for an easier triumph, and a result less fundamental and astounding. Both read the same Bible and pray to the same God, and each invokes His aid against the other. It may seem strange that any men should dare to ask a just God's assistance in wringing their bread from the sweat of

other men's faces, but let us judge not, that we be not judged.[13] The prayers of both could not be answered. That of neither has been answered fully. The Almighty has His own purposes. "Woe unto the world because of offenses; for it must needs be that offenses come, but woe to that man by whom the offense cometh."[14] If we shall suppose that American slavery is one of those offenses which, in the providence of God, must needs come, but which, having continued through His appointed time, He now wills to remove, and that He gives to both North and South this terrible war as the woe due to those by whom the offense came, shall we discern therein any departure from those divine attributes which the believers in a living God always ascribe to Him? Fondly do we hope, fervently do we pray, that this mighty scourge of war may speedily pass away. Yet, if God wills that it continue until all the wealth piled by the bondsmen's two hundred and fifty years of unrequited toil shall be sunk, and until every drop of blood drawn with the lash shall be paid by another drawn with the sword, as was said three thousand years ago, so still it must be said "the judgments of the Lord are true and righteous altogether."[15]

With malice toward none, with charity for all, with firmness in the right as God gives us to see the right, let us strive on to finish the work we are in, to bind up the nation's wounds, to care for him who shall have borne the battle and for his widow and his orphan—to do all which may achieve and cherish a just and lasting peace among ourselves and with all nations.[16]

## Lincoln Knew the Bible Almost by Heart

As was his custom, Lincoln quoted Scripture in his address, specifically Matthew 7:1; 18:7 and Revelation 16:7. Many references to God, the Bible and prayer were also incorporated. In the book, *The Religion of Abraham Lincoln*, William W. Wolf wrote:

> No president has ever had the detailed knowledge of the Bible that Lincoln had. No president has ever woven its thoughts and its rhythms into the warp and woof of his state papers as he did.[17]

## Sixteen-Year-Old Sculptress Vinnie Ream's Recollections of the Real Abraham Lincoln

Perhaps one of the most intimate sketches of Abraham Lincoln, the real man, has been passed down to us by a young sculptress of the day – Vinnie Ream. In 1864, Senator James S. Rollins of Missouri approached President Lincoln with an unusual request: he asked permission for a 16-year-old girl to have the benefit of personal sittings to make sketches for a statue of the president.[18]

He declined the petition with the candid question: "Why would anyone want to picture a man so homely?" The senator pointed out that the girl was young, talented, ambitious and would be disappointed. Lincoln remained unswerved. "But," said the senator, "she's very poor." This motivated Lincoln to respond: "She is poor, is she? Well, that is nothing against her. I will sit for the model."[19]

Following are her recollections from the daily sittings with him in the months prior to his tragic death: In her *Personal Recollections of Lincoln* Vinnie Ream relates her own story of a young girl's eyewitness impressions of the Great Emancipator:

The opportunity that I had to study Abraham Lincoln, was, indeed, unusual, because of its intimacy and because of the unusual conditions under which I saw him. There were a good many people who were rather closely acquainted with Lincoln and who, I think, appraised his character rather correctly. Most of them are, however, long since dead.

When I knew him and spent half an hour daily with him while modeling my statue, he was nearing that greatest of tragedies in American history, the assassination in the theater. So I knew the ultimate man. I met him also as an impressionable young girl of sixteen and the intuitions of such a child as I was are very apt to be correct. The mind at that age is as plastic as clay and receives an impression as readily, and that impression is likely to harden and be permanently retained. At sixteen I was mature enough to very well grasp the character of the man...

Lincoln had been painted and modeled before, and when friends of mine first asked him to sit for me he dismissed them wearily until he was told that I was but an ambitious girl, poor and obscure. He granted me sittings for no other reason than that I was in need. Had I been the greatest sculptor in the world, I am quite sure I would have been refused.

I came for half an hour every day. I was the merest slip of a child, weighing less than ninety pounds, and the contrast between the raw-boned man and me was indeed great. I sat demurely in my corner and begged Mr. Lincoln not to allow me to disturb him. It seemed that he used this half hour as a time for relaxation, for he always left instructions that no one was to be admitted during that time.

He seemed to find a strange sort of companionship in being with me, although we talked but little. His favorite son, Willie, had but just died, and this had been the greatest personal sorrow in a life that was mostly sorrowful. I made him think of Willie. He often said so and as often wept.

I think that history is particularly correct in writing Lincoln down as the man of sorrow. The one great, lasting, all-dominating impression that I have always carried of Lincoln has been that of unfathomable sorrow, and it was this that I tried to put into my statue.

*Vinnie Ream*

When he sat for me I believe he let himself go and fell into the mood that was ever within him, but against which he struggled. He never told a funny story to me. He rarely smiled.

I remember him especially in two attitudes. The first of these was his great form slouched into the chair at his desk, his huge feet extended, his head bowed on his chest, deeply thoughtful. I think he was, during those moments, following in mind some such thing as the operation of the army of Grant about Richmond, appraising the horrible sacrifices that every day brought upon the people of his nation feeling that all the deaths that wisdom and forethought might prevent would and should be laid at his door. He was hearing the cries of suffering that were coming from the prisons and the sobs of the mothers for sons, lost like his own.

The second attitude he most often assumed was by the window that looked out upon the White House lawn. I always thought that when he stood by the window he was looking out for Willie, for he had watched the boy play many an afternoon from that very window. It was as he stood by the window that the great tears would course down his hollow cheeks, and he would be forced to dry them with his handkerchief. On two or three occasions he was so broken with his grief that he sank into a chair by the window and wept aloud. A big, strong man broken by grief is always a tragic thing to see, but never was there grief equal to Lincoln's.

In all the months that I had my daily half hour with Lincoln the order that we were not to be interrupted was broken but twice, and in each of these interruptions the breach was strangely illustrative of the character of the man. The first person who intruded upon the rest hour was a woman of middle age. She was the mother of a boy who had worn the gray and who had been captured and was in the old Capitol prison.

The mother wanted a pass to see her boy, and such a pass required the signature of the President. Lincoln listened graciously to the woman's plea, wrote a pass with his own hand and apologized that the boy was being kept from his home. The second woman was young and pretty, and she blushed when she started, falteringly, to state her mission. The President anticipated her request, said that he knew by her blushes that she wanted to see a sweetheart, and granted her request in advance.

These visits to the White House continued for five months. Through all this time the personality of Lincoln was gradually sinking deeper and deeper into my soul. I was modeling the man in clay, but he was being engraven more deeply upon my heart.

Then, finally, came the great tragedy. I was in our home on Capitol Hill that terrible night. My parents had been out for the evening. They returned about midnight, and as they were entering the house some one hurrying past called out to them that the President had been murdered. The murder of a President of a great nation is a most terribly tragic thing at best…

So, of course, I was moved beyond measure at the death of Lincoln. I was prostrated… The success of the statue that I subsequently made was attributed to its trueness to the actual Lincoln. My ability to produce it was unquestionably due to those half hours in the quiet of the President's office, and to the searing in of the image by the great tragedy.[20]

ABRAHAM LINCOLN PRAYER WINDOW

*Original stained-glass window in the New York Avenue Presbyterian Church, Lincoln's parish church, two blocks from the White House.*

## Lincoln's Pastor Testifies to the President's Godliness and Life of Prayer

Reverend Phineas Gurley, his pastor at the New York Avenue Presbyterian Church in Washington, D.C. delivered this eulogy at Abraham Lincoln's funeral, summarizing the life of a man who was loved by the people and who, in turn, loved his God and relied upon Him for everything in prayer.

Rev. P.D. Gurley, D.D.
Pastor of the New York Avenue Presbyterian Church,
Washington, D.C.

As we stand here today, mourners around this coffin and around the lifeless remains of our beloved chief magistrate, we recognize and adore the sovereignty of God. His throne is in the heavens, and His kingdom ruleth over all. He hath done, and He hath permitted to be done, whatsoever He please.

…The people confided in the late lamented President with a full and loving confidence. Probably no man since the days of Washington was ever so deeply and firmly embedded and enshrined in the very hearts of the people as Abraham Lincoln. Nor was it a mistaken confidence and love. He deserved it—deserved it well—deserved it all. He merited it by his character, by his acts, and by the whole tenor, and tone, and spirit of his life. He was simple and sincere, plain and honest, truthful and just, benevolent and kind. His perceptions were quick and clear, his purposes were good and pure beyond question. Always and everywhere he aimed and endeavored to be right and to do right…

He saw his duty as the Chief Magistrate of a great and imperilled people, and he determined to do his duty, and his whole duty, seeking the guidance and leaning upon the arm of Him of whom it is written, "He giveth power to the faint, and to them that have no might He increaseth strength." Yes, he leaned upon His arm, He recognized and received the truth that the "kingdom is the Lord's, and He is the governor among the nations." He remembered that "God is in history," and felt that nowhere had His hand and His mercy been so marvelously conspicuous as in the history of this nation. He hoped and prayed that that same hand would continue to guide us, and that same mercy continue to abound to us in the time of our greatest need. I speak what I know, and testify what I have often heard him say, when I affirm that that guidance and mercy were the props upon which he humbly and habitually leaned; they were the best hope he had for himself and for his country. Hence, when he was leaving his home in Illinois, and coming to this city to take his seat in the executive chair of a disturbed and troubled nation, he said to the old and the tried friends who gathered tearfully around him and bade him farewell, "I leave you with this request: pray for me." They did pray for him; and millions of other people prayed for him; nor did they pray in vain. Their prayer was heard, and the answer appears in all his subsequent history; it shines forth with a heavenly radiance in the whole course and tenor of his administration, from its commencement to its close. God raised him up for a great and glorious mission, furnished him for his work, and aided him in its accomplishment. Nor was it merely by strength of mind, and honesty of heart, and purity and pertinacity of purpose, that He furnished him; in addition to these things, he gave him a calm and abiding confidence in the overruling Providence of God and in the ultimate triumph of truth and righteousness through the power and the blessing of God...

Never shall I forget the emphasis and the deep emotion with which he said in this very room, to a company of clergymen and others, who called to pay him their respects in the darkest days of our civil conflict: "Gentlemen, my hope of success in this great and terrible struggle rests on that immutable foundation, the justice and goodness of God. And when events are threatening, and prospects very dark, I still hope that in some way which man cannot see all will be well in the end, because our cause is just, and God is on our side..."

He is dead; but the God in whom he trusted lives, and He can guide and strengthen his successor, as He guided and strengthened him...but the cause he so ardently loved survives his fall, and will survive it...[21]

## Lincoln's 1847 Family Bible

Abraham Lincoln's 1847 family Bible, one of the gems of America's Christian heritage, is in the custody of the Rare Book Collection of the Library of Congress. It displays the wording HOLY BIBLE upon its spine, and contains these beautiful illustrations: Rebecca at the Well; and Samuel Praying, showing the godly Old Testament hero kneeling in prayer at his bedside; and the baby Moses and his mother, captioned: "She took for Him an ark of Bulrushes and put the Child therein." (Exodus 11:3). The editor's preface to Lincoln's family Bible reads:

> ...The sacred text is that of the Authorized Version, commonly called King James Bible, and is printed from the edition revised, corrected and improved, by Dr. Blayney, which from its accuracy, has been considered the Standard Edition, to which subsequent impressions should be made conformable. Forming an analysis and compendium of the Sacred Scriptures, of the Authenticity of the Scriptures: of the Inspiration of the Scriptures; of the Manuscripts and the Early Printed Editions of the Scriptures; of the Apostolic and Primitive Fathers; of the Jewish Sects; of the measures, weights and coins; of the modes of computing time in Scripture; Geography and History of the nations mentioned in Scripture...[22]

Four interior pages within this Bible contain Abraham Lincoln's *Family Record*, which includes this entry:

> Abraham Lincoln and Mary Todd, married November 4, 1842.[23]

### The Lincoln Marriage Certificate reads:

> The people of the state of Illinois—To any Minister of the Gospel, or other authorized person—Greetings. These are to license and permit you to join in the holy bands of Matrimony Abraham Lincoln and Mary Todd of the County of Sangman and State of Illinois, and for so doing, this shall be your sufficient warrant.

Given under my hand and seal of office, at Springfield, in said County, this
4th day of November, 1842.

(signed) N.W. Matheny, Clerk.[24]

## "There is a Fountain Filled with Blood" and "Rock of Ages Cleft for Me" Among Abraham Lincoln's Favorite Hymns

It was reported that Lincoln had favorite hymns that ministered to
him. These old hymns glorified Jesus Christ, Son of God, Savior of the
world. Among these are: "There is a Fountain Filled with Blood";
"When Shall I See Jesus and Reign with Him Above"; "Father What
E'er of Earthly Bliss Thy Sovereign Will Denies"; and "Rock of Ages."[25]

## His Maxims and Short Sayings

Lincoln had written his own Maxims and Short Sayings for practical daily living, and for living life at its highest. Following is a collection
of some of them:

- All in that one word, Thorough!
- I'm nothing, but Truth is everything.
- Freedom is the last, best hope of earth.
- Let us have faith that right makes might.
- I am free from any taint of personal triumph.
- Wealth is a superfluity of what we don't need.
- Many have got into a *habit* of being dissatisfied.
- Let them laugh as long as the thing works well.
- I know I am right, because I know Liberty is right.
- God bless my mother! All I am or hope to be I owe to her.
- Faith in God is indispensable to successful statesmanship.
- When you have written an wrathful letter—*put it in the stove.*
- Suspicion and jealousy never did help any man in any situation.
- If men never began to drink, they would never become drunkards.
- Don't shoot too high – aim low and the common people will understand.
- I do not think much of a man who is not wiser to-day than he was yesterday.
- Gold is good in its place; but, loving, brave, patriotic men are better than gold.
- The Lord must love the common people – that's why He made so many of them.
- Now, sonny, keep that (temperance) pledge and it will be the best act of your life.
- A man has no time to spend in quarrels. If any man ceases to attack me, I never remember the past against him.
- You may fool all of the people some of the time, and some of the people all of the time, but you cannot fool all of the people all of the time.
- If all that has been said in praise of woman were applied to the women of America, it would not do them justice for their conduct during this war. God bless the women of America![26]

Abraham Lincoln's short, two-page autobiography sheds further light upon the true Lincoln—a humble, sincere man, who was almost self-taught:

## Lincoln's Autobiography—Springfield, December 20, 1859

J. W. Fell, Esq.
My Dear Sir:

Herewith is a little sketch, as you requested. There is not much of it, for the reason, I suppose, that there is not much of me. If anything be made of it, I wish it to be modest, and not to go beyond the material.

I was born February 12, 1809, in Hardin County, Kentucky. My parents were both born in Virginia, of undistinguished families – second families, perhaps I should say. My mother, who died in my tenth year, was of a family by the name of Hanks. My paternal grandfather, Abraham Lincoln, emigrated to Kentucky about 1781 or 1782, where, a year or two later, he was killed by the Indians, not in battle, but by stealth, when he was laboring to open a farm in the forest. His ancestors, who were Quakers, went to Virginia from Berks County, Pennsylvania.

My father, at the death of his father, was but six years of age, and grew up literally without education. He removed from Kentucky to what is now Spencer County, Indiana, in my eighth year. There I grew up. There were some schools, so called, but no qualification was ever required of a teacher beyond "readin', writin', and cipherin' to the rule of three." There was absolutely nothing to excite ambition for education. Of course, when I came of age I did not know much. I have not been to school since. The little advance I now have upon this store of education I have picked up from time to time under the pressure of necessity.

I was raised to farm work, which I continued until I was twenty-two. At twenty-one I came to Illinois, Macon County. Then I got to New Salem, where I remained a year as a sort of clerk, in a store. Then came the Black Hawk War; and I was elected a captain of volunteers, which gave me more pleasure than any I have had since. I went to the campaign, was elated, ran for the Legislature the same year (1832) and was beaten–the only time I was ever beaten by the people. The next and three succeeding biennial elections, I was elected to the Legislature. I was not a candidate afterward. During this legislative period I had studied law, and removed to Springfield to practise it. In 1846 I was elected to the Lower House of Congress. Was not a candidate for re-election. From 1849 to 1854, both inclusive, practised law more assiduously than ever before. Always a Whig in politics, and generally on the electoral tickets, making active canvasses. I was losing interest in politics when the repeal of the Missouri Compromise aroused me again. What I have done since is pretty well known.

If any personal description is thought desirable, it may be said I am, in height, six feet four inches, nearly; lean in flesh, weighing on an average one hundred and eighty pounds; dark complexion, with coarse black hair and gray eyes. No other marks and brands recollected.

Yours truly,
A. LINCOLN[27]

## Tad Lincoln's Death

The death of Lincoln's youngest son, Tad, took place about six years later. The obituary, from the Evening Post, is printed below for its intimate portrayal of Lincoln as a devoted and loving father:

Evening Post
OBITUARY
Saturday, July 15, 1871

Death of "Tad" Lincoln, this Morning, at the Clifton House.
An Epitome of His Life.

...Thomas Lincoln, better known by the familiar subriquet of "Tad,' bestowed upon him by the genial President, was born in the capital of this State in 1853, being at the time of his death, at eight o'clock this morning, eighteen years old. He was a bright, precious boy, and, from his earliest infancy, was noted for his affectionate and winning disposition. After the death of his elder brother, William, he became the pet of the house and was almost inseparable from the company of his distinguished father, who delighted in the juvenile pranks and amusing prattle of the boy. Whenever Lincoln went to any public gathering or to the courts of law in Springfield, little "Tad" would be sure to accompany him, unless unwillingly detained at home to study his lessons. He became quite a public character while yet almost an infant in years, and was known to the inhabitants of his native city almost as much as was Abraham Lincoln himself.

Soon after President Lincoln was inaugurated, in 1861, the family removed from Springfield to the capital of the United States. In Washington little "Tad" was destined to become quite as much of a favorite as he had been in the Illinois capital. During his moments of relaxation, the toil-worn and patriotic President would, for the time, forget the tremendous responsibility that rested upon him, to enjoy himself in the bosom of his family, of which the subject of this sketch was the chiefest attraction. The President always devoted his leisure hours—which through all that exciting time were not many—to the instruction of his children. Robert was then nearly grown to man's estate, and was, consequently, more removed from the paternal anxiety, but "Tad" was, in a measure, the special pupil of the best-natured President that ever occupied the White House. He inherited much of his lamented father's character. He had the same predisposition to melancholy, and the same genial spirit beaming from his features. The assassination of that beloved parent was a terrible shock to the poor boy; he never afterward regained the same elasticity of spirit, and the shadow of his father's doom clung to him through all his after life."[28]

The Civil War began just weeks after Lincoln took office, and ended only days before his death. Though he had longed to see the rebuilding of the nation, it would seem that God had specifically chosen and destined him for the task of guiding the young nation through the Civil War, its darkest days.

As his pastor said about Lincoln,

...He is dead; but the God in whom he trusted lives...

*After the original bronze masterpiece in Statuary Hall,*
*U.S. Capitol, Washington, D.C.*

# ROBERT E. LEE
## Servant of God—Leader of Men
## (1807 - 1870)

General Robert E. Lee, the great leader of the Confederate army in the Civil War, was a military genius. Considered to be in the ranks of the greatest military leaders in all history, he was also loved and respected as a Christian gentleman in the north, as well as in his native Virginia and the southern states.

## Robert's Background

Born in 1807, he was the fourth son of Major General Henry "Light Horse Harry" Lee, a Revolutionary War hero, and Anne Hill Carter, a direct descendant of Robert "King" Carter, one of the most noble and significant figures of Virginia's Golden age in the early 18th century.[1] He grew up in his family home built in 1795, an outstanding example of federal architecture. It stands as a unique landmark at 607 Oronoco Street in Alexandria, and is open to the public.

## Anne Hill Carter, Robert's Mother—
## An Example of Christian Virtue

When Robert was six, his father, ill, penniless and broken in spirit, left the family for Barbados and never returned. The former hero died on his way back when Robert was 11, so that he was raised by his mother from age six. Anne Hill Carter, one of the little-celebrated heroines of America, brought up her five children almost single-handedly, giving them a magnificent example of Christian virtue, and molding their characters upon Scripture truth.

## The Unselfishness, Generosity, Purity and Faithfulness
## of the Virginia Carters Passed Down to Robert

Fitzhugh Lee, a distinguished contemporary, wrote the following regarding Lee's early life:

> If he inherited much from a long and illustrious line of paternal ancestors, he no less fell heir to the strong characteristics of his mother's family, one of the oldest and best in Virginia. The unselfishness, generosity, purity, and faithfulness of the Virginia Carters are widely known, and they have always been "true to all occasions true." In his mother was personified all the gentle and sweet traits of a noble woman. Her whole life was admirable, and her love for her children beyond all other thoughts. To her watchful care they were early confided by the long absence and death of her distinguished husband.

Robert was four years old when his father removed the family to Alexandria, six when he visited the West Indies for his health, and eleven when he died. If he was early trained in the way he should go, his mother trained him. If he was "always good," as his father wrote, she labored to keep him so. If his principles were sound and his life a success, to her, more than to any other, should the praise be given... As Robert grew in years he grew in grace; he was like the young tree whose roots, firmly imbedded in the earth, hold it straight from the hour it was first planted till it develops into majestic proportions. With the fostering care of such a mother the son must go straight, for she had planted him in the soil of truth, morality, and religion, so that his boyhood was marked by everything that produces nobility of character in manhood. The handsome boy was studious and sedate, was popular with other boys, stood high in the estimation of his teachers, and his early inspiration was good, for his first thoughts were directed upon subjects by an excellent mother.[2]

At age 18, Lee entered the United States Military Academy, West Point, as a cadet to train for his distinguished career. In the 1830's he became a lieutenant. Lee married Mary Ann Randolph, only surviving child of George Washington Parke Custis, who was George Washington's adopted grandson. They had seven children.

Though deeply devoted to his family, Lee's military career required long separations from his loved ones, taking him to many parts of the country. In 1846, when the United States declared war on Mexico, Lee was called into active duty, and his bravery and military skills won him recognition and promotion.

Lee greatly loved the Union, having devoted his adult life to its service as a soldier. He was opposed to secession. The following excerpt is from a letter he wrote from Texas where he was stationed, to his favorite cousin, Martha Custis Williams, on January 22, 1861, just months before the Civil War began:

God alone can save us from our folly, selfishness & shortsightedness. The last accounts seem to show that we have barely escaped anarchy to be plunged into civil war. What will be the result I cannot conjecture. I only see that a federal calamity is upon us, & fear that the country will have to pass through for its sins a fiery ordeal. I am unable to realize that our people will destroy a government inaugurated by the blood & wisdom of our patriot fathers, that has given us peace & prosperity at home, power & security abroad, & under which we have acquired a colossal strength unequalled in the history of mankind. I wish to live under no other government, & there is no sacrifice I am not ready to make for the preservation of the Union save that of honour. If a disruption takes place, I shall go back in sorrow to my people & share the misery of my native state, & save in her defence there will be one solider less in the world than now. I wish for no other flag than the "Star Spangled Banner," & no other air than "Hail Columbia." I still hope the wisdom & patriotism of the nation will yet save it.[3]

## Robert E. Lee States His Reasons for Joining the Confederacy

In February, Texas voted to secede from the Union, and Lee was ordered to report to General Winfield Scott, Commander-in-Chief of the United States Army. On March 28, he accepted a promotion to full colonel in the U.S. Army; the commission was signed by Abraham Lincoln. He still hoped that efforts to preserve the Union would be successful. However, on April 17th, Virginia seceded. On April 18, the command of the U.S. Army was offered to Lee. Lee turned it down, resigning from the army and shortly after joined the Confederacy. In a letter to his sister, he wrote:

> With all my devotion to the union and the feeling of loyalty and duty of an American citizen, I have not been able to make up my mind to raise my hand against my relatives, my children, my home.[4]

Lee accepted command of the forces of the state troops of Virginia two days later. A year later, he was made General of the Confederate Army in Virginia, and not until near the close of the war was he made General-in-Chief of all the Confederate forces. The South entered the war lacking an already existing army and navy, together with basic resources. Through four desperate years of war, Lee frequently faced unfavorable odds against him.

## Robert E. Lee—
## "My Heart is Filled with Gratitude to Almighty God"
On Christmas day, 1862, Lee wrote to his wife from Fredericksburg:

> My heart is filled with gratitude to Almighty God for His unspeakable mercies with which He has blessed us in this day, for those He has granted us from the beginning of life, and particularly for those He has vouchsafed us during the past year. What should have become of us without His crowning help and protection? Oh, if our people would only recognize it and cease from self-boasting and adulation, how strong would be my belief in final success and happiness to our country! But what a cruel thing is war; to separate and destroy families and friends, and mar the purest joys and happiness God has granted us in this world; to fill our hearts with hatred instead of love for our neighbors, and to devastate the fair face of this beautiful world! I pray that, on this day when only peace and good-will are preached to mankind, better thoughts may fill the hearts of our enemies and turn them to peace. Our army was never in such good health and condition since I have been attached to it. I believe they

share with me my disappointment that the enemy did not renew the combat on the 13th. I was holding back all day and husbanding our strength and ammunition for the great struggle, for which I thought I was preparing. Had I divined that was to have been his only effort, he would have had more of it. My heart bleeds at the death of every one of our gallant men.[5]

## Lee Announces Stonewall Jackson's Death— "His Unshaken Confidence in God as Our Hope and Strength"

When General Stonewall Jackson was shot in the arm in the Spring of 1863, it was expected that he would fully recover. Lee told an officer to give him the message "to make haste and get well, and come back to me as soon as he can. He has lost his left arm, but I have lost my right." Later in announcing Jackson's unexpected death, Lee issued this word to the troops:

> ...The daring, skill, and energy of this great and good soldier, by the decree of an All-wise Providence, are now lost to us. But, while we mourn his death, we feel that his spirit still lives, and will inspire the whole army with his indomitable courage and unshaken confidence in God, as our hope and strength. Let his name be a watchword to his corps, who have followed him to victory on so many fields. Let his officers and soldiers emulate his invincible determination to do everything in defence of our beloved country.[6]

## The Battle of Gettysburg

The Battle of Gettysburg in July of 1863 was the greatest battle of the Civil War. The Southern army of 75,000 men met the North's 90,000 in Union territory. Lasting three days, the Confederates had the advantage for the first two days, pushing the Union back, but on the third day the Union gained the victory, and the Confederate troops were left with no choice but to retreat back to Virginia in a dreary rainstorm, having lost over 20,000 men, dead or wounded. Lee accepted full responsibility for the defeat as shown in this letter to Jefferson Davis, written on July 31 from Camp Culpepper:

> No blame can be attached to the army for its failure to accomplish what was projected by me, nor should it be censored for the unreasonable expectations of the public—I am alone to blame, in perhaps expecting too much of its prowess & valor. It however in my opinion achieved under the guidance of the Most High a general success, though it did not win a victory. I thought at the time that the latter was practicable. I still think if all things could have worked together it would have been accomplished. But with the knowledge I then had, & in the circumstances I was then placed, I do not know what better course I could have pursued. With my present knowledge, & could I have foreseen that the attack on the last day would have failed to drive the enemy from his position, I should certainly have tried some other course. What the ultimate result would have been is not so clear to me. Our loss has been very heavy, that of the enemy's is proportionately so. His crippled condition

enabled us to retire from the Country, comparatively unmolested...[7]

## Robert E. Lee Proclaims a Day of Fasting, Humiliation and Prayer—"Soldiers, We Have Sinned Against Almighty God"

Gettysburg marked a turning point in the war; the South no longer had the battle against the North. Though there would be another two years of fighting, the North began getting an upper hand with their superior resources and manpower. On August 21, Jefferson Davis called for a day of fasting and prayer. Lee issued the following order regarding it:

> General Order No. 83
> Headquarters Army Northern Virginia, August 13, 1863
> The President of the Confederate States has, in the name of the people, appointed the 21st day of August as a day of fasting, humiliation, and prayer. A strict observance of the day is enjoined upon the officers and soldiers of this army. All military duties, except such as are absolutely necessary, will be suspended. The commanding officers of brigades and regiments are requested to cause divine services, suitable to the occasion, to be performed in their respective commands.
> Soldiers! We have sinned against Almighty God. We have forgotten his signal mercies, and have cultivated a revengeful, haughty, and boastful spirit. We have not remembered that the defenders of a just cause should be pure in his eyes; that "our times are in his hands;" and we have relied too much on our own arms for the achievement of our independence. God is our only refuge and our strength. Let us humble ourselves before Him. Let us confess our many sins, and beseech Him to give us a higher courage, a purer patriotism, and more determined will; that He will convert the hearts of our enemies; that He will hasten the time when war, with its sorrows and sufferings, shall cease, and that He will give us a name and place among the nations of the earth.[8]

## The Results of Prayer—"A Precious Revival Was in Progress—15,000 Professions of Faith in Christ"

Chaplain Jones of the Confederate Army reported the following regarding the spiritual revival which resulted from this day of fasting, humiliation and prayer:

> We can never forget the effect produced by the reading of this order at the solemn services of that memorable fast day. A precious revival was already in progress in many of the commands. The day was almost universally observed; the attendance upon preaching and other services was very large; the solemn attention and starting tear attested the deep interest felt; and the work of grace among the troops widened and deepened, and went gloriously on until there had been at least *fifteen thousand* professions of faith in Christ as a personal Saviour. How far these grand results were due to this fast-day, or to the quiet

influence and fervent prayers of the commanding general, eternity alone shall reveal.[9]

## Lee's Superior Military Genius

In March, 1864, Lincoln gave Ulysses S. Grant command of the entire Union army, giving the North the advantage of a coordinated effort. Lee's superior military genius was, however, evident in his great resourcefulness, his strategy and tactical skill.

## Lee's Surrender

In February, 1865, Lee was made commander-in-chief of the Confederate army, and his strategy was to join forces with General Johnston and attack the North's troops led by Sherman. However, due to poor roads and lack of transportation facilities, Grant overtook him at the end of March and inflicted a crushing defeat with troops numbering four to one against the South. Lee, knowing that continued fighting would only lead to the needless sacrifice of his men, was faced with no alternative but to surrender.

## Two Great Generals, Lee and Grant, Meet at Appomattox

The two great generals, Grant and Lee, met on April 9, 1865 at Appomattox. Grant offered generous terms of surrender, which Lee accepted.

## The Confederate Troops Cheer Lee

Lee then had to face his own troops with the news of the surrender, here described by Brigadier General E.P. Alexander:

He had hardly reached the line, however, when someone started a cheer, which was taken up by others, and then both infantry and artillery broke their line and crowded about his horse in the road. The general stopped and made a short address. Briefly, it was about as follows:

' I have done for you all that it was in my power to do. You have done all your duty. Leave the result to God. Go to your homes and resume your occupations. Obey the laws and become good citizens as you were soldiers.'

There was not a dry eye in the crowd that heard him, and even he seemed deeply moved. The men crowded around to try and shake his hand or touch his horse, and some appealed to him to get us all exchanged and try it again; but he made no reply to such remarks. Then he rode on to his camp, and the crowd broke up, and then ranks were formed once more and marched off to bivouac, and the Army of Northern Virginia was an army no longer, but a lot of captives awaiting their paroles. But it had written its name in history, and no man need be ashamed of its record, though its last chapter is a story of disaster. And surely those qualities in its commander for which men are loved and admired by friend and foe shone out here with no less luster than on any other field.[10]

## Robert E. Lee, President of Washington College, Devotes His Life to Educating Youth

In August 1865, Lee was offered the presidency of Washington College. At the same time, he had a number of offers which would bring him fame and affluence both in this country and abroad. In his own words, his answer was:

> No; I am grateful, but I have a self-imposed task, which I must accomplish. I have led the young men of the South in battle; I have seen many of them fall under my standard. I shall devote my life now to training young men to do their duty in life.[11]

## Lee and Jackson—"Great Readers of the Bible—Practicing Virtues of Humility, Purity, Peacemaking and Love of Righteousness"

Author Benjamin Howell Griswold, Jr. in his book, *The Spirit of Lee and Jackson*, wrote:

> ...Lee and Jackson were both professing Christians—most men of their day were that—but on the premise that these men not only professed Christianity, but actually practised it and endeavored in every way to live according to its much neglected tenets. They were great readers of the Bible, and nearly every act of their lives was directed by their interpretation of its maxims. This was true of their actions not only at home toward their family and neighbors, but even in the camp and on the battlefield toward their enemies...Humility, Purity, Peacemaking, Love of Righteousness—virtues neglected—if not a little despised today, seem to have exalted these men and lifted them from the depths of defeat to the pinnacle of fame...[12]

## Robert E. Lee's Death— "Leaning Trustfully Upon the All-sustaining Arm— He Passed from this World to the Realities of the Hereafter"

Robert E. Lee's last days were written by Colonel William Preston Johnston for Reverend J.W. Jones in his *Personal Reminiscences of General Robert E. Lee, 1874*. Colonel Johnston was an intimate friend of the general and a distinguished member of the faculty of his college. He was one of those at the bedside of the dying general. It is being excerpted below in order to shed further light on Lee's true character and Christian comportment:

The death of General Lee was not due to any sudden cause, but was the result of agencies dating as far back as 1863...In October, 1869, he was again attacked by inflammation of the heart-sac, accompanied by muscular rheumatism of the back, right side, and arms. The action of the heart was weakened by this attack...His decline was rapid, yet gentle; and soon after nine o'clock on the morning of October 12th, he closed his eyes, and his soul passed peacefully from earth...General Lee's closing hours were consonant with his noble and disciplined life. Never was more beautifully displayed how a long and severe education of mind and character enables the soul to pass with equal step through this supreme ordeal; never did the habits and qualities of a lifetime, solemnly gathered into a few last sad hours, more grandly maintain themselves amid the gloom and shadow of approaching death. The reticence, the self-contained composure, the obedience to proper authority, the magnanimity and the Christian meekness, that marked all his actions, still preserved their sway, in spite of the inroads of disease and the creeping lethargy that weighed down his faculties...Leaning trustfully upon the all-sustaining Arm, the man whose stature, measured by mortal standards, seemed so great, passed from this world of shadows to the realities of the hereafter.[13]

# STONEWALL JACKSON
## "Prayer in Stonewall Jackson's Camp"
### (1824-1863)

The great military leader for the Confederate Army, Thomas Jonathan Jackson, is more commonly known as Stonewall Jackson. He was born in 1824 in Clarksburg, West Virginia. His lawyer father died when he was very young.

## Stonewall's Mother—Zealous for Christian Values

His mother is reputed to have been a woman of faith in God and of biblical understanding, bringing this zeal and fervor for Christian values into the life of young Stonewall and his siblings. Jackson never forgot his mother, always referring to her in later years with deep love and gratitude.[1]

## Stonewall Jackson Excels During the Civil War

The election of Abraham Lincoln to office on March 4, 1861, as President of the United States, brought an opponent of slavery in the White House. On April 13, the Confederate capture of the Federal Fort Sumter at Charleston, South Carolina, led to a state of war. The Confederates, or Southerners, numbered about six million whites. The command of the sea gave considerable advantage to the Union armies, giving them the usual benefit of an extensive base. It was thus almost impossible to completely intercept them.[2]

On April 29, 1861, Colonel Jackson took command of 4,500 men at Harper's Ferry. On November 1, 1861, Jackson, with the rank of Major-General, was appointed to the command of the Shenandoah Valley, in which position he fully realized the importance of controlling the Baltimore and Ohio Railway.[3]

Jackson excelled in "secrecy and surprise" of which Napoleon, Hannibal and Wellington were masters. His superiority of the regulars in battle appeared in the Mexican campaign, and at the two battles of Bull Run and at Gaines' Mill. He also understood the value and importance of using initiative. His expertise in the use of cavalry, the strategic arm before battle, were: scouting, screening, pursuing, charging and perhaps raiding. Jackson made it his constant practice to study his opponent's character. He was well versed in the use of strategic positions in warfare, thereby gaining frequent advantage over his adversary.[4]

*After the painting by Vizetelly, "Prayer in Stonewall Jackson's Camp."*
*Original in the Library of Congress Collection.*

## Stonewall Jackson's Faith in Christ

Behind his military prowess and boldness, however, was the quiet strength of one who walked humbly before God, with a deep faith and trust in the Lord Jesus Christ, and a zeal for His Word. Following is an excerpt from a 1938 public school history book on these two aspects of his character:

> ...He was extremely religious. He prayed before battle; he prayed during a battle; he prayed again after it was over. He would fight on Sunday, because he believed he was engaged in a holy cause; but he would not open a letter or write one, or read anything except the Bible until Monday. Yet he was a genius on the battlefield. He gave the Union commanders more unpleasant surprises than any other southern leader. His soldiers were called "foot cavalry," so swiftly did they march. They had complete confidence in him as did General Lee...[5]

Another history book gives the following description of Stonewall Jackson:

> ...He was of truly heroic mould, brave, generous, devout. His military perception was unerring; his decision swift as lightning. He rose early in the morning to read the Scriptures and pray. He gave a tenth part of his income for religious uses. He taught a Sunday school class of negro children. He delivered lectures on the authenticity of Scripture. When he dropped a letter into the post office, he prayed for a blessing on the person to whom it was addressed. As his soldiers marched past his erect, unmoving figure, to meet the enemy, they saw his lips move, and knew that their leader was praying for them to Him who "covereth the head in the day of battle...[6]

## Jackson Promises Chaplains and Missionaries for His Troops

Not only did Jackson pray for his men, but he did all he could to make certain that their spiritual welfare was provided for, as described below:

> ...The following winter and spring, Jackson spent in improving the organization, discipline and efficiency of the corps, and as in his judgment, a most important means of accomplishing this, he labored to have chaplains in every regiment and missionaries to visit the army, and did everything in his power to promote the religious welfare of his soldiers. It was largely through his influence that a chaplains' association was formed, and he had regular prayer meetings at his headquarters during the week and preaching on Sundays...[7]

## Jackson: "A Herald of the Cross the Most Noble of all Professions"

In the following excerpt from a letter he wrote to his aunt, he reveals his heart's desire to do battle for God's army as a herald of the cross, as he described it:

> Lexington, Virginia 1852
> To his Aunt
> Mrs. Clementine (Alfred) Neale:
> ...The subject of becoming herald of the cross has often seriously engaged my attention, and I regard it as the most noble of all professions. It is the profession of our divine Redeemer, and I should not be surprised were I to die upon a foreign field, clad in ministerial armor, fighting under the banner of Jesus. What could be more glorious? But my conviction is that I am doing good here; and that for the present I am where God would have me. Within the last few days I have felt an unusual religious joy. I do rejoice to walk in the love of God...[8]

## Jackson's Tragic Death

The great hero's life drew to a tragic end following one of his victorious surprise attacks in which the enemy withdrew. At twilight, as Jackson and his staff were examining the results of the battle, he was mistaken for the enemy, and fired upon by soldiers from the South:

> ...Jackson fell from his horse, with two bullets in his left arm and one through his right hand. They placed him on a litter to carry him from the field. One of the bearers was shot down by the enemy, and the wounded general fell heavily to the ground. The sound of musketry wakened the Federal artillery, and for some time Jackson lay helpless on ground swept by the cannon of the enemy. When his men learned the situation of their beloved commander, they rushed in and carried him from the danger. Jackson sunk under his wounds. He bore patiently his great suffering. "If I live, it will be for the best,"he said, "and if I die, it will be for the best. God knows and directs all things for the best." He died eight days after the battle, to the deep sorrow of his countrymen...[9]

## General Lee Wishes "To Have Been Disabled in His Stead"

General Lee, when hearing Jackson had been wounded, wrote to him, "Could I have dictated events I should have chosen for the good of the country to have been disabled in your stead." Jackson's left arm had been amputated and recovery was expected, but pneumonia set in, and he died on May 10, 1863.[10]

## Jackson Mourned by 7,000,000 People in the South

It is reported that at General Jackson's death, seven million people throughout the South went into mourning. Says Colonel R.P. Chew, Chief of Horse Artillery, Army of Northern Virginia, in his address delivered at the Virginia Military Institute on June 19, 1912:

> He was a Christian without fanaticism, a Christian in the open; one who did not hesitate in the presence of assembled thousands to pause on the eve of some great enterprise and raise his hand aloft, invoking the blessing of Divine Providence upon his efforts and those of his soldiers. He rose superior to human infirmity and was proof against the temptations of this life...while his strategy was as brilliant, his tactics as effective, he had achieved a victory that could be accorded to no one of these great commanders, (Caesar, Bonaparte, Marlborough and Wellington), he had made himself complete and absolute master of himself. Possessed of perfect poise of mind and temperament, his character adorned with every moral and manly attribute, and endowed with every Christian virtue....[11]

## Stonewall Jackson on the Battlefield, Reading His Bible

Our National Cathedral in Washington, D.C., immortalizes the life of Stonewall Jackson with an inspiring stained-glass window. It depicts this American son kneeling on the battlefield, reading his Bible. The caption engraved upon the wall beneath it reads:

> To the glory of the Lord of Hosts whom he so zealously served and in honored memory of Thomas Jonathan Jackson, Lieutenant General C.S.R. Like a Stone Wall in his steadfastness, swift as lightning and mighty in battle, he walked humbly before his Creator, whose Word was his guide. This Bay is erected by the United Daughters of the Confederacy and his admirers from South and North.

# SAM HOUSTON
## Texas' Greatest Hero
## (1793 - 1863)

Sam Houston was born on March 2, 1793, at Timber Ridge in Rockbridge County, Virginia, seven miles from Lexington.[1] His father, a planter, physician and colonel in the Revolutionary War, died when he was 13. His mother, with her six sons and three daughters, subsequently settled near Knoxville, Tennessee.[2] Sam attended a country school in Virginia, and took a short course at an academy in Tennessee. For one summer term, he also taught in a country school.[3]

## Sam Houston's Mother's Advice:
## "Take this Rifle, and Never Disgrace it"

At the outset of his military career, his mother took down her husband's rifle and, with tear-filled eyes, handed it to her son, "Here my boy," she said courageously, "take this rifle and never disgrace it. Remember that I would rather that all my sons should lie in honorable graves than that one of them should turn his back to save his life. Go, and God be with you, but never forget that, while my door is always open to brave men, it is always shut to cowards."[4]

## Houston the Congressman,
## Major-General of the Tennessee Militia, and Governor

At age 30, Houston was both member of the U.S. House of Representatives and Major-General of the Tennessee Militia. He served two terms as Congressman, and was inaugurated governor of Tennessee on October 1, 1827 in the Old Baptist Church at Nashville.[5]

## Sam Houston's Marriage

He married Eliza Allen a year later. She was the polished and lovely daughter of Colonel John Allen, of Summer County, Tennessee — a family known for its integrity and accomplishments.[6] A few months after his marriage, however, Eliza left him. He sought her out, pleading with her to return, to no avail. Brokenhearted, Houston wrote to a family member exemplifying Christian character traits of forebearance and charity:

> Eliza stands acquitted by me. I have received her as a virtuous, chaste wife and as such I pray God I may ever regard her, and I trust I ever shall. She was cold to me and I thought did not love me; she owned that that was one cause of my unhappiness. You can think how unhappy I was united to a woman that

SAMUEL HOUSTON
TEXAS

*After the original marble statue in Statuary Hall,*
*U.S. Capitol, Washington, D.C.*

did not love me. That time is now past...[7]

Years later, in 1840, Houston married Margaret Lea, with whom he had six children.

## Commander-in-Chief of the Texas Army, President of Texas, Senator and Governor

After moving to Texas, Houston was appointed as the Commander-in-Chief of the Texas army in the war for its liberation from Mexico, and was the outstanding hero of the battle of San Jacinto in 1836, which sealed Texas' independence. He was the first elected president of Texas (1836-38); its third president (1841-44); a Senator representing Texas in Congress (1846-59); and finally, governor of Texas from 1859 to 1861 until he was deposed for opposing the secession of Texas from the Union.[8]

Houston has been described as "the greatest single leader in Texan history and one of the greatest in the westward expansion of the United States to the Pacific."[9]

## Sam Houston and the Alamo

Sam Houston's fame comes chiefly from his association with one of the foremost epics of courage in the history of America — and the world — that of the *Alamo*. This is vividly related for us in the *Pilgrimage Address at the Alamo*, given by Lt. General William W. Momyer, USAF, to the House of Representatives, on April 18, 1966:

FROM THE ORIGINAL IN OIL AT THE
ALAMO
LT. COL. WILLIAM B. TRAVIS

## Pilgrimage Address at the Alamo

We are assembled here to give tribute to the men who defended the Alamo. Some 130 years ago, a group of almost 200 men gave their lives in one of the most stirring battles of our history. The men of Colonel Travis' command fought off a superior force of more than 2,500 troops for 13 days. The gallant defense of the Alamo stands as a living memorial to all men of courage. Knowing that no help could reach them in time, *these men laid down their lives so Sam Houston might have time to gather additional forces for other battles to be fought.* We know the valuable time the defense of the Alamo gave Sam Houston permitted him to defeat Santa Anna at San Jacinto and, thereby, established the Republic of Texas. American history is punctuated with the outstanding courage of its fighting men. When men fight in defense of their freedom, courage and dedication to their fellow men are characteristic. The strength of our country is in our people and the willingness to fight for those ideals that have made us the greatest country on earth. Whenever our ideals have been threatened we have responded with heroic self-sacrifice in defense of those precious things... Our fighting men have faced difficult battles in the past and shall face even more difficult ones in the future. Sam Houston didn't become discouraged because of the severity of the struggle. His cause and determination to succeed swept all obstacles aside. Our fighting men are led by the same dedicated leadership today... I think we need have no fear of the strength and will of our fighting men. We can all be proud of the example set by that heroic group of volunteers at the *Alamo.* Their display of self-sacrifice for a more noble cause should be a source of inner strength for all of us as we face the future, and an individual determination that we will courageously defend our freedom no matter how small or great the challenge. Yes, we

THE ALAMO SAN ANTONIO, TEXAS

remember the *Alamo*, because without the strength of character displayed by men like Travis, Crockett, Bowie, and Bonham there would be no freedom to defend...[10]

## Houston's Christian Character Traits

From the above, we glean Houston's courage, self-sacrifice, optimism, determination, perseverance and strength of character in the face of great obstacles. Housed in the Rare Book Collection of the Library of Congress, *The Life of General Samuel Houston* gives us the true historic record of the surrender of Mexican General Santa Ana to Sam Houston, in its recorded dialogue between Houston and his prisoner:

...Houston asked the prisoner to be seated on a box nearby and sent for Almonts to interpret, when the following conversation took place between the two generals, Houston resting on his elbow upon the ground:

| | |
|---|---|
| Santa Ana: | The conqueror of the Napoleon of the West is born to no common destiny and he can afford to be generous to the vanquished. |
| Houston: | You should have remembered that Sir, at the Alamo! |
| Santa Ana: | The Alamo was taken by storm, and the usages of war justified the slaughter of the vanquished. |
| Houston: | Such usages do not now prevail among civilized nations. |
| Santa Ana: | I was acting under the orders of my government. |
| Houston: | You are the government yourself, Sir. |
| Santa Ana: | I have such orders in my possession. |
| Houston: | A dictator, Sir, has no superior. |
| Santa Ana: | My orders were to exterminate every man found in arms in Texas, to treat all such as pirates, because they have no government and are fighting under no recognized flag. |
| Houston: | I have no doubt you have found out by this time that Texans have both a government and a flag, but admitting the force of your plea for the San Antonio massacre, you have no excuse for the Fannin slaughter, for he had capitulated on the terms offered by your General, and yet his whole command was murdered without arms in their hands. |
| Santa Ana: | I knew nothing of their capitulation, but ordered their execution upon the representation of General Urrea, that he had conquered them in battle. |
| Houston: | I know, Sir, that the command had capitulated. |
| Santa Ana: | Then I was ignorant of the fact, and if ever I get Urrea into my hands, I will execute him for his duplicity, for he had no authority to receive their capitulation at all. |

Here the conversation ended for a while, and Santa Ana asked for opium, which was given him...[11]

The above testify to the dignity, caliber, integrity and strength of character exemplified by this great leader. That Sam Houston fulfilled his widowed mother's admonishments about bravery and self-sacrifice are evident from these words taken from a speech that he delivered to the U.S. Senate on August 1, 1854:

> ...one arm and one leg I have given to be crushed in the defense of my country. I have yet one arm and one leg which I can sacrifice, if necessary, in the defense of my person...[12]

## Texas' Declaration of Independence

On the second day of March 1836, Texas' future was sealed, when the Texan Declaration of Independence was made by the delegates of the people of Texas, in General Convention, Washington, D.C. It reads thus, excerpted:

> When a government has ceased to protect the lives, liberty and property of the people, from whom its legitimate powers are derived, and for the advancement of whose happiness it was instituted; and so far from being a guarantee for their inestimable and inalienable rights, becomes an instrument in the hands of evil rulers for their oppression... It denies us the right to worship the Almighty, according to the dictates of our own conscience, by the support of a National Religion, calculated to promote the temporal interests of its human functionaries rather than the glory of the true and living God.[13]

## Sam Houston's Acceptance of Jesus Christ as his Personal Savior

Houston's strength and bravery as a military leader did not deter him from his need for a personal Savior. He accepted Jesus Christ as his Lord and Redeemer in early November 1854, during a revival conducted in his hometown by Independence Church. It is reported that Houston responded to the minister's appeal, and, weeping for his sins, professed his faith in Christ.[14] ...On Sunday, November 19, the father of Texas was baptized by Pastor Rufus Burleson of Independence Church in Little Rocky Creek, two miles south of the town.[15]

The above is but a glimpse of the life, words and character of Sam Houston, a great American son, one who was proud to lead Texas out of the slavery of an alien power into the freedom and liberties of a government established under God. It is fitting that the citizens of Texas chose him to be included among this nation's noble statesmen and heroes represented in the U.S. Capitol's Hall of Fame.

# JOHN WANAMAKER
## The Prayers of John Wanamaker
## (1838 - 1922)

In the late 1800's and early 1900's, John Wanamaker became foremost in the history of merchandising, with the development of his innovative department store in the city of Philadelphia. To this day, one may still do personal shopping in the national historic landmark.

## The Unique 33,000-Pipe Organ
## in Wanamaker's Department Store

Upon entering the Wanamaker Department Store opposite City Hall, one is greeted by a spectacular sight—that of a 33,000-pipe organ encircling the upper gallery of the main floor. And, if one should be there during a concert, it's like being in a magnificent worship service or a classical organ recital. In addition, a 10-foot bronze eagle stands proudly in the center of the court, symbolizing our national emblem. If one visited the department store prior to 1988 at Easter time, this store rivaled any art gallery with its two irreplaceable oil paintings: "Christ before Pilate" and "Christ on Calvary"—annually displayed with the story of Jesus Christ's mock trial, humiliating death, and glorious resurrection three days later, a 60-year-old Philadelphia tradition. Who, and what is behind this unique enterprise? Simply, a godly man.

## Young John Wanamaker—An Errand Boy at Age 14

John Wanamaker was the man who built this impressive store. Born in Philadelphia on July, 11, 1838, he attended public schools, and at age 14, began his career in business as an errand boy in a store.[1]

## "The Finest Organ in the World"
## Plays on Every Business Day

It was John's brother, Rodman, who had the idea of utilizing the grand court of the new edifice as a music center, and he set out to obtain the finest organ in the world and acquired the Louisiana Purchase exposition organ, in Festival Hall, St. Louis. The instrument had been played by Alexander Guilmont and nearly every other noted organist of that day. It took 13 freight cars to ship it to Philadelphia, where it was rebuilt and heard publicly for the first time on June 22, 1911. Unlike most organs, the Wanamaker organ has been played every business day since its installation.

*John Wanamaker, after an original painting*

Marcel Dupré, organist at Notre Dame Cathedral in Paris and one of many world-renowned organists who played this instrument, made his American debut at Wanamakers in November 1921.

## The Organ—"An Orchestra in Itself"

The great French Classicist, Honoré de Balzac, said of the organ:

> The organ is in truth the grandest, the most daring, the most magnificent of all instruments invented by human genius. It is a whole orchestra in itself. It can express anything in response to a skilled touch. Surely it is, in some sort, a pedestal on which the soul poises for a flight forth into space, essaying on her course to draw picture after picture in an endless series to paint human life, to cross the infinite that separates Heaven from earth![2]

## Wanamaker's Remarkable Business Accomplishments

Wanamaker brought merchandising into the 20th century with his modern concept of the department store, expanded use of advertising truth and honesty in retailing, and profit-sharing for his employees. He took a prominent part in the movement to secure pure water in the city of Philadelphia. In 1889, Wanamaker entered President Harrison's cabinet as Postmaster-General.[3]

## The Source of Wanamaker's Success—God's Word

Behind Wanamaker's outward success as a financier and a business tycoon, was a man who was firmly established upon the truth of God's Word. He was president of the Young Men's Christian Association in Philadelphia for a number of years.[4] In 1858, he organized a small Sunday school, beginning with 27 pupils, which he expanded to an enrollment of 5000, one of the largest in the country, and which became Bethany Presbyterian Sunday School of Philadelphia. He was active superintendent of the Sunday school for over 60 years.

## Pastor MacLennan Reveals "Wanamaker's Great Childlike Faith"

The most poignant insight into John Wanamaker comes from his pastor, A. Gordon MacLennan of Bethany Presbyterian Church. The following is excerpted from the introduction to *Prayers of John Wanamaker*, published a year after his death in 1922:

> In the prayers contained in this volume, there is revealed the loftiness of soul, the catholicity of spirit, the perfect standing of human need, and the great childlike faith of John Wanamaker. He was truly a man of prayer and the place of prayer was precious to him. He always approached the Throne of

Grace with great reverence and deep humility, as though he, too, had heard the command, "Put off thy shoes from off thy feet, for the place whereon thou standest is holy ground."

His regular church prayer meeting always found him in his place, and many times he has said: "I like to be present at the meeting, in the middle of the week, feeling, as I sit among the people gathered, some of them deaf, hearing hardly a spoken word and others with failing sight, that as the Lord passed around amongst them He might give me a blessing too." He was present always, as leader of a little meeting of men at 9 o'clock in the morning, for prayer and meditation, known as the John Wesley Class Meeting. At 9:30 he attended the Brotherhood Meeting, leading and inspiring the men with his unique personality and deep spiritual insight and constant interest in the lives of the 300 or more men who met there. From the Brotherhood Meeting he went to regular morning church service, taking a full part in all the worship. At 2:30 in the afternoon, he was present to superintend the great Sunday School which he, with the same uniqueness which built the greatest merchandising establishment in America, developed from a class of 27 pupils to an enrollment of 5,000!

But his activity in connection with the church and school did not cease with the services on Sunday, for wherever there was trouble, or sickness, or death he always found time to be present giving words of counsel and help and always to lead the distressed ones to the Throne of Grace where he had found One able to help in all times of need.

## The Prayers of John Wanamaker
Following are prayers excerpted from *Prayers of John Wanamaker*:

Ever-living God, our Father, we have come into Thy house again through Thy mercy which has kept us alive. We would worship Thee with reverence. We hallow Thy name, O God, our Father, the name which is above every other name. We Worship Thee, O Christ, God manifest in the flesh. We hear Thee speak, O Christ, who walked the pathways of this very earth and talked and did things like a man, and left the earth richer for the charity of thy words and the work of Thy dear, kindly hands. Thou hast written Thy name on so much of daily life that we cannot walk or talk or open the doors of our homes without thinking of Thee and Thy ways in Galilee.

Oh Lord, Thou hast told us how to pray. Help us to shut the door, shutting out the world, and the enemy and any fear or doubt which spoils prayer. May there be no distance between our souls and Thee.

Our Father, we have come to sit down together to rest, after a busy week, and to think. We are not satisfied with ourselves for we all, like sheep, have gone astray. What we have done is what we ought not to have done. We are stung to the quick with disappointment, sorrow and desolation. It seems as though there were a cankerworm eating at the core of our hearts, and there is no rest for our souls day or night. Have pity upon us, Lord, and cut us not down in Thy displeasure. We confess our sin and bring it to Thee. Let our prayers prevail in Heaven, and do Thou heal and help us to a new life in Christ Jesus. Amen.[5]

## Unanswered Prayers. Why?

Due to the magnificence of the first volume of Wanamaker's heartfelt prayers to Almighty God, a second volume was printed, *Prayers at Bethany Chapel* by John Wanamaker. It included the following thoughts on unanswered prayer by Wanamaker:

UNANSWERED PRAYERS. WHY?

The positiveness of Sacred Scriptures about praying puzzles many Bible believers when they find their prayers have not been answered according to their asking.

'If ye shall ask anything of the Father, in my Name, He will give it.'

'If two of you shall agree on earth as touching anything that ye shall ask, it shall be done for you of my Father which is in heaven.'

The promises to be heard are made to God's children; they are not to everybody. Nor can a believer pray for harm to be visited upon another believer. The right to pray is bestowed on a believer, and no one has the right to pray for that which is contrary to the loving nature and known will of God.

The promises of the Bible are made to God's children as His children; they are not to everybody, or regardless of the attitude of the person praying.

The petitioner may be disqualified by his conduct, or by his asking for what he has no actual right to ask; such as to be helped to do what he ought not to do, or to be protected in a danger he has no right to incur; we may pray for protection when God has given us a special mission, or when doing a known duty. God does not want us to yield to temptation—in such cases we can ask nothing doubting... "Oh! I have faith in mother's prayers," someone says. The Bible says, "Have faith in God." Man's hopes in prayers, beyond the promises of God, are always liable to disappointment.[6]

## Wanamaker's Prayers at Bethany Chapel

Following are some of Wanamaker's communications with God at Bethany Chapel:

Father Almighty, at Thy command we come to Thee. If we were shut off from prayer, we would not know where to turn for true wisdom. We thank Thee for the Sabbath Day in which we are free to become acquainted with Thee. Thou hast placed us in this world. We are young and weak, unskilled and ask Thee to keep us from mistakes, and the blindness of folly. Help us to rest our souls in Thy keeping, O Wondrous Father, Loving God, Redeeming Christ. May this earth be a step to Heaven, and each day find us more obedient to Thy Will. Make us truly Thy children, and may others see Christ in us.

Amen.[7]

We remember, Lord, that while John was preaching by Jordan a humble, silent, industrious Man at Nazareth was working at the carpenter's bench. But the day that closed the door of that carpenter's shop was when the Man went to the synagogue and opened the Scriptures and read, "The Spirit of the Lord is upon me because he hath anointed me to preach the gospel to the poor; he hath sent me to heal the broken hearted, to preach deliverance to the captives, and recovering of sight to the blind, to set at liberty them that are bruised, to preach the acceptable year of the Lord"; and He added, "This day is this Scripture fulfilled in your ears." We thank Thee that John heard and saw and said, "Behold the Lamb of God, who taketh away the sin of the world." We thank Thee for the voice out of the sky at Jordan—"This is my beloved Son, hear him." May we begin to prepare the way of the Lord in our lives and by our service. In His Name, we pray. Amen.[8]

Our Father and Our God, Thou dost ordain a day of worship and call us to the sanctuary to speak to us. Speak in Thine own way by a mighty wind or a still small voice out of Thy Great Book. Speak with angelic interpreters or through a light like that which Saul saw on the road to Damascus. Give us seeing eyes, and hearing ears; appoint us our work and inspire us not to challenge it but to go in Thy strength. "We can do all things through Him which strengtheneth us." May we learn that it is "not by might, nor by power, but by Thy Spirit." Through Jesus Christ, our Lord, we pray. Amen.[9]

O God, Creator and Sustainer of Life, we are taking from Thee, now, the breath we breathe that enables us to live. The life we live is a vanishing life. Pardon, we humbly beseech Thee in the Sanctuary, that spirit which takes from Thee all and gives so little back. Thunder with a great thunder upon us, that we may hear Thy call to no longer refuse to repent and yield ourselves to Thee. Thou didst lay the foundations of earth and the heavens are the work of Thy hands. Father, God, King of the silver stars and maker of the golden Sun, the earth is Thine and the fulness thereof. We are tenants with a short lease. We take air and sunshine and light to use brain and body and eyes and ears. Make us to remember that we must render our account to Thee as any servant does to his Master. Make us faithful stewards. In Jesus' Name, we pray. Amen.[10]

Living and loving God, God of life and God of love, we worship Thee as our heart's only God. We are sinners. God be merciful unto us. We have had a festival of hunger and a dance of shame. We have had spasms of consciousness and went straight on in willful, stubborn, disobedience. We tried to drown them in liquor and wrong doing, but we are determined not to play the devil's game any longer. We come in through the door of unworthiness and the door of helplessness. We see a nail-scarred Hand reaching down to us, and a little ladder marked Faith. We pull ourselves together and place our sore and unfit feet upon it to climb to the Hospital of Mercy, to put our case in the Friendly Physician's hands. Eternal Father so pitiful; Eternal Christ so tender; Eternal Spirit so patient; heal and help and hold on to us with mighty love, full pardon, and abounding grace. Amen.[11]

O Lord, we know what it is to come to the end of our strength. We know Thou hast a purpose in making us little to reveal Thy strength. We have discovered by Thy Spirit, the way of the Lord. Once we thought our way better, or just as good. We were grievously wrong. Make us to be students of Thy Word, and full of hunger for Divine Bread. Deliver us from small ideas, warped judgments, cowardly indolence; lighten us with Thy smile, and break in upon us with great surprises of Thy love, and set us wondering at Thy overflowing grace. Pity this poor wilderness-world, and for Christ's sake turn it into heaven's garden-land. Amen.[12]

We thank Thee, our Father, that there is a place always accessible to make our prayers together. After the dark week, we bless Thee for the Sabbath light. In Thy tender Providence we are here waiting in hope, as the child comes to its mother with names of love. We come to Thee, our Father, to speak Thy names:—The God of grace and all comfort; The Father of mercies; the God and Father of our Lord Jesus Christ. Touch and heal heartaches, sorrows, distresses, bind up wounds. We know that none are righteous, not one. We have sinned and plead guilty; have done what we should not and left undone what we ought to have done. We are witnesses against ourselves. We cannot boast, our self-confidence is done. We see Jesus; He alone is our sufficiency and our souls cry out in need, "God be merciful to me, a sinner." Amen.[13]

## Wanamaker's Secret of Success—His Faith in God

From the above moving prayers, we see that Wanamaker's secret of success stems from his faith in Almighty God and his love and adherence to Jesus Christ, His unfailing words being ever before him. What a testimony to the Christian character and wisdom which have made the name *"John Wanamaker"* a household word in business and finance in America.

# CONCLUSION

In the twelve years since I began researching and writing about America's true history and heritage from original sources, I found myself continually being thwarted and opposed with obstacles and hindrances. What seemed to me would be considered a purely patriotic and non-threatening endeavor to any American, resulted in a stirring up of the ire and resentment of officials, whose cooperation was needed in this task. Gradually, over the years, as I met with the same spirit of opposition, again and again, it came to be my belief through evidence presented, that this was a well-orchestrated, master-minded agenda to destroy America through the eradication of Christianity from her history, culture and civilization.

Fellow Americans, at this juncture of our nation's history, there is a need more than ever before, for critical analysis and keen discernment in rightly dividing truth from falsehood. We are living in an era of high deception and undercover intrigue, as proven in my previous book, *The Rewriting of America's History.*

For those of you who wish to pursue and understand the revisionist historians' insidious agenda to undo America from within her ranks, I would refer you to this book. For a people who do not know where they came from, also do not know where they are going, thus they become easy prey for a conquering nation. As God tells us in His Word:

> My people perish for lack of knowledge.
> Hosea 4:6a

*For those of you who*, in reading the pages of this book, have realized the need for the Savior and a new lease on life, please pray this silent prayer with me:

Father in Heaven, I come to you humbly, as a child, accepting your free gift of salvation through your Son Jesus' sacrificial death and atonement for my sins. I now accept Him as my Lord and Savior, and I thank you, Father, for this priceless gift of a Messiah. I now repent and turn my life over to you, Lord Jesus, in order to serve you all the days of my life in Spirit and in Truth. I accept your unconditional forgiveness, Father, through Christ's sacrifice on Calvary's cross, and realize that through your grace and mercy, I am now translated into the Kingdom of Eternal Life, have become your beloved child, and that I am sealed with the Holy Spirit of promise forever; for You tell me that if I confess with my mouth Jesus as Lord, and believe in my heart that God raised Him from the dead, I shall be saved. (Romans 10:9) Lead me, I pray, into all truth through your Holy Word, Lord Jesus. Amen.

## Chapter I

(i)   [1]Kling, August J. "Columbus —A Layman Christ-bearer to Uncharted Isles." *The Presbyterian Layman.* October, 1971.

[2]Columbus, Christopher. *Concerning the Islands Lately Discovered. The Epistle of Christopher Colon to Lord Raphael Sanxis, Treasurer of King Ferdinand of Spain.* May 3, 1493. Rare Manuscript Division of Library of Congress, Washington, D.C.

[3]Columbus, Christopher. *Translation of Manuscript copy of a Letter written by Christopher Columbus to the King and Queen of Spain, dated on the Island of Jamaica, July 7, 1503.* Rare Manuscript Division of Library of Congress , Washington, D.C. pp. 8-10.

[4]David, Maurice. *Who Was Christopher Columbus?* Letter from Don Cristobal Colon to his son, Don Diego, published by the Duchess of Berwick y Alba. New York: The Research Publishing Company, 1933, p. 92.

(ii)   [1]*Letter of Hernando de Soto, in Florida, to the Justice and Board of Magistrates in Santiago de Cuba, July 9th, 1539.* Translated from the Spanish by Buckingham Smith, Washington, 1854. Library of Congress Rare Book Collection, Washington, D.C. pp. 7-10.

[2]*Memoir of Hernando de Escalante Fontaneida, respecting Florida, written in Spain, about the year 1575.* Translated from the Spanish by Buckingham Smith, Washington, 1854. Library of Congress Rare Book Collection, Washington, D.C., pp. 22-31.

[3]Ibid., pp. 51-53.

[4]*A Narrative of the Expedition of Hernando de Soto into Florida by a Gentleman of Elvas,* published at Evora in 1557. Translated from the Portuguese by Richard Hackluyt, London, 1609. Library of Congress Rare Book Collection, Washington, D.C., pp. 117; 171.

(iii)   [1]Commager, Henry Steele (ed.) *Documents of American History.* New York: F.S. Crofts and Company, 1934, p. 8.

[2]Keith, Sir William. *The History of the British Plantations in America. Part I containing the History of Virginia.* London: Printed at the expense of the Society for the Encouragement of Learning by S. Richardson, 1738, pp. 66-71.

[3]Ibid., p. 96.

[4]Smith, Captain John. *The Generall Historie of Virginia, New England and the Summer Isles,* from their first beginning AN: 1584 to this present 1626. London: Edward Blackmore. 1632, p. 36.

[5]Ibid., p. 34.      [6]Ibid., pp. 32-34.      [7]Ibid.

[8]Inscription upon the bronze plaque, Robert Hunt Memorial, Jamestown Island, Virginia.

[9]Smith, Captain John. *The Generall Historie of Virginia, New England*

*and the Summer Isles,* from their first beginning AN: 1584 to this present 1626. London: Edward Blackmore, 1632, pp. 11-12.

(iv)   [1]Keith, Sir William. *The History of the British Plantations in America. Part I Containing the History of Virginia.* London: Printed at the expense of the Society for the Encouragement of Learning by S. Richardson, 1738, p. 129.

[2]Mace, William H. *A Primary History — Stories of Heroism.* New York: Rand McNally and Company, 1909, p. 63.

## Chapter II

(i)   [1]Millard, Catherine. *The Rewriting of America's History.* Camp Hill: Horizon House Publishers, 1991, pp. 14-17.

[2]Winsor, Justin. *The Surrender of the Bradford Manuscript.* Cambridge: John Wilson and Son, University Press, 1897.

[3]Commager, Henry Steele (ed.) *Documents of American History.* New York: F.S. Crofts and Company, 1934, pp. 14-15.

[4]Bradford, William. *Of Plimoth Plantation.* Library of Congress Rare Book Collection, Washington, D.C.

[5]Adams, John Quincy. *An Oration Delivered at Plymouth, December 22, 1802, at the Anniversary Commemoration of the First Landing of our Ancestors at the Place.* Boston: Russell and Cutler, 1802, pp. 17, 18, 20.

(ii)   [1]Hooker, Thomas. *A Survey of the Summe of Church Discipline.* Boston: Old South Leaflets No. 55, 1896, p. 15.

[2]Ibid.   [3]Ibid.   [4]Ibid.   [5]Ibid.

[6]Hooker, Thomas. (Late pastor of the Church at Hartford upon Connecticut, in N.E.) *A Survey of the Summe of Church Discipline, wherein the Way of Churches of New England is warranted out of the Word and all exceptions of weight, which are made against it, answered.* London: A.M. for John Bellamy, 1648, Preface.

[7]Hooker, Thomas. (Reverend and faithful Minister of the Gospel) *The Covenant of Grace Opened.* London: G. Dawson, 1649.

[8]Hooker, Thomas. *A Survey of the Summe of Church Discipline,* Old South Leaflets, No. 55, 1896, p. 16.

(iii)   [1]Brandeis, Louis D. *True Americanism – Thoughts on American Liberties.* An Oration delivered before the city government and citizens of Boston in Faneuil Hall, on the one hundred and thirty-ninth anniversary of the Declaration of Independence of these United States, July 5, 1915. Library of Congress Collection.

[2]*Sketch of the Life of Roger Williams.* Collections of the Rhode Island Historical Society (Vol. 1) Providence: John Miller, 1827, p. 9.

[3]Ibid.   [4]Ibid.   [5]Ibid., p. 10.   [6]Ibid., pp. 10-11.

[7]Easton, Emily. *Roger Williams – Prophet and Pioneer.* Boston: Houghton Mifflin Co., 1930, pp. 287-288.

[8]Ibid., p. 288.

[9]*Sketch of the Life of Roger Williams.* Collections of the Rhode Island Historical Society (Vol. 1) Providence: John Miller, 1827, p. 11.

[10]Ibid., p. 12.    [11]Ibid., pp. 12-13.

[12]Williams, Roger. *A Discourse – The Hireling Ministry.* London: Christina Contributor Office, 1652, pp. 158-159.

[13]Williams, Roger. *A Key into the Language of America* or an help to the language of Natives in that part of America called New England. London: Gregory Dexter, 1643, p. 23.

[14]Ibid., pp. 114-115.    [15]Ibid., p. 162.    [16]Ibid., p. 163.

[17]Smyth, Clifford. *Roger Williams and the Fight for Religious Freedom.* New York: Funk and Wagnalls Company, 1931, p. 76.

[18]Williams, Roger. *The Bloudy Tenent of Persecution, for Cause of Conscience,* discussed, in a Conference betweene Truth and Peace. Who, in all tender affection, present to the High Court of Parliament. Printed by Gregory Dexter, 1644, Preface.

(iv)  [1]*The Encyclopedia Americana.* (Vol. 21). Americana Corporation, 1940, p. 512.

[2]Millard, Catherine. *The Rewriting of America's History.* Camp Hill: Horizon House Publishers, 1991, p. 37.

[3]*The Encyclopedia Americana.* (Vol. 21). Americana Corporation, 1940, p. 513.

[4]Cope, Thomas Pryn (ed.) *Passages from the Life and Writings of William Penn.* Philadelphia: Friends Bookstore, 1882.

[5]Ibid.

[6]Muzzey, David Saville. *A History of Our Country. A Textbook for High School Students.* New York: Ginn and Company, 1936, p. 71.

[7]Ibid., pp. 71, 72.

[8]*Penn Mutual Archives Collection.* Philadelphia.

[9]Muzzey, David Saville. *A History of Our Country,* p. 72.

[10]*Original in the Pennsylvania Historical Society Collection.* Philadelphia.

[11]*Original in the Philosophical Society of Pennsylvania Collection.* Philadelphia.

[12]*The Encyclopedia Americana.* (Vol. 21). Americana Corporation, 1940, pp. 513, 514.

[13]Cope, Thomas Pryn (ed.) *Passages from the Life and Writings of William Penn.* Philadelphia: Friends Bookstore, 1882.

[14]William Penn's Original 1684 Prayer for Philadelphia in the Historical Society of Pennsylvania. Philadelphia, PA.

(v)  [1]Morton, Louis. *Robert Carter of Nomini Hall, A Virginia Tobacco*

*Planter of the 18th Century*. Williamsburg: Colonial Williamsburg, Inc., 1941, p. 63.

[2]Ibid., p. 9.    [3]Ibid.

[4]Robert Carter to Francis Lee, 15 July 1702. *Wormeley Estate Papers, 1701-1716*. Lancaster County, VA: Christ Church Parish.

[5]Wright, Louis B., (ed.) *Letters of Robert Carter, 1720-1727*. San Marino: The Hunting Library, 1940, p. 25.

[6]Ibid., p. 34.    [7]Ibid., p. 37.

[8]Morton, Louis. *Robert Carter of Nomini Hall*, p. 11.

[9]Ibid., p. 12.    [10]Ibid.    [11]Ibid., p. 13.

[12]Ibid.    [13]Ibid., p. 20.    [14]Ibid., pp. 23-24.

# Chapter III

(i)    [1]Porter, Edward G. *An Address on the Life and Character of Samuel Adams*, delivered in the Old South Meeting House, Boston, Sunday, October 26, 1884. On the occasion of the erection of tablets in the church, commemorative of its line of ministers, and of Samuel Sewall and Samuel Adams. Boston: Press of David Clapp and Son, 1885, p. 3.

[2]Ibid.    [3]Ibid., p. 46.    [4]Ibid., p. 44.

[5]Ibid., p. 3.    [6]Ibid.    [7]Ibid.    [8]Ibid., p. 12.

[9]Adams, Samuel. *An Oration Delivered at the State-House in Philadelphia* to a very numerous audience, on Thursday the 1st of August, 1776; member of the General Congress of the United States of America. Philadelphia: E. Johnson. 1776, pp. 1-6; 17-18; 32.

[10]Ibid., p. 42.

[11]Porter, Edward G. *An Address on the Life and Character of Samuel Adams*, delivered in the Old South Meeting House, Boston, Sunday, October 26, 1884. Boston: Press of David Clapp and Son, 1885, p. 14.

(ii)    [1]Montague, Mary Louise. *Witherspoon, Signer of the Declaration of Independence*. Washington, D.C.: H.C. and J.B. McQueen, Inc., 1932, p. 1.

[2]Ibid.    [3]Ibid., p. 2.    [4]Ibid., pp. 2-3.    [5]Ibid., p. 3.

[6]Ibid.    [7]Ibid., p. 4.    [8]Ibid., p. 5.    [9]Ibid.

[10]Ibid., pp. 5-6. [11]Ibid., p. 9.    [12]Ibid.    [13]Ibid., p. 10.

[14]Ibid.    [15]Ibid., pp. 10-11.

[16]Wilson, Woodrow. *Dedication Speech* at unveiling of John Witherspoon's statue.

[17]Witherspoon, Rev. John, D.D., L.L.D., late President of the College at Princeton, New Jersey. *A Serious Inquiry into the Nature and Effects of the State: and a Letter respecting Play Actors*. New York: Whiting and Watson, 1812, pp. 6-7.

[18]Woodward, William W. *The Miscellaneous Works of the Rev. John*

Witherspoon, D.D., L.L.D., Late President of the College of New Jersey. Philadelphia: William W. Woodward, 1803, pp. 227-229.

(iii)  [1]*George Washington's Rules of Civility and Decent Behaviour in Company and Conversation.* Cambridge: Riverside Press, 1926.

[2]*The Encyclopedia Americana.* (Vol. 28) New York: Americana Corporation, 1940, p. 749.

[3]Ibid.      [4]Ibid.

[5]Burk, William Herbert, D.D. *The Washington Window in the Washington Memorial Chapel of Valley Forge.* Pennsylvania: Norristown Press, 1926, p. 25.

[6]Washington, George. *General Orders.* Archives of Mount Vernon, Virginia.

[7]Padover, Saul K. (ed.) *A Jefferson Profile.* New York: J. Day and Company, 1956, p. 227.

[8]Millard, Catherine. *God's Signature over the Nation's Capital.* Officially Recorded Presidential Inaugural Scriptures compiled by Author. West Wilmington, PA: Sonrise Publications, 1988, p. 171.

[9]Commager, Henry Steele. *Documents of American History.* F.S. Crofts and Company, 1934, pp. 151-152.

[10]Washington's Last Will. *Shanahan's Guide to Washington and its Environs.* William M. Wright, 1894.

[11]Adams, John. *Address to the U.S. Senate on the Death of Washington.* December 22, 1799 Newspaper article.

(iv)  [1]Seymour, George Dudley. *Documentary Life of Nathan Hale,* comprising all available Official and Private Documents bearing on the Life of the Patriot. New Haven: Printed by the Author, 1941, p. XXV.

[2]Ibid.          [3]Ibid., p. XXVI. [4]Ibid., p. XXVII. [5]Ibid.
[6]Ibid., p. XXVIII. [7]Ibid.          [8]Ibid.          [9]Ibid., p. XXIX.
[10]Ibid., p. XXX.  [11]Ibid.         [12]Ibid.
[13]Ibid., p. XXXI. [14]Ibid.         [15]Ibid., p. XXXIII.

[16]*History of New London,* 1860, p. 515.

[17]Seymour, George Dudley. *Documentary Life of Nathan Hale,* comprising all available Official and Private Documents bearing on the Life of the patriot. New Haven: Printed by the Author, 1941, p. 160.

[18]Ibid., p. 158.

(v)  [1]Adams, Charles Francis. *Familiar Letters of John Adams and his wife Abigail Adams,* during the Revolution, with a memoir of Mrs. Adams. New York: Hurd and Houghton, 1876, p. IX.

[2]Ibid.

[3]Bonnell, John Sutherland. *Presidential Profiles, Religion in the Life of American Presidents*. Philadelphia: Westminster Press, 1971, p. 28.

[4]Adams, Charles Francis. *Familiar Letters of John Adams and His Wife Abigail Adams*. New York: Hurd and Houghton, 1876, p. IX.

[5]Ibid.

[6]Fuller, Edmund and Green, David. *God in the White House, the Faiths of American Presidents*. New York: Crown, 1968, p. 20.

[7]Bonnell, John Sutherland. *Presidential Profiles, Religion in the Life of American Presidents*. p. 28.

[8]Fuller, Edmund and Green, David. *God in the White House, the Faiths of American Presidents*. New York: Crown, 1968, p. 27.

[9]Arnold, Richard K (ed.) *Adams to Jefferson/Jefferson to Adams — a Dialogue from their Correspondence*. San Francisco: Jerico Press, 1975, p. 25.

[10]Ibid., p. 30.

[11]Adams, Charles Francis. *Familiar Letters of John Adams and His Wife Abigail Adams*. p. 65.

[12]Adams, Abigail. *Letters of Abigail Adams to Her Husband*, Old South Leaflets, No. 6. Fourth Series, 1866, pp. 1-3.

[13]Thomson, Charles. First Secretary to Congress. *Journals of Congress*, September 7, 1774, p. 27. Library of Congress Rare Book Collection, Washington, D.C.

[14]*Congressional Record*, April 13, 1965. U.S. House of Representatives, Washington, D.C.

[15]Adams, Charles, Francis. *Familiar Letters of John Adams and His Wife Abigail Adams during the Revolution*. pp. 37, 38.

[16]Adams, John. *Speech Delivered to Congress, July 2, 1776*. Library of Congress Collection.

[17]Bonnell, John Sutherland. *Presidential Profiles, Religion in the Life of American Presidents*, p. 28.

(vi)     [1]Longshore, Joseph, M.D. and Knowles, Benjamin. *The Centennial Liberty Bell, Independence Hall – Its Traditions and Associations*. Philadelphia: Claxton, Reuben and Haffelfinger, 1876, pp. 67-68.

[2]Ibid.     [3]Ibid.     [4]Ibid.     [5]Ibid.     [6]Ibid.

[7]Montague, Mary Louise. *John Witherspoon, Signer of the Declaration of Independence*. Washington, D.C.: H.L. and J.B. McQueen, Inc., 1932, p. 1.

[8]Adams, John. *Speech delivered to Congress July 2, 1776*. Library of Congress Collection.

[9]Wanamaker, John. *The Wanamaker Primer on Abraham Lincoln*. New York: John Wanamaker, 1909, pp. 98-100.

[10]Commager, Henry Steele. (ed.) *Documents of American History*. F.S. Crofts and Company, 1934, pp. 125-126.

[11]Lipscomb, Andrew A. (ed.) *The Writings of Thomas Jefferson*. vol. XVI. The Thomas Jefferson Memorial Association of the United States, Washington, D.C.: 1904, pp. 281-282.

[12]Rayner, B.L. (ed.) *Sketches of the Life, Writings and Opinions of Thomas Jefferson*, with selections of the most valuable portions of his voluminous and unrivalled private correspondence. New York: A.W. Boardman, 1832, p. 518.

[13]Ibid., p. 516.     [14]Ibid., p. 398.     [15]Ibid., p. 518.

[16]Letters of Thomas Jefferson on Religion. (Compiled for Senator A. Willis Robertson, April 27, 1960). The Williamsburg Foundation, Williamsburg, Virginia.

[17]Jefferson, Thomas. *Catalogue of Paintings, etc. at Monticello*. Library of Congress Rare Book Collection, Washington, D.C.

[18]Rayner, B.L. (ed.) *Sketches of the Life, Writings and Opinions of Thomas Jefferson, with selections of the most valuable portions of his voluminous and unrivalled private correspondence.* New York: A.W. Boardman, 1832, p. 518.

[19]Ibid., pp. 526-527.

[20]Jefferson, Thomas. *A Summary View of the Rights of British America*, set forth in some Resolutions intended for the inspection of the present Delegates of the people of Virginia, now in Convention. By a native, and member of the House of Burgesses. Williamsburg: Printed by Clementinarind, 1774, pp. 15-16.

[21]Jefferson, Thomas. *Autobiography*. Original in the Library of Congress Rare Manuscript Division, Washington, D.C.

[22]Ibid.

[23]Rayner, B.L. (ed.) *Sketches of the Life, Writings and Opinions of Thomas Jefferson*, p. 556.

[24]Ibid., p. 556.

(vii)   [1]Seeley G. Mudd Manuscript Library, Princeton University Archives, File #54-1771, Princeton: New Jersey, p. 1.

[2]Ibid., p. 2.

[3]*The Encyclopedia Americana*. (Vol. 18). New York: Americana Corporation, 1940, p. 99.

[4]Madison, James. *A Memorial and Remonstrance*. (Presented by the General Assembly of the State of Virginia). 1785. Library of Congress Rare Book Collection, Washington, D.C.

[5]Ibid.     [6]Ibid.     [7]Ibid.

[8]*The Encyclopedia Americana*. (Vol. 18), p. 99.

[9]Ibid.     [10]Ibid.

[11]Adams, John Quincy. *A Eulogy on the Life and Character of James Madison*, September 27, 1836. Boston: John H. Eastburn City Printers, 1836, p. 18.

(viii)    [1]*The Encyclopedia Americana.* (Vol. 12) New York: Americana Corporation, 1940, p. 8.

[2]Ibid.

[3]Millard, Catherine. *The Rewriting of America's History.* Camp Hill: Horizon House Publishers, 1991, p. 125.

[4]Rogers, George L. (ed.) Benjamin Franklin. *The Art of Virtue.* Minnesota: Acorn Publishing Company, 1990, pp. 69-70.

[5]Ibid., p. 68.

[6]Rice, Wallace. *The Franklin Year Book – Maxims and Morals from the Great Philosopher.* Chicago: A.C. McClurg and Company, 1907, n.p.

[7]*The Encyclopedia Americana.* (Vol. 12) New York: Americana Corporation, 1940, p. 8-12.

(ix)    [1]Mace, Williams, H. *A Primary History – Stories of Heroism.* New York: Rand McNally and Company, 1909, p. 143.

[2]*The Encyclopedia Americana.* (Vol. 14) New York: Americana Corporation, 1940, p. 106.

[3]Millard, Catherine. *The Rewriting of America's History.* Camp Hill: Horizon House Publishers, 1991, p. 138.

[4]*The Encyclopedia Americana.* (Vol. 14) New York: Americana Corporation, 1940, p. 107.

[5]Drinkard, William R. *An Oration on the Life and Character of Patrick Henry,* delivered before the Patrick Henry Society of the William and Mary College on May 29, 1940. Richmond: P.D. Bernard, 1840.

[6]Mace, William H. *A Primary History – Stories of Heroism.* pp. 141-142.

[7]Millard, Catherine. *The Rewriting of America's History.* p. 138.

[8]Adams, Charles Francis. *Familiar Letters of John Adams and His Wife Abigail Adams, during the Revolution.* Letter dated 16 September, 1774. Hurd and Houghton, 1876, pp. 37-38.

[9]Veterans of Foreign Wars of the United States. *Patrick Henry – Statesman, Patriot.* Issued by the Americanization Department: Veterans of Foreign Wars of the United States. 1927, pp. 3-4.

[10]Ibid., pp. 5-8.

(x)    [1]Millard, Catherine. *The Rewriting of America's History.* Camp Hill: Horizon House Publishers, 1991, p. 143.

[2]*Encyclopedia Americana.* (Vol. 18). New York: Americana Corporation, 1940, p. 380.

[3]Ibid.      [4]Ibid.      [5]Ibid.

[6]Mason, Robert C. *George Mason of Virginia (Citizen, Statesman and Philosopher).* An Address Commemorative of the launching of the S.S. Gunston Hall at Alexandria, Virginia, January, 1919. New York: Oscar Aurelius Morgnor, p. 18.

[7]Machen, Lewis H. *An Address: George Mason of Virginia* (1725-1792). Presenting a portrait to Fairfax County. May 20, 1901.

[8]*Encyclopedia Americana*, p. 380.

[9]Ibid.          [10]Ibid.          [11]Ibid., p. 381.

[12]Mason, George. Eulogy on Ann Mason, inscribed within his original 1759 Bible. Gunston Hall Plantation, Lorton, Virginia.

[13]Mason, Robert C. *George Mason of Virginia (Citizen, Statesman and Philosopher)*, p. 10.

(xi)   [1]Religious News Service. April 1, 1976. *Memorial in Capital Planned to Honor "Fighting Parson."*

[2]Hocher, Edward W. *The Fighting Parson of the American Revolution – a Biography of General Peter Muhlenberg, Lutheran Clergyman, Military Chieftain and Politcal Leader.* Philadelphia: Published by the Author, 1936, p. 63.

[3]Ibid., p. 64.          [4]Ibid., p. 65.

[5]*Decennial Register of the Pennsylvania Society of Sons of the Revolution* (1888-1898) Philadelphia: J.B. Lippincott Company, 1898.

[6]Dictionary of American Biography. *Peter von Muhlenberg.* 1933 edition, p. 312.

[7]Ayres, Philip Wheelock. *Peter Muhlenberg – Pennsylvania.* Office of the Architect of the Capitol, Washington, D.C., p. 1.

[8]Ibid., p. 2.          [9]Ibid., p. 3.          [10]Ibid., p. 4.

(xii)   [1]Murdock, Myrtle Cheney. *"Statuary Hall" – Delaware – Caesar Rodney.* Office of the Architect of the Capitol, Washington, D.C.

[2]Lord, Frank B. *Little Sung Heroes of Independence.* The Washington Post, June 28, 1931, p. 3.

[3]Dictionary of American Biography. *Caesar Rodney.* 1933 edition, p. 81.

[4]Lord, Frank B. *Little Sung Heroes of Independence.* The Washington Post, June 28, 1931, p. 3.

[5]Ibid.          [6]Ibid., p. 11.          [7]Ibid., p. 3.          [8]Ibid.

[9]Dictionary of American Biography. *Caesar Rodney.* 1933 edition, p. 81.

[10]*The Works of John Adams.* (Vol. II), *with a Life of the Author, Notes and Illustrations* by his grandson, Charles Francis Adams. Boston: Charles C. Little and James Brown, 1850, p. 364.

[11]Dictionary of American Biography. *Caesar Rodney.* 1933 edition, p. 82.

[12]Lord, Frank B. *Little Sung Heroes of Independence.* p. 3.

[13]*Proceedings of the Convention of the Delaware State, held at New Castle, on Tuesday, August 27, 1776 – Delaware Constitutional Convention, 1776, Delaware State.* Printed by James Adams, 1776.

[14]A Declaration of Rights and Fundamental Rules of the Delaware State. Delaware Constitutional Convention, 1776, Delaware State. Printed by James Adams, 1776.

(xiii) [1]The Encyclopedia Americana. (Vol. 20) New York: Americana Corporation, 1940, p. 66.

[2]Ibid.

[3]Address Delivered to the General Assembly of the Commonwealth of Virginia, by the heirs and representatives of General Thomas Nelson of Yorktown. Library of Congress Rare Book Collection, Washington, D.C.

[4]Ibid.

[5]Inscription on the base of the Victory Monument, Yorktown, Virginia.

[6]Address Delivered to the General Assembly of the Commonwealth of Virginia. Library of Congress Rare Book Collection, Washington, D.C.

(xiv) [1]The Christian Statesmen of America. Boston: Massachusetts Sabbath School Society, 1861, p. 34.

[2]Ibid., p. 80  [3]Ibid., p. 81.  [4]Ibid., p. 37.  [5]Ibid., p. 38.
[6]Ibid.  [7]Ibid., p. 46.  [8]Ibid.  [9]Ibid., p. 54.
[10]Ibid.  [11]Ibid.  [12]Ibid., p. 65.  [13]Ibid., p. 86.

[14]Some Conversations of Dr. Franklin and Mr. Jay, being the first publication of a manuscript written by John Jay in Paris during 1783-1784, with an introductory essay on Dr. Franklin and Mr. Jay by Frank Monaghan of Yale University. New Haven: The Three Monks Press, 1936, p. 5.

[15]Ibid., pp. 6-7.  [16]Ibid., p. 8.

[17]Jay, John. An Address to the People of the State of New York, on the subject of the Constitution, agreed upon at Philadelphia, the 17th September, 1787. New York: Samuel and John Loudoun, Printers to the State, 1788, pp. 4; 18.

[18]Ibid., p. 19.

[19]The Christian Statesmen of America, p. 113.

[20]Ibid., p. 115.  [21]Ibid., p. 116.
[22]Ibid., pp. 117-118.  [23]Ibid., p. 118.

(xv) [1]The Encyclopedia Americana. (Vol. 29) New York: Americana Corporation, 1940, p. 151.

[2]Millard, Catherine. The Rewriting of America's History. Camp Hill: Horizon House Publishers, 1991, p. 153.

[3]The Encyclopedia Americana (Vol. 29) New York: Americana Corporation, 1940, p. 151.

[4]Millard, Catherine. The Rewriting of America's History, p. 159.

[5]Ibid.

[6]Webster, Noah, LL.D. *Introduction to An American Dictionary of the English Language*. (Revised and Enlarged by Chauncy A. Goodrich, Professor at Yale College). Springfield, MA: George and Charles Merriam, 1828.

[7]Ibid.

[8]Memoir of the Author by the Editor. *An American Dictionary*. 1847.

[9]*The Encyclopedia Americana*. (Vol. 29). New York: Americana Corporation, 1940, p. 151.

[10]Leavitt, Robert Keith. *Noah's Ark, New England Yankees and Endless Quest. A Short History of the Original Webster Dictionaries, with Reference to their First Hundred Years as publications of G. & C. Merriam Company*. Springfield, MA: G. & C. Merriam Co., 1947, p. 76.

[11]Millard, Catherine. *The Rewriting of America's History*, p. 159.

[12]Ibid.

[13]Ibid.

[14]Webster, Noah, LL.D. *The Holy Bible*, Containing the Old and New Testament in the Common Version. New Haven: Durrie and Peck, 1833.

## Chapter IV

(i)     [1]Library of Congress documentation.

[2]Ibid., p. 211.          [3]Ibid., p. 214.          [4]Ibid., p. 217.

[5]Ibid., pp. 218-219.          [6]Ibid., p. 219.

[7]Webster, Daniel. *Oration at Plymouth, December 22, 1820*.

[8]Library of Congress documentation.

[9]Ibid., p. 236.          [10]Ibid., p. 235.          [11]Ibid., p. 236.          [12]Ibid.

[13]Webster, Daniel. *Oration at Plymouth, December 22, 1820*.

[14]Library of Congress documentation.

[15]Ibid.

(ii)     [1]Tanner, Virginia. *"What hath God Wrought!" Celebrating one hundred years of Telegraphing*. Baltimore and Ohio Magazine, published monthly at Baltimore, Maryland by the Baltimore and Ohio Railroad to improve its service to the public and to promote efficiency and community of interest among its employees. May, 1944.

[2]Ibid.

[3]Page and Lord. *Story of a Nation's Capital*, 1932. Office of the Architect of the Capitol, Washington, D.C.

[4]Tanner, Virginia. *"What hath God Wrought!" Celebrating one hundred years of Telegraphing*.

[5]Ibid.

[6]Ibid., p. 62.      [7]Ibid.              [8]Ibid.

[9]Ibid.              [10]Ibid.

[11]Collins, A.C. *The Story of America in Pictures. Samuel F.B. Morse.*
Office of the Architect of the Capitol, Washington, D.C.

[12]America and the Future. *The Hero as Inventor: Samuel F.B. Morse.*
Office of the Architect of the Capitol, Washington, D.C.

[13]Bronze Plaque on the wall of Small Rotunda, Senate side, U.S.
Capitol, Washington, D.C.

(iii)    [1]*The World Encyclopedia.* (Vol. 11), Chicago: Field Enterprises, Inc.,
1949, p. 4667.

[2]Ibid., pp. 4667-8.        [3]Ibid., p. 4668.        [4]Ibid.

[5]Smith, William Earnest. *About the McGuffeys.* Oxford, OH: Cullen
Printing Company, 1963, Title Page.

[6]Westerhoff, John H., III. *McGuffey and his Readers - Piety, Morality
and Education in 19th Century America.* Nashville: Abington Press,
n.d., p. 13.

(iv)    [1]Weigle, Luther A. (ed.) *The Pageant of America.* (Vol. X)
American Idealism. New Haven: Yale University Press, 1925.

[2]Harding, Warren Gamaliel. *A Government Document.*
Washington, D.C.: Government Printing Office, 1923.

[3]Hanna, Rev. Joseph A. *Dr. Whitman and His Ride to Save Oregon.*
(Read before the Association of Presbyterian Ministers of Los
Angeles, April 8, 1903.) Los Angeles, 1903.

[4]Maxey, Chester Collins. *Marcus Whitman, 1802-1847: His Courage, His Deeds, and His College.* New York: Newcomon Society in
North America, 1950, p. 38.

(v)    [1]Barker, Burt Brown. *Oregon, Prize of Discovery, Exploration,
Settlement.* Salem: State Printing Section, 1952, p. 33.

[2]Ibid.              [3]Ibid., p. 34.    [4]Ibid.              [5]Ibid.

[6]Ibid., p. 35.     [7]Ibid.            [8]Ibid., pp. 35-36.  [9]Ibid., p. 36.

[10]Ibid., p. 37.     [11]Ibid., p. 38.   [12]Ibid.

[13]*House Joint Resolution*, No. 1., concurred by the Senate, February
16, 1921. Adopted by the House of Representatives, February 11,
1921. U.S. Congress, Washington, D.C.

(vi)    [1]Millard, Catherine. *The Rewriting of America's History.* Camp Hill:
Horizon House Publishers, 1991, p. 215.

[2]Ibid.

[3]Tibesar, Antoine, OFM (ed.) *Writings of Junipero Serra.* (Vol. IV.)
Washington, D.C.: Academy of American Franciscan History,
1966.

[4]Morgado, Martin J. *Junipero Serra's Legacy.* Pacific Grove,
California: 1987, p. 25.

[5]"Carmel Mission Bible to be used by Reagan," Monterey Peninsula Herald, 28 December, 1966, p. 1.

[6]Morgado, Martin J. *Junipero Serra's Legacy*. p. XIX.

[7]Ibid., p. 101.

[8]Geiger, *The Life and Times of Fray Junipero Serra*, O.F.M., 2:392.

(vii)  [1]Bingham, Hiram, A.M. (Member of the American Oriental Society and Late Missionary of the American Board). *Residence of Twenty-one years in the Sandwich Islands; or the Civil, Religious and Political History of those Islands:* Comprising a particular view of the missionary operations connected with the introduction and progress of Christianity and Civilization among the Hawaiian people. New York: Herman Converse, 1848. p. 57.

[2]Ibid.        [3]Ibid. p. 58.        [4]Ibid.        [5]Ibid. pp. 58-59.

[6]Humphrey, Heman. (Pastor of the Congregational Church at Pittsfield, Massachusetts). *The Promised Land, a Sermon delivered at Goshen, Connecticut at the Ordination of the Reverend Messrs. Hiram Bingham and Asa Thurston, as Missionaries to the Sandwich Islands, September 29, 1819.* Boston: Samuel T. Armstrong, 1819.

[7]Ibid., p. XVI.

[8]Bingham, Hiram, A.M. *Residence of Twenty-one years in the Sandwich Islands.* pp. 69-70.

[9]Ibid. pp. 48-49.        [10]Ibid. p. 113.        [11]Ibid.

[12]Ibid. pp. 114-115.        [13]Ibid. p.117.        [14]Ibid. p.104.

[15]Sturdevant, C.V. *Hawaii, General Information by a Citizen.* 1898, pp. 42-43.

[16]Taylor, Albert Pierce. *Under Hawaiian Skies.* Honolulu: Advertiser Publishing Company, Ltd., 1926, pp. 264-265.

[17]Ibid.        [18]Ibid.

[19]*Hawaii in Pictures, Visual Geography Series.* London: Sterling Publishing Company, Inc. 1961, p. 30.

(viii)  [1]*Congressional Record* – U.S. Senate, April 23, 1926. Acceptance speech for the United States by Senator William J. Harris of Georgia, p. 7991.

[2]Ibid.

[3]Ayres, Phillip Wheelock. *Crawford Williamson Long – Georgia.* Office of the Architect of the Capitol, Washington, D.C.

[4]*Congressional Record* – U.S. Senate, April 23, 1926. p. 7988.

[5]Ibid.

(ix)  [1]*Letter addressed to the Honorable Otis F. Glenn,* Senate Office Building, Washington, D.C. by Earnest Fremont Tittle, Minister of the First Methodist Episcopal Church, Evanston, Illinois. Dated January 10, 1933. Office of the Architect of the Capitol, Washington, D.C.

[2]*Congressional Record* – U.S. Senate, April 23, 1926. p. 2095.

[3]*The Evening Star,* Washington, D.C. April 6, 1892, p. 4, column 2.

[4]*Congressional Record* – House of Representatives, February 17, 1939. Speech of the Honorable Stephen Bolles of Wisconsin, p. 2365.

[5]*Congressional Record* – U.S. Senate, February 17, 1939. Address by Mr. Sheppard – Centenary of the birth of Frances E. Willard, pp. 2199-2200.

[6]*Congressional Record* – U.S. Senate, February 16, 1939, p. 2095.

(x)   [1]*The Encyclopedia Americana.* (Vol. 15) New York: Americana Corporation. 1940, p. 574.

[2]Ibid.

[3]Bancroft, George. *Oration delivered at the Commemoration, in Washington, of the death of Andrew Jackson, June 27, 1845.* Library of Congress Rare Book Collection, Washington, D.C. pp. 1-8.

[4]*The Encyclopedia Americana,* p. 574.

[5]Bancroft, George. *Oration delivered at the Commemoration, in Washington, of the death of Andrew Jackson.*

[6]*The Encyclopedia Americana,* p. 575.

[7]Bancroft, George. *An Oration delivered at the Commemoration, in Washington, of the death of Andrew Jackson.*

[8]Scott, Walter Dill. (ed.) *The American People's Encyclopedia.* (Vol. 11) Chicago: Spencer Press, Inc., 1957, p. 11-481.

[9]Ibid.

[10]Bancroft, George. *An Oration delivered at the Commemoration, in Washington, of the death of Andrew Jackson.*

[11]Ibid.

[12]Eulogy on Andrew Jackson given in the U.S. Senate, June 8, 1845. Library of Congress Rare Book Collection, Washington, D.C.

[13]Letter written by Andrew Jackson to Commodore Jesse D. Elliott, USN dated March 27, 1845. Displayed in front of the sarcophagus at the Smithsonian Institution, in 1966.

(xi)   [1]*The Encyclopedia Americana.* (Vol. 17) New York: Americana Corporation. 1940. p. 409.

[2]Millard, Catherine. *The Rewriting of America's History.* Camp Hill: Horizon House Publishers, 1991, p. 165.

[3]*The Encyclopedia Americana.* (Vol. 17) New York: Americana Corporation. 1940. p. 409.

[4]Ibid.          [5]Ibid.          [6]Ibid.

[7]Ibid., p. 410.     [8]Ibid.          [9]Ibid.

[10]Wanamaker, John. *The Wanamaker Primer of Abraham Lincoln.* New York: John Wanamaker, 1909, pp. 98-100.

[11]Lincoln, Abraham. *Gettysburg Address.* Inscribed upon the inner South Wall, Lincoln Memorial, Washington, D.C.

[12]Millard, Catherine. *The Rewriting of America's History.* Camp Hill: Horizon House, 1991, p. 167.

[13]Matthew 7:1

[14]Matthew 18:7

[15]Revelation 16:7

[16]Lincoln, Abraham. *Second Inaugural Address.* Inscribed upon the inner North Wall, Lincoln Memorial, Washington, D.C.

[17]Wolf, William J. *The Religion of Abraham Lincoln.* New York: Seabury Press, 1963.

[18]Herndon, Ann. *The Teenage Girl who Sculptured Abraham Lincoln.* The Sunday Star Magazine, February 10, 1957, Washington, D.C., p. 15.

[19]Ibid.

[20]Hoxie, Vinnie Ream. *Personal Recollections of Lincoln.* Office of the Architect of the Capitol, Washington, D.C.

[21]Millard, Catherine. *The Rewriting of America's History.* Camp Hill: Horizon House, 1991, pp. 181-182.

[22]Abraham Lincoln's 1847 Family Bible. Library of Congress Rare Book Collection, Washington, D.C.

[23]Ibid.

[24]*The Lincoln Reader,* Edited, with an Introduction by Paul M. Angle. Rutgers University Press, 1947, p. 116.

[25]Bernard, Kenneth A. *Lincoln and Music. The American Story Radio Program – Abraham Lincoln, 1809-1865,* pp. 2-3; 5-6. Library of Congress Collection.

[26]Wanamaker, John. *The Wanamaker Primer on Abraham Lincoln.* New York: John Wanamaker, 1909, pp. 101-102.

[27]Ibid, 96-97.

[28]*The Evening Post.* Obituary. Saturday, July 15, 1871.

(xii) [1]Millard, Catherine. *The Rewriting of America's History.* Camp Hill: Horizon House Publishers, 1991, p. 183.

[2]Lee, Fitzhugh. *General Lee.* New York: D. Appleton and Company, 1894, pp. 20-22.

[3]Lattimore, Ralston B. (ed.) *The Story of Robert E. Lee, as told in his own Words and those of his Contemporaries.* Washington, D.C.: Colortone Press, 1964, p. 24.

[4]*American Peoples Encyclopedia.* (Vol. 12) Chicago: Spencer Press, Inc., 1954, p. 120317.

[5]Lattimore, Ralston B. (ed.) *The Story of Robert E. Lee,* p. 47.

[6]Ibid., p. 49.       [7]Ibid., p. 60.       [8]Ibid., p. 12.       [9]Ibid., p. 13.

[10]Alexander, Brigadier General E.P. "Lee at Appomattox, Personal Recollections of the Break-up of the Confederacy." Century Magazine, Vol. 63, No. 6 (April, 1902), p. 930.

[11]Banks, Louis Albert, D.D. *Capital Stories about Famous Americans.* New York: The Christian Herald, 1905, p. 361.

[12]Griswold, Benjamin Howell. *The Spirit of Lee and Jackson.* Baltimore: The Norman Remington Company, 1927, pp. 12-13; 18.

[13]Lee, Robert E., Captain. *Recollections and Letters of General Robert E. Lee by his Son.* New York: Doubleday, Page and Company, 1924, pp. 88, 89.

(xiii) [1]Millard, Catherine. *The Rewriting of America's History.* Camp Hill: Horizon House Publishers, 1991, p. 190.

[2]Ibid., p. 191.  [3]Ibid.  [4]Ibid.

[5]Freeman, Melville, A.M. *The Story of Our Republic,* (by the Head of History Department, High School of Practical Arts, Boston, Lecturer on Biographical and Historical Subjects; formerly President, New England History Teachers' Association). Philadelphia: F.A. Davis Company, Publishers, 1938, p. 36.

[6]Butterworth, Hezekiah. (ed.) *History of the United States.* New York: The Saalfield Publishing Company, 1904, p. 423.

[7]*The Encyclopedia Americana.* (Vol. 15). New York: Americana Corporation, 1940, p. 583.

[8]Gittings, John G. *Personal Recollections of Stonewall Jackson.* Cincinnati: The Editor Publishing Company, 1899, p. 32.

[9]Butterworth, Hezekiah. (ed.) *History of the United States.* New York: The Saalfield Publishing Company, 1904, p. 443.

[10]*The Encyclopedia Americana.* (Vol. 15). New York: Americana Corporation, 1940, p. 583.

[11]Chew, Colonel, R.P. *An Address on Stonewall Jackson.* (Delivered at the Virginia Military Institute, Lexington, on the unveiling of Ezekiel's Statue of General T.J. Jackson, June 19, 1912). Lexington: Rockbridge County News Print, 1912, pp. 61, 62.

(xiv) [1]Dictionary of American Biography. *Samuel Houston.* 1933 edition, p. 262.

[2]Ayres, Philip Wheelock. *Samuel Houston – Texas.* Office of the Architect of the Capitol, Washington, D.C., p. 1.

[3]Ibid.

[4]Powell, Alexander E. *Some Forgotten Heroes and their Place in American History.* New York: Charles Scribner's Sons, 1913, p. 115.

[5]Ibid., p. 3.

[6]Moore, John Trotwood. *Houston – Greatest Comeback in American History.* The Saturday Evening Post, May 19, 1928, p. 26.

[7]Ibid.

[8]*Congressional Record* – House of Representatives. *Sam Houston, Hero of the Great Southwest: An Outstanding Memorialization,* May 31, 1966, pp. 11;274.

[9]Ibid.

[10]*Congressional Record* – House of Representatives. *Pilgrimage Address at the Alamo,* April 18, 1966. Address by Lt. Gen. William W. Momyer, USAF, p. A2367.

[11]*The Life of General Sam Houston.* Washington, D.C.: J.T. Powers, 1856, Library of Congress Rare Book Collection, Washington, D.C.

[12]*Speech of the Honorable Sam Houston of Texas in the Senate of the United States – on Texan affairs.* Washington, D.C.: Thomas Jefferson Green, 1854. Library of Congress Rare Book Collection, Washington, D.C.

[13]*The Declaration of Independence made by the Delegates of the people of Texas, in General Convention, at Washington on March 2, 1836.* p. 48. Library of Congress Rare Book Collection, Washington, D.C.

[14]Musacchio, George. Dean, College of Arts and Sciences, University of Mary Hardin, Hardin - Baylor, Belton. *Born 200 Years Ago, Houston Became Faithful Baptist Layman.*, The (Texas) Baptist Standard, 3 March 1993: 12; 14.

[15]Ibid.

(xv) [1]*The Encyclopedia Americana.* (Vol. 28). New York: Americana Corporation, 1940, p. 253.

[2]*The Great Organ and the Grand Court.* John Wanamaker, Philadelphia, n.d.

[3]*The Encyclopedia Americana.* (Vol. 28). New York: Americana Corporation, 1940, p. 253.

[4]Ibid.

[5]Wanamaker, John. *The Prayers of John Wanamaker.* New York: Fleming H. Revell Company, 1923.

[6]Wanamaker, John. *Prayers at Bethany Chapel.* New York: Fleming H. Revell Company, 1925, pp. 5-8.

[7]Ibid., p. 15.    [8]Ibid., p. 14.    [9]Ibid., p. 16.

[10]Ibid., p. 18.    [11]Ibid., p. 22.    [12]Ibid., p. 80.    [13]Ibid., p. 24.

Notation

All dates of births and deaths of *Great American Statesmen and Heroes* taken from *Dictionary of American Biography.* New York: Charles Scribner's Sons, 1933 edition.

### Christian Heritage Week
#### –A History–

The first "Christian Heritage Week" took place in Albuquerque, New Mexico, November 10-16, 1991. Citizens for Excellence in Education and Christian Heritage Ministries worked hand-in-hand to make this week a true revival of the Christian principles, values and virtues upon which **this nation under God** was founded.

The event was extremely significant for our nation, as it is the first official proclamation signed by a State Governor, recognizing the Christian principles upon which our country was founded, and thus glorifying the God of our fathers and resuscitating the historical, biblical legacy which is ours.

More than one thousand Christian (and non-Christian) students, teachers, homeschoolers, parents and educators attended the seminars and slide presentations which I conducted. One non-Christian private school had two hundred and fifty students, teachers and parents in attendance. We were able to minister to numerous young people who had important and pressing questions pertaining to the true history of America, as opposed to its modern, revised versions permeating our nation's school system. The breakthroughs for Christ were gratifying and encouraging. As our Lord Jesus says in John's gospel, Chapter 8 verses 31 and 32: "If you abide in my Word . . . the Truth shall make you free." And again: "Where the Spirit of the Lord is, there is liberty." (II Cor. 3:17).

Upon returning to Washington, God gave me the task to research each of the 50 State Constitutions at the International Law Library of the Library of Congress. The Preamble to all 50 State Constitutions glorifies God as the Father and sustainer of our liberties as Americans. All State Proclamations were then formulated, citing each State's Christian heritage, followed by the founding fathers' use of Scripture and their reliance upon Almighty God in prayer. These were then put into the hands of Christian Heritage Ministries' state co-ordinators at God's appointed time for each state Governor's signature, in order to celebrate their first "Christian Heritage Week."

Schools, both public and Christian, homeschoolers, ministries, churches, and the public-at-large are thus impacted with historic fact from the original documents of our founders.

Christian Heritage Ministries begins our youth-oriented, grassroots, community-involved "Christian Heritage Week" celebrations in early

September of each academic school year, through May of the successive year, **precluding** summer holidays, Thanksgiving and Christmas weeks, when the schools of America are closed. We have celebrated "Christian Heritage Week" on a statewide level in 27 individual states to date, to include California, Missouri, Colorado, South Carolina, Illinois, Idaho, Michigan and South Dakota; resuscitating, restoring, reviving and teaching anew our nation's rich Christian history and heritage from original sources. The states of California, Wisconsin, Delaware, Virginia, Hawaii and Arkansas have celebrated their second annual "Christian Heritage Week."

We have given our four slide presentations and talks to many public schools, who have welcomed the exciting experience of learning about America's authentic history from original records. We intend to cover all 50 states with a statewide "Christian Heritage Week" in the years to come. Some of the State Governors' signed proclamations designating their first "Christian Heritage Week" are hereunder reprinted for your edification.

Catherine Millard

State of New Mexico — Office of the Governor

# BRUCE KING, Governor

## Proclamation

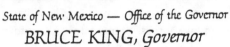

**WHEREAS,** THE GOVERNOR OF THE STATE OF NEW MEXICO DESIRES TO RECOGNIZE AND COMMEMORATE THE CHRISTIAN HERITAGE OF THE UNITED STATES OF AMERICA; AND

**WHEREAS,** THE CHRISTIAN HERITAGE OF OUR NATION IS RECOGNIZED IN THE ACCOMPLISHMENTS OF SUCH RENOWNED INDIVIDUALS AS CHRISTOPHER COLUMBUS, WILLIAM BRADFORD, GEORGE WASHINGTON, JOHN HANCOCK, ABIGAIL ADAMS, NOAH WEBSTER, ABRAHAM LINCOLN, AND WOODROW WILSON; AND

**WHEREAS,** TEACHING CHILDREN ABOUT THE HISTORICAL CHRISTIAN HERITAGE OF OUR NATION FROM ITS DISCOVERY, AND CONCEPTION TO ITS CONTINUAL APPLICATION IS BENEFICENT EDUCATIONALLY AND VIRTUOUSLY; AND

**WHEREAS,** THE RIGHTS OF CITIZENS TO BE FULLY EDUCATED AS TO THE CHRISTIAN HERITAGE OF OUR NATION IS RECOGNIZED BY THE UNITED STATES AS A VOLUNTARY EXERCISE OF THE FREEDOM OF EDUCATIONAL CHOICE; AND

**WHEREAS,** THE CHRISTIAN FAITH HAS BEEN HISTORICALLY DOCUMENTED AS A FOUNDATIONAL INFLUENCE ON THE INCEPTION, FORMATION, STRUCTURE AND CULTURE OF OUR NATION;

**NOW, THEREFORE,** I, BRUCE KING, GOVERNOR OF THE STATE OF NEW MEXICO, DO HEREBY PROCLAIM NOVEMBER 10 THROUGH NOVEMBER 16, 1991 AS:

## "CHRISTIAN HERITAGE WEEK"

IN NEW MEXICO.

ATTEST

*Stephanie Gonzales*

SECRETARY OF STATE

DONE AT THE EXECUTIVE OFFICE THIS 25TH DAY OF SEPTEMBER, 1991.

WITNESS MY HAND AND THE GREAT SEAL OF THE STATE OF NEW MEXICO.

*Bruce King*

BRUCE KING
GOVERNOR

STATE OF ALABAMA

# PROCLAMATION

## BY THE GOVERNOR

WHEREAS, the Preamble to the state Constitution says "We, the people of the state of Alabama, in order to establish justice, insure domestic tranquility, and secure the blessings of liberty to ourselves and to our posterity, invoking the favor and guidance of Almighty God, do ordain and establish the following Constitution and form of government for the state of Alabama;" and

WHEREAS, Benjamin Franklin, at the Constitutional Convention in 1787 said, "It is impossible to build an empire without our Father's aid. I believe the sacred writings which say that 'Except the Lord build the house, they labor in vain that build it'" (Psalm 127:1); and

WHEREAS, George Washington enunciated "animated alone by the pure spirit of Christianity, and conducting ourselves as the faithful subjects of our free government, we may enjoy every temporal and spiritual felicity;" and

WHEREAS, Thomas Jefferson, author of the Declaration of Independence, wrote: "Can the liberties of a nation be secure when we have removed the conviction that these liberties are the gift of God?" and

WHEREAS, James Madison, father of the U.S. Constitution, advocated "the diffusion of the light of Christianity in our nation" in his memorial and remonstrance; and

WHEREAS, Patrick Henry quoted Proverbs 14:34 for our nation: "Righteousness alone can exalt a nation, but sin is a disgrace to any people;" and

WHEREAS, George Mason, in his Virginia Declaration of Rights, forerunner to our U.S. Bill of Rights, affirmed: "That it is the mutual duty of all to practice Christian forbearance, love and charity toward each other;" and

WHEREAS, these and many other great men and women of America, giants in the structuring of American history, were Christian statesmen of caliber and integrity who did not hesitate to express their faith:

NOW, **THEREFORE**, I, Guy Hunt, Governor of the State of Alabama, do hereby proclaim March 14 through March 20, 1993, as

## CHRISTIAN HERITAGE WEEK

in Alabama.

GIVEN UNDER MY HAND, and the Great Seal of the Governor's Office at the State House in the City of Montgomery on this the 23rd day of December, 1992.

GUY HUNT

STATE OF TENNESSEE

# PROCLAMATION

BY THE GOVERNOR

**WHEREAS,** the Constitution of the State of Tennessee states that "All power is inherent in the people, and all free governments are founded on their authority, and instituted for their peace, safety, and happines...That all men have a natural and indefeasible right to worship Almighty God according to the dictates of their own conscience; that no man can of right be compelled to attend, erect, or support any place of worship, or to maintain any minister against his consent..."; and

**WHEREAS,** Benjamin Franklin, at the Constitutional Convention in 1787 stated: "It is impossible to build an empire without our Father's aid. I believe the sacred writings which say that 'Except the Lord build the house, they labor in vain that build it' (Psalm 127:1); and

**WHEREAS,** George Washington enunciated: "animated alone by the pure spirit of Christianity, and conducting ourselves as the faithful subjects of our free government, we may enjoy every temporal and spiritual felicity;" and

**WHEREAS,** Thomas Jefferson, author of the Declaration of Independence, wrote: "Can the liberties of a nation be secure when we have removed the conviction that these liberties are the gift of God?" and

**WHEREAS,** James Madison, father of the U.S. Constitution, advocated "the diffusion of the light of Christianity in our nation" in his Memorial and Remonstrance; and

**WHEREAS,** Patrick Henry quoted Proverbs 14:34 for our nation: "Righteousness alone can exalt a nation, but sin is a disgrace to any people;" and

**WHEREAS,** George Mason, in his Virginia Declaration of Rights, forerunner to our U.S. Bill of Rights, affirmed: "that it is the mutual duty of all to practice Christian forbearance, love and charity towards each other"; and

**WHEREAS,** these, and many other truly great men and women of America, giants in the structuring of American history, were Christian statesmen of calibre and integrity who did not hesitate to express their faith;

**NOW THEREFORE,** I, Ned McWherter, as Governor of the State of Tennessee do hereby proclaim August 29 through September 4, 1993, as

**CHRISTIAN HERITAGE WEEK**

in Tennessee and urge all citizens to join me in this worthy observance.

IN WITNESS WHEREOF, I HAVE HEREUNTO SET MY HAND AND CAUSED THE GREAT SEAL OF THE STATE OF TENNESSEE TO BE AFFIXED AT NASHVILLE ON THIS 21ST DAY OF JUNE, 1993.

_Ned McWherter_
GOVERNOR

_Riley C. Darnell_
SECRETARY OF STATE

## The State of Wisconsin

## OFFICE OF THE GOVERNOR

### A PROCLAMATION

WHEREAS, the Preamble to the Constitution of the State of Wisconsin states that "We, the people of Wisonsin, grateful to Almighty God for our freedom, domestic tranquility and promote the general welfare, do establish this Constitution"; and

WHEREAS, Benjamin Franklin, at the Constitutional Convention in 1787 stated: "It is impossible to build an empire without our Father's aid. I believe the sacred writings which say that 'Except the Lord build the house, they labor in vain that build it'" (Psalm 127:1); and

WHEREAS, George Washington enunciated: "animated alone by the pure spirit of Christianity, and conducting ourselves as the faithful subjects of our free government, we may enjoy every temporal and spiritual felicity"; and

WHEREAS, Thomas Jefferson, author of the Declaration of Independence, wrote: "Can the liberties of a nation be secure when we have removed the conviction that these liberties are the gift of God?"; and

WHEREAS, James Madison, father of the U.S. Constitution, advocated "the diffusion of the light of Christianity in our nation" in his Memorial and Remonstrance; and

WHEREAS, Patrick Henry quoted Proverbs 14:34 for our nation: "Righteousness alone can exalt a nation, but sin is a disgrace to any people"; and

WHEREAS, George Mason, in his Virginia Declaration of Rights, forerunner to our U.S. Bill of Rights, affirmed: "That it is the mutual duty of all to practice Christian forbearance, love and charity towards each other"; and

WHEREAS, these, and many other truly great men and women of America, giants in the structuring of American history, were Christian statesmen of calibre and integrity who did not hesitate to express their faith;

NOW, THEREFORE, I, TOMMY G. THOMPSON, Governor of the State of Wisconsin, do hereby proclaim October 3 through October 9, 1993

### CHRISTIAN HERITAGE WEEK

in the State of Wisconsin, and I commend this observance to all citizens.

IN TESTIMONY WHEREOF, I have hereunto set my hand and caused the Great Seal of the State of Wisconsin to be affixed. Done at the Capitol in the City of Madison this twentieth day of September in the year one thousand nine hundred ninety-three.

TOMMY G. THOMPSON

By the Governor:

DOUGLAS LA FOLLETTE
Secretary of State

**STATEMENT**
**IN OBSERVANCE OF**
**CHRISTIAN HERITAGE WEEK**

*Whereas,* our Nation was founded on the belief that religious freedom was an inherent right of all citizens; and

*Whereas,* the Constitution of the State of Delaware states that "Through Divine Goodness, all men have by nature the rights of worshipping and serving their Creator according to the dictates of their consciences..."; and

*Whereas,* Benjamin Franklin, at the Constitutional Convention in 1787 stated: "It is impossible to build an empire without our Father's aid. I believe the sacred writings which say that 'Except the Lord build the house, they labor in vain that build it'" (Psalm) 127:1); and

*Whereas,* George Washington enunciated: "animated alone by the pure spirit of Christianity, and conducting ourselves as the faithful subjects of our free government, we may enjoy every temporal and spiritual felicity"; and

*Whereas,* Thomas Jefferson, author of the Declaration of Independence, wrote: "Can the liberties of a nation be secure when we have removed the conviction that these liberties are the gift of God?"; and

*Whereas,* James Madison, father of the U.S. Constitution, advocated "the diffusion of the light of Christianity in our nation" in his Memorial and Remonstrance; and

*Whereas,* Patrick Henry quoted Provers 14:34 for our nation: "Righteousness alone can exalt a nation, but sin is a disgrace to any people"; and

*Whereas,* George Mason, in his Virginia Declaration of Rights, forerunner to our U.S. Bill of Rights, affirmed: "That it is the mutual duty of all to practice Christian forbearance, love and charity towards each other"; and

*Whereas,* these, and many other truly great men and women of America, giants in the structuring of American history, were Christian statesman of calibre and integrity who relied on their religious beliefs for guidance, strength and comfort.

*Now, Therefore, We, Thomas R. Carper, Governor, and Ruth Ann Minner, Lieutenant Governor,* of the State of Delaware, do hereby declare November 14-20, 1993, as:

**CHRISTIAN HERITAGE WEEK**

in the State of Delaware, and urge all citizens to recognize the importance of this event.

*Thomas R. Carper, Governor*

*Ruth Ann Minner, Lieutenant Governor*

# *Proclamation*

WHEREAS, the Preamble to the Constitution of the State of Hawaii states, "We, the people of Hawaii, Grateful for Divine Guidance...;" and

WHEREAS, the State Motto, *"Ua mau ke ea o ka `aina i ka pono"* -- The Life of the Land is Perpetuated in Righteousness -- was first uttered by Queen Ke`opuolani as she was baptized into the Christian faith before her death in 1825; and

WHEREAS, King Kamehameha III reiterated his mother's dying words, *"Ua mau ke ea o ka `aina i ka pono,"* as he gave thanks to God at Kawaiaha`o Church for the return of his kingdom in 1843; and

WHEREAS, the first Hawaiian Christian, Henry Opukahai`a's zeal for Christ and love for the Hawaiian people inspired the first American Board mission to Hawaii in 1820; and

WHEREAS, amid much solemnity and rejoicing the remains of Henry Opukahai`a were returned to Hawaii in 1993, 175 years after his death in Connecticut, and were reinterred at Napo`opo`o, Kona, Hawaii; and

WHEREAS, the influence of Christianity helped to bring about medical aid, public health policies, public education, law and order, political stability and the principles of democracy to the Hawaiian Kingdom; and

WHEREAS, the founding fathers of the United States and many of the leaders who shaped the modern history of Hawaii readily acknowledged their Christian religious heritage as a guiding force in their daily lives and in the conduct of their professional and personal pursuits; and

WHEREAS, the Hawaii Association of Evangelicals has set aside a period in February, 1994, for activities and events to educate the public about the Christian roots of our country and our state; and

WHEREAS, this period -- designated as Christian Heritage Week -- has been chosen because it is between the birthdays of Presidents Lincoln and Washington, deeply religious leaders who drew great strength and inspiration from their Christian beliefs, and within this period also falls the anniversary of the death of Henry Opukahai`a, recognized as one of the pivotal persons in Hawaii's history;

NOW, THEREFORE, I, JOHN WAIHEE, Governor of the State of Hawaii, do hereby proclaim the period February 12 through February 22, 1994, to be

## CHRISTIAN HERITAGE WEEK IN HAWAII

DONE at the State Capitol, in the Executive Chambers, Honolulu, State of Hawaii, this Thirtieth day of December, 1993.

# STATE OF ARKANSAS
## EXECUTIVE DEPARTMENT

---

# PROCLAMATION

### TO ALL TO WHOM THESE PRESENTS SHALL COME – GREETINGS:

WHEREAS,     The Preamble to the Constitution of the State of Arkansas states that "We the people of the State of Arkansas, *grateful to Almighty God for the privilege of choosing our own form of government, for our civil and religious liberty, and desiring to perpetuate its blessings and secure the same to ourselves and posterity,* do ordain and establish this Constitution."; and

WHEREAS,     Benjamin Franklin, at the Constitutional Convention in 1787 stated: "It is impossible to build an empire without our Father's aid. I believe the sacred writings which say that 'Except the Lord build the house, they labor in vain that build it'" (Psalm 127:1); and

WHEREAS,     George Washington enunciated: "animated alone by the pure spirit of Christianity, and conducting ourselves as the faithful subjects of our free government, we may enjoy every temporal and spiritual felicity"; and

WHEREAS,     Thomas Jefferson, author of the Declaration of Independence, wrote: "Can the liberties of a nation be secure when we have removed the conviction that these liberties are the gift of God?"; and

WHEREAS,     James Madison, father of the U.S. Constitution, advocated "the diffusion of the light of Christianity in our nation" in his Memorial and Remonstrance; and

WHEREAS,     Patrick Henry quoted Proverbs 14:34 for our nation: "Righteousness alone can exalt a nation, but sin is a disgrace to any people"; and

WHEREAS,     George Mason, in his Virginia Declaration of Rights, forerunner to our U.S. Bill of Rights, affirmed: "That it is the mutual duty of all to practice Christian forbearance, love and charity towards each other"; and

WHEREAS,     These, and many other truly great men and women of America, giants in the structuring of American history, were Christian statesmen of calibre and integrity who did not hesitate to express their faith;

NOW, THEREFORE,     I, Mike Huckabee, Acting Governor of the State of Arkansas, do proclaim **February 27th** through **March 5th, 1994,** as:

## CHRISTIAN HERITAGE WEEK

in the State of Arkansas.

IN WITNESS WHEREOF, I have hereunto set my hand and caused the Great Seal of the State of Arkansas to be affixed at the Capitol in Little Rock on this 1st day of February in the year of our Lord nineteen hundred and ninety-four.

_____
ACTING GOVERNOR

_____
SECRETARY OF STATE

# COMMONWEALTH of VIRGINIA

## Office of the Governor

George Allen
Governor

### CHRISTIAN HERITAGE WEEK

**WHEREAS,** the Constitution of the Commonwealth of Virginia states *"That religion or the duty which we owe to our creator, and the manner of discharging it, can be directed only by reason and conviction;* not by force or violence; and, therefore, all men are equally entitled to the free exercise of religion, according to the dictates of conscience; *and that it is the mutual duty of all to practice Christian forbearance, love, and charity towards each other;"* and

**WHEREAS,** Benjamin Franklin, at the Constitutional Convention in 1787 stated: "It is impossible to build an empire without our Father's aid. I believe the sacred writings which say that 'Except the Lord build the house, they labor in vain that build it'" (Psalm 127:1); and

**WHEREAS,** George Washington enunciated: "animated alone by the pure spirit of Christianity, and conducting ourselves as the faithful subjects of our free government, we may enjoy every temporal and spiritual felicity;" and

**WHEREAS,** Thomas Jefferson, author of the Declaration of Independence, wrote: "Can the liberties of a nation be secure when we have removed the conviction that these liberties are the gift of God?" and

**WHEREAS,** James Madison, father of the U.S. Constitution, advocated "the diffusion of the light of Christianity in our nation" in his Memorial and Remonstrance; and

**WHEREAS,** Patrick Henry quoted Proverbs 14:34 for our nation: "Righteousness alone can exalt a nation, but sin is a disgrace to any people;" and

**WHEREAS,** George Mason, in his Virginia Declaration of Rights, forerunner to our U.S. Bill of Rights, affirmed: "That it is the mutual duty of all to practice Christian forebearance, love and charity towards each other;" and

**WHEREAS,** these, and many other truly great men and women of America, giants in the structuring of American history, were Christian statesmen of calibre and integrity who did not hesitate to express their faith;

**NOW, THEREFORE,** I, George Allen, Governor, do hereby recognize March 13 - 19, 1994 as **CHRISTIAN HERITAGE WEEK,** in the **COMMONWEALTH OF VIRGINIA,** and I call this observance to the attention of all our citizens.

_____
**Governor**

_____
**Secretary of the Commonwealth**

## STATE OF MISSISSIPPI

*Office of the Governor*

A PROCLAMATION
BY GOVERNOR
**KIRK FORDICE**

*Whereas, in 1994, we again reflect on the goals set forth in past years to understand and recapture our Christian Heritage and to reestablish our original freedom of religious concepts; and*

*Whereas, we are reminded of the words of James Madison who in 1778 said, "We have staked the whole future of American civilization, not upon the power of government, far from it. We have staked the future...upon the capacity of each and all of us to govern ourselves, to sustain ourselves, according to the Ten Commandments of God"; and*

*Whereas, James Madison also advocated, "The diffusion of the light of Christianity in our nation" in his Memorial and Remonstrance; and*

*Whereas, let us now refrain from excluding from our teachings, our textbooks and our thoughts the importance of religious values and activities in America's private, public and political life; and*

*Whereas, may we also remember the words in the Declaration of Independence when the Framers noted, "And for the support of this Declaration, with a firm reliance on the protection of Divine Providence, we mutually pledge to each other our Lives, our Fortunes and our sacred Honor":*

*Now, therefore, I, Kirk Fordice, Governor of the State of Mississippi, hereby proclaim September 18 through September 24, 1994,*

### *CHRISTIAN HERITAGE WEEK*

*in the State of Mississippi and encourage our citizens to join in remembering that individual faith is the power that inspires men of goodwill to lay foundations and to pursue noble goals for themselves and their country.*

*IN WITNESS WHEREOF, I have hereunto set my hand and caused the Great Seal of the State of Mississippi to be affixed.*

*DONE at the Capitol, in the City of Jackson, September 6, 1994, in the two hundred and nineteenth year of the United States of America.*

**KIRK FORDICE**
GOVERNOR

BY THE GOVERNOR

SECRETARY OF STATE

# STATE OF OKLAHOMA

**EXECUTIVE DEPARTMENT**

# Proclamation

**Whereas,** the Preamble to the Constitution of the State of Oklahoma states that "*Invoking the guidance of Almighty God, in order to secure and perpetuate the blessing of liberty,...*we, the people of the State of Oklahoma, do ordain and establish this Constitution, " and

**Whereas,** Benjamin Franklin, at the Constitutional Convention in 1787 stated: "It is impossible to build an empire without our Father's aid. I believe the sacred writings which say that "Except the Lord build the house, they labor in vain that build it" (Psalm 127:1), and

**Whereas,** George Washington enunciated: "animated alone by the pure spirit of Christianity, and conducting ourselves as the faithful subjects of our free government, we may enjoy every temporal and spiritual felicity: " and

**Whereas,** Thomas Jefferson, author of the Declaration of Independence, wrote: " Can the liberties of a nation be secure when we have removed the conviction that these liberties are the gift of God?" and

**Whereas,** James Madison, father of the U.S. Constitution, advocated "the diffusion of the light of Christianity in our nation" in his Memorial and Remonstrance; and

**Whereas,** Patrick Henry quoted proverbs 14:34 for our nation: "Righteousness alone can exalt a nation, but sin is a disgrace to any people;" and

**Whereas,** George Mason, in his Virginia Declaration of Rights, forerunner to our U.S. Bill of Rights, affirmed: "That it is the mutual duty of all to practice Christian forbearance, love and charity towards each other," and

**Whereas,** these, and many other truly great men and women of America, giants in the structuring of American history, were Christian statesmen of calibre and integrity who did not hesitate to express their faith,

**Now, Therefore, I** Frank Keating, Governor of the Great State of Oklahoma, do proclaim and announce April 2 through April 8, 1995 in Oklahoma as:

## Christian Heritage Week

in the state of Oklahoma.

*In Witness Whereof, I have hereunto set my hand and caused the Great Seal of the State of Oklahoma to be affixed.*

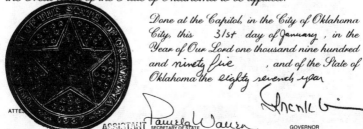

*Done at the Capitol, in the City of Oklahoma City, this 31st day of January, in the Year of Our Lord one thousand nine hundred and ninety five, and of the State of Oklahoma the eighty sevenths year*

ATTE

ASSISTANT SECRETARY OF STATE Pamela Warren

GOVERNOR

# STATE OF KANSAS

# PROCLAMATION BY THE GOVERNOR

TO THE PEOPLE OF KANSAS, GREETINGS:

WHEREAS, The Preamble to the Constitution of the State of Kansas states that, "We, the people of Kansas, *grateful to Almighty God* for our civil and religious privileges . . ."; and

WHEREAS, Benjamin Franklin, at the Constitutional Convention in 1787 stated: "It is impossible to build an empire without our Father's aid. I believe the sacred writings which say that 'Except the Lord build the house, they labor in vain that build it.'" (Psalm 127:1); and

WHEREAS, George Washington enunciated: "animated alone by the pure spirit of Christianity, and conducting ourselves as the faithful subjects of our free government, we may enjoy every temporal and spiritual felicity"; and

WHEREAS, Thomas Jefferson, author of the Declaration of Independence, wrote: "Can the liberties of a nation be secure when we have removed the conviction that these liberties are the gift of God?"; and

WHEREAS, James Madison, father of the U.S. Constitution, advocated "the diffusion of the light of Christianity in our nation" in his Memorial and Remonstrance; and

WHEREAS, Patrick Henry quoted Proverbs 14:34 for our nation: "Righteousness alone can exalt a nation, but sin is a disgrace to any people"; and

WHEREAS, George Mason in his Virginia Declaration of Rights, forerunner to our U.S. Bill of Rights, affirmed: "That it is the mutual duty of all to practice Christian forbearance, love and charity towards each other"; and

WHEREAS, these, and many other truly great men and women of America, giants in the structuring of American history, were Christian statesmen of calibre and integrity who did not hesitate to express their faith:

NOW, THEREFORE, I, BILL GRAVES, GOVERNOR OF THE STATE OF KANSAS, do hereby proclaim the week of April 23-29,1995 as

## *Christian Heritage Week*

in Kansas, and urge that all citizens join in the observance.

DONE    At the Capitol in Topeka
under the Great Seal of
the State this 2nd day of
February, A.D. 1995

BY THE GOVERNOR:

Ron Thornburgh
Secretary of State

Assistant Secretary of State

# CERTIFICATE of RECOGNITION

*By virtue of the authority vested by the Constitution*
*in the Governor of the Commonwealth of Virginia,*
*there is hereby officially recognized:*

### CHRISTIAN HERITAGE WEEK

**WHEREAS,** the Constitution of the Commonwealth of Virginia states: "That religion or the duty which we owe to our creator, and the manner of discharging it, can be directed only by reason and conviction; not by force or violence; and, therefore, all men are equally entitled to the free exercise of religion, according to the dictates of conscience; and that it is the mutual duty of all to practice Christian forbearance, love, and charity towards each other"; and

**WHEREAS,** Benjamin Franklin, at the Constitutional Convention in 1787 stated: "It is impossible to build an empire without our Father's aid. I believe the sacred writings which say that 'Except the Lord build the house, they labor in vain that build it'" (Psalm 127:1); and

**WHEREAS,** George Washington enunciated: "animated alone by the pure spirit of Christianity, and conducting ourselves as the faithful subjects of our free government, we may enjoy every temporal and spiritual felicity"; and

**WHEREAS,** Thomas Jefferson, author of the Declaration of Independence, wrote; "Can the liberties of a nation be secure when we have removed the conviction that these liberties are the gift of God?"; and

**WHEREAS,** James Madison, father of the U.S. Constitution, advocated "the diffusion of the light of Christianity in our nation" in his Memorial and Remonstrance; and

**WHEREAS,** Patrick Henry quoted Proverbs 14:34 for our nation: "Righteousness alone can exalt a nation, but sin is a disgrace to any people"; and

**WHEREAS,** George Mason, in his Virginia Declaration of Rights, precedent for our U.S. Bill of Rights, affirmed: "That it is the mutual duty of all to practice Christian forbearance, love and charity towards each other"; and

**WHEREAS,** these, and many other truly great men and women of America, giants in the structuring of American history, were founders of our country of liberty, who with honor and dignity did not hesitate to express their faith;

**NOW, THEREFORE, I,** George Allen, Governor, do hereby recognize March 12 - 18, 1995 as the **SECOND ANNUAL CHRISTIAN HERITAGE WEEK,** in the **COMMONWEALTH OF VIRGINIA,** and I call this observance to the attention of all our citizens.

*George Allen*

Governor

*Betsy Davis Beamer*

Secretary of the Commonwealth

**The Birmingham News**                    March 20, 1993

# Erasing Religion in Texts Called Part of Morals Loss

by Roy Williams
News staff writer

Taking religion out of school textbooks has helped lead to a decline in the "moral fiber" of the nation, the head of the Christian Heritage Ministries said Friday.

"They (children) have lost sight of it (religion) because they haven't studied it," said Catherine Millard, president of the ministry based in the Washington, D.C. suburb of Springfield, Va.

Ms Millard has been in Birmingham this week as part of Christian Heritage Week, a celebration of the role of Christianity.

Alabama is one of eight states to celebrate the week.

Since arriving in Birmingham Tuesday, Ms. Millard has addressed students at Huffman Middle School, Arrington Middle School, Phillips High School, Forrest Hill Middle School, Cross Valley Academy and Briarwood Christian School.

She also spoke at Covenant Presbyterian Church and Friday night appeared at the Radisson Hotel for the state convention of the Eagle Forum.

"My purpose is to celebrate, restore and revive the Christian history and heritage of America," Ms. Millard said.

She focuses her talks on educating people about the important role Christianity played in the lives of the nation's founding fathers.

She has conducted extensive research on America's Christian heritage and has written two books, *God's Signature Over the Nation's Capital: Evidence of your Christian Heritage* and *The Rewriting of America's History.*

"All the original documents had strong Biblical principles behind them," Ms. Millard said of her research.

"That's where the source of their strength came from. Unfortunately, beginning in the 1930s they (writers) took God out of the textbooks and have virtually rewritten history," she said.

As a result, schoolchildren from age 5 to 18 grow up learning nothing about God, resulting "in a decline of the moral fiber of our nation," she said.

She advises young people during her speeches to learn as much about the nation's Christian heritage as possible.

Parents, she said, should pray with their children and live their lives "so that they can give them strong Christian moral examples."

She said anyone wanting information about Christian Heritage should write the ministry at 6597 Forest Dew Court, Springfield, Va 22152.

𝕮𝖑𝖆𝖗𝖎𝖔𝖓 𝕷𝖊𝖉𝖌𝖊𝖗, 𝕵𝖆𝖈𝖐𝖘𝖔𝖓, 𝕸𝖎𝖘𝖘𝖎𝖘𝖘𝖎𝖕𝖕𝖎   September 21, 1994

# Christian Heritage Week
## A Time to Remember Nation's Historic Roots
*God wasn't a minor topic in our nation's history that many would apparently like to make Him today.*

by Matt Friedman, Columnist

To read this nation's original documents, writings and quotations of our Founding Fathers; to peruse early American paintings and sculptures; to read Noah Webster's original dictionary and behold so many of the great landmarks of the earliest colonies is to drink deeply of this nation's strong faith in God.

And yet, if one were to scan this nation's textbooks today, an accurate portrayal of such history has been excised and thus hidden from this nation's children and from future remembrance. Catherine Millard, head of Christian Heritage Ministries who is visiting Jackson this week, considers this historical loss unsatisfactory and has spent years trying to address the deletions.

"Children have lost sight of religion because they haven't studied it," says Millard. "Unfortunately, beginning in the 1930s writers took God out of the textbooks and have virtually rewritten history." The result, of course, is a generation almost wholly ignorant – even antagonistic towards – the Judeo-Christian influence on this nation and the biblical foundations that stand behind the democratic principles upon which America stands.

Millard, author of *God's Signature over the Nation's Capital* – a book used when she conducts teaching tours of biblical history using the nation's capital – a stunning rebuttal to the notion that this nation was reared on secularity. As the book follows Millard's tour through the National Archives, the memorials and monuments, the White House, Supreme Court and Capitol; the Cathedrals, national and historic churches; the national museums, and galleries of art, the multitudinous national landmarks and monuments to preachers and, of course, the memorials, it is quite clear that God wasn't a minor topic in our nation's history that most scholars and educationists would apparently like to make Him today.

In her most recent book, *The Rewriting of America's History*, Millard demonstrates exactly how removal of religion has, and continues to be, expunged from the accounts of history.

Those interested that we have, for the next generation, an accurate account of history will be shocked.

"We have been the recipients of the choicest bounties of heaven," said Abraham Lincoln on the proclamation for a National Day of Fasting, Humiliation and Prayer. "We have been preserved, these many years in peace and prosperity. We have grown in numbers, wealth and power, as no other nation has ever grown. But we have forgotten God. We have forgotten the gracious hand which preserved us in peace, and multiplied and enriched and strengthened us; and we have vainly imagined, in the deceitfulness of our hearts, that all these blessings were produced by some superior wisdom and virtue of our own. Intoxicated with unbroken success, we have become too self-sufficient to feel the necessity of redeeming and preserving grace, too proud to pray to the God that made us!"

Christian Heritage Week ought to be about rediscovering a reliable rendering of history and a recognition that "forgetting," as Lincoln called it, will spell a certain end to this once great nation.

Remembering, there is hope.

Catherine Millard will make a media presentation of the nation's historic roots at Christ United Methodist Church Thursday at 7 p.m., sponsored by Home Educators of Central Mississippi. Everyone welcome.

The following State Joint House and Senate Resolution was a result of our proclamation for "Christian Heritage Week — Colorado, April 24-30, 1994:"

## Senate Joint Resolution 93S-3

By Senators Roberts, Meiklejohn, Mutzebaugh, and Tebedo; also Representatives Martin, Duke, and Sullivan.

Concerning The Encouragement Of Educators To Incorporate Concepts Of Ethics And Morality Into The Daily Education Of Our Youth.

WHEREAS, Many areas of Colorado have recently experienced an unprecedented increase in incidents of crime and violence among the youth of this state; and

WHEREAS, A special session of the General Assembly has been convened to focus on the youth of our state and to combat the corruptive influences of crime and violence; and

WHEREAS, The nature of the violent crimes being committed by our youth, such as drive-by shootings, crimes involving handguns, and other crimes of senseless violence evidence an ethical and moral depravity which is contrary to the heritage of our nation and to the ethical and moral principles of our forebears; and

WHEREAS, We, the General Assembly, believe that part of the cause underlying the increasing trend toward the commission of such crimes is the lack of ethics and moral principles among our youth; and

WHEREAS, Legislation alone cannot directly address the lack of ethics and morality which has resulted in the prevalence of crime and violence among our youth; and

WHEREAS, If we are to successfully attack the root cause of our present crisis, it is imperative that we instill in our youth a sense of ethics and generally accepted morality; and

WHEREAS, The influence of generally accepted moral concepts has been documented as having a foundational influence on the inception, formation, structure, and culture of our nation; and

WHEREAS, The teachers of the school districts in this state stand in a unique position to make a significant contribution to the future of our society by incorporating such concepts into the daily education of our youth; and

WHEREAS, By emphasizing ethics and generally accepted morality in the daily lessons of our youth and teaching the application of such principles from an early age, we can begin to guide our youth away from the specter of violence and crime; now, therefore,

Be It Resolved by the Senate of the Fifty-ninth General Assembly of the State of Colorado, the House of Representatives concurring herein:

(1) That we, the members of the General Assembly, encourage the teachers of the school districts of the state to work diligently to instill in our youth a sense of principled ethics and generally accepted morality by incorporating such concepts into the daily education of our youth.

(2) That the teachers of the school districts of this state will look to the spoken and written words of men and women who, in the founding and developing of this country, helped to shape the thinking that makes this country great in the eyes of the world; and that these words shall reflect the vast contributions of all who helped to make us a consistently dynamic and successful republic.

*Be It Further Resolved,* That a copy of this resolution be presented to the superintendent of each school district in Colorado.

Tom Norton
*President Of The Senate*

Charles Berry
*Speaker Of The House Of Representatives*

Joan Albi
*Secretary Of The Senate*

Lee Bahrych
*Chief Clerk Of The House Of Representatives*

After the original bronze statue of
"The Statue of Liberty Enlightening the World"
by Auguste Bartholdi, New York.

# About the Author

Catherine Millard, B.A., M.A., D. Min. in Christian Education, is the founder and president of Christian Heritage Tours, Inc. and Christian Heritage Ministries. She is also the author of *God's Signature Over the Nation's Capital*, *The Rewriting of America's History* and *A Children's Companion Guide to America's History*. Catherine won the 1990 George Washington Honor Medal, sponsored by the Freedoms Foundation at Valley Forge, in recognition of excellence in individual achievement for her many patriotic activities; and the 1992 Faith and Freedom Religious Heritage of America award for her outstanding contributions in strengthening the biblical principles and moral values in America.

She is the writer and producer of four video documentaries, *The Christian Heritage of our Nation*; and editor of *Christian Heritage News*, the quarterly newsletter of Christian Heritage Ministries. For additional information, contact Christian Heritage Tours, Inc. 6597 Forest Dew Ct., Springfield, VA 22152, or call, (703) 455-0333.

Catherine Millard is also available to provide lectures, seminars and multimedia presentations to your organization on the subject of America's Christian heritage. You may contact her through the above address.

Notes

Notes